Cinematic perspectives on international law

Manchester University Press

Melland Schill Perspectives on International Law

General editors
Jean d'Aspremont
Iain Scobbie
Sufyan Droubi

Building on the history of Melland Schill Classics and Melland Schill Studies at Manchester University Press, Melland Schill Perspectives on International Law was established to reflect the diversity of international legal scholarship worldwide. This inclusive, accessible series aims to offer a platform for scholars from different regions who adopt innovative approaches to new and old topics.

Melland Schill Perspectives on International Law is founded on the idea that every international legal issue should be debated from various and, at times, incommensurable perspectives. Though there is a great deal of diversity in international legal debates and practice, this diversity is often obfuscated by prevailing Euro-centric and positivist narratives, which not only creates difficulties for non-Western scholars to be heard but hinders the development of different approaches.

Previously published

African perspectives in international investment law

Edited by Yenkong Ngangjoh Hodu and Makane Moïse Mbengue

International organisations, non-State actors and the formation of customary international law

Edited by Sufyan Droubi and Jean d'Aspremont

Cinematic perspectives on international law

Edited by
Olivier Corten and François Dubuisson

Assistant Editor
Martyna Fałkowska-Clarys

MANCHESTER UNIVERSITY PRESS

Copyright © Manchester University Press 2021

While copyright in the volume as a whole is vested in Manchester University Press, copyright in individual chapters belongs to their respective authors, and no chapter may be reproduced wholly or in part without the express permission in writing of both author and publisher.

Published by Manchester University Press
Oxford Road, Manchester M13 9PL

www.manchesteruniversitypress.co.uk

British Library Cataloguing-in-Publication Data
A catalogue record for this book is available from the British Library

ISBN 978 1 5261 4991 6 hardback
ISBN 978 1 5261 9571 5 paperback

First published 2021
Paperback published 2026

The publisher has no responsibility for the persistence or accuracy of URLs for any external or third-party internet websites referred to in this book, and does not guarantee that any content on such websites is, or will remain, accurate or appropriate.

EU authorised representative for GPSR:
Easy Access System Europe – Mustamäe tee 50,
10621 Tallinn, Estonia
gpsr.requests@easproject.com

Typeset by Newgen Publishing UK

Contents

Notes on contributors   vi

1. International law on the screen: determining the methodology – Olivier Corten and François Dubuisson   1
2. International law, guardian of the galaxy? – Marco Benatar   20
3. Interspecies relations in science fiction movies and human international law – Vincent Chapaux   40
4. The UN Charter in action movies – Olivier Corten   58
5. The Israeli–Palestinian conflict: a cinematic saga – François Dubuisson   78
6. Is cinema the handmaid of international criminal justice? – Anne Lagerwall   104
7. The fog of law in the fog of war: international humanitarian law in war movies – Martyna Fałkowska-Clarys and Vaios Koutroulis   128
8. Science fiction cinema and the nature of international law – Nicolas Kang-Riou   153
9. War on film: gender trouble in Siddiq Barmak's *Osama* – Gabrielle Simm   166
10. *Shut the fuck up, Suarez!* Necroethics and rights in a world of shit – Mario Prost   181
11. Presentations and representations of international law in films and TV series – Serge Sur   199
12. Cine-legality: international law at the movies – Gerry Simpson   217

Index   225

Notes on contributors

Marco Benatar is an Associate Legal Officer at the International Tribunal for the Law of the Sea. Before joining the Tribunal, he was a Research Fellow at the Max Planck Institute Luxembourg for Procedural Law and the Research Foundation Flanders.

Vincent Chapaux is the Research Manager of the Maison des Sciences Humaines and a Research Fellow at the Center for International Law of the Université libre de Bruxelles.

Olivier Corten is Professor of International Law at the Université libre de Bruxelles.

François Dubuisson is Professor of International Law at the Université libre de Bruxelles.

Martyna Fałkowska-Clarys is an attaché at the Belgian Judicial Training Institute (IGO-IFJ). Before joining the Institute, she was a Senior Research Fellow at the Max Planck Institute Luxembourg for Procedural Law.

Nicolas Kang-Riou is a senior lecturer at the University of Lincoln.

Vaios Koutroulis is Professor of Public International Law at the Université libre de Bruxelles.

Anne Lagerwall is Professor of International Law at the Université libre de Bruxelles.

Mario Prost is a senior lecturer and programme director of the LLM in International Law at the Keele Law School.

Gabrielle Simm is a senior lecturer in the Faculty of Law at the University of Technology, Sydney.

Gerry Simpson is Professor of Public International Law at the London School of Economics and Political Science.

Serge Sur is Emeritus Professor of International Law at Panthéon-Assas University, Paris.

1

International law on the screen: determining the methodology

Olivier Corten and François Dubuisson

In *The Bridge on the River Kwai* (David Lean, UK, 1957), whose action takes place during the Second World War, British soldiers are captured by the Japanese army, the occupying power of Burma at the time. Colonel Saito plans to construct a bridge that would be decisive for the army's communications. He wants all the detained prisoners, soldiers and officers alike, to participate in the construction of the bridge. In a scene taking place in the middle of the prisoners' camp, in full view, the head of the contingent of British prisoners, Lieutenant Colonel Nicholson, invokes article 27 of the 1929 Geneva Convention relating to the protection of prisoners of war, according to which '[b]elligerents may employ as workmen prisoners of war who are physically fit, *other than officers*'.[1] This is the dialogue that follows:

Colonel Saito: Give me the book.
Lt Col. Nicholson: By all means. You read English I take it.
Colonel Saito: Do you read Japanese?
Lt Col. Nicholson: I'm sorry, no. But if it is a matter of precise translation, I'm sure that can be arranged. You see the code specifically states that the ...

Colonel Saito then violently slaps the Lieutenant Colonel in the face with the text of the convention, wounding him slightly on the lips: 'You speak to me of code? What code? The cowards' code!' He throws the text of the convention on the ground. 'What do you know of the soldier's code? Of bushido? Nothing! You are unworthy of command.' Lieutenant Colonel Nicholson steps over and, in a dignified way, picks up the text of the convention, before the eyes of his soldiers standing at attention, apparently stoic. He cleans the text from the dust, folds it almost ceremoniously, and says in a calm but firm voice: 'Since you refuse to abide by the laws of the civilised world, we must consider ourselves absolved from our duty to

---

1 Emphasis added.

obey you. My officers will not do manual labour.' 'We shall see' replies Colonel Saito.

The renowned international humanitarian law specialist Eric David explains that this scene, which he saw when he was an adolescent, remained engraved in his memory, particularly as an expression of the Japanese official's contempt for the law.[2] This anecdote has inspired a section dedicated to 'International Law and Cinema' on the website of the International Law Centre of the Free University of Brussels (Université libre de Bruxelles, ULB).[3] The section was created in January 2013 and contains numerous commentaries of films or TV series, alongside the scene from *The Bridge on the River Kwai* presented above. Given the interest, not to say the enthusiasm, for this initiative, the ULB International Law Centre took up this theme for the conference celebrating the Centre's fiftieth anniversary in 2014, and published a book containing the contributions presented at the conference: *Du droit international au cinéma*.[4] The timeliness of the project is further illustrated by the fact that, in the 10th Anniversary Conference of the European Society of International Law, held in September 2014 in Vienna, an Agora was dedicated to 'International Law and Film: The Power of Pictures'.[5] In 2015, the International Law Centre launched a more global online publishing project, covering various aspects of the relationship between pop culture and international law: in addition to cinema, analyses focus on music, literature, comics, theatre, video games and the visual arts.[6]

In the years that followed, several studies on the representation of international law in film were published, but they remained relatively rare and isolated (see below). This book is thus conceived as a first, more global and coherent approach to the analysis of the issue of the representation

---

2 Eric David, 'Le Pont de la rivière Kwaï (David Lean, 1957): le droit international existe-t-il?', http://cdi.ulb.ac.be/le-pont-de-la-riviere-kwai/, accessed 1 December 2019.
3 'Pop Culture & International Law: International Law and Cinema', http://cdi.ulb.ac.be/category/cinema/, accessed 1 December 2019. A webpage named 'International Law and Films' was created in 2007 on the website of New York University (http://iiljfilms.blogspot.be). However, it seems that the webpage has been inactive since 2008. Moreover, the commentaries of films contained therein are of a more general character; they are not (or, in any case, not primarily) focused on international law.
4 Olivier Corten and François Dubuisson (eds), *Du droit international au cinéma. Présentations et représentations du droit international dans les films et les séries télévisées* (Paris: Pedone, 2015).
5 https://esil2014.univie.ac.at/programme/ and https://esil2014.univie.ac.at/call-for-papers/agora-11/, accessed 1 December 2019.
6 Centre de droit international ULB, 'Pop culture et droit international', cdi.ulb.ac.be/culture-pop-et-droit-international/, accessed 1 December 2019.

of international law in film, in English. The innovative nature of this research project requires, as a first step, the definition and formulation of a methodological framework. This is the object of this introductory chapter. The methodological indications set out here have guided the contributors to this book in the analysis of their respective subjects, but they are also intended to contribute to the conduct of other future research in this area.

International law and cinema: a subject still little explored

For social sciences, cinema has been a subject of research for some time now. However, it must be noted that the place of international law in film productions has not yet been much studied. Existing analyses mainly focus either on the application of domestic law in a national context or on international relations from a political science perspective.

First, some legal experts have reflected on the relationship between law and cinema, mostly in the context of domestic law.[7] Indeed, a number of studies seek to analyse specific scenes or entire movies by confronting them to existent positive law, in what could be termed a 'legal critic' analysis. An example in this respect is the book *Reel Justice: The Courtroom Goes to the Movies*. In this book, the contributors comment critically on a large number of films, by comparing the cinematographic representation included therein to existent law and jurisprudence.[8] Sometimes, as illustrated by Bruno Dayez's *Justice et cinéma*, such comments are accompanied by information concerning the context relating to a film's theatrical release or by an evaluation of the technical or aesthetic qualities of a film.[9] Aside from books adopting this cross-sectional approach, others focus on one specific issue. This is for example the case of *Framed: Women in Law and Films*.[10] In this context, the relationship between law and cinema can be considered as being part of a school of thought like the *Cultural Studies*,[11] which largely

---

7 See, for example, Stefan Machura and Peter Robson (eds), *Law and Film* (Malden: Blackwell, 2001).
8 Paul Bergman and Michael Asimow, *Reel Justice: The Courtroom goes to the Movies* (Kansas City: Andrews McMeel, 2006).
9 Bruno Dayez, *Justice et cinéma* (Bruxelles: Anthemis, 2008).
10 Orit Kamir, *Framed: Women in Law and Films* (Durham, NC: Duke University Press, 2006).
11 See, for example, Jerry D. Leonard (ed.), *Legal Studies as Cultural Studies: A Reader in (Post)Modern Critical Theory* (New York: State University of New York Press, 1995); Austin Sarat and Jonathan Simon (eds), *Cultural Analysis, Cultural Studies and the Law: Moving Beyond Legal Realism* (Durham, NC: Duke University Press, 2003); Naomi Mezey, 'Approaches to the Cultural Study of Law: Law as Culture' (2001) 13 *Yale Journal of Law & the Humanities* 35ff.

departs from positive law in order to study the representations of law in cultural phenomena: literature, comics, music, cinema and TV series, and video-games, to cite but a few.[12] These developments around the subject of 'law and cinema' can be explained by various factors, amongst which the existence of a rich cinematographic production of legal films seems to be one of the most important. Indeed, such films, particularly courtroom movies, have become a film genre of their own. On a methodological plane, another factor is the success of schools of legal thought such as the *Critical Legal Studies*, whose aim is to study the general discourse and reveal those representations which are inclined to foster the reproduction of conformist intellectual frameworks, as well as, in certain cases, power relations.[13]

Moreover, a large number of scholars have associated cinema with international relations.[14] Several studies have focused on the relationship between Hollywood and the Pentagon, particularly between cinema and US foreign relations.[15] However, in those studies, international law is only marginally invoked, if at all.[16] This can be explained, at least partly, by

---

12 Austin Sara and Jonathan Simon, 'Beyond Legal Realism? Cultural Analysis, Cultural Studies, and the Situation of Legal Scholarship' (2001) 13 *Yale Journal of Law & the Humanities* 3–31; James Daily and Ryan Davidson, *The Law of Superheroes* (New York: Gotham, 2012) (chapter 11 focuses on international law); Ben Clarke, Christian Rouffaer and François Sénéchaud, 'Beyond the Call of Duty: Why Shouldn't Video Game Payers Face the Same Dilemmas as Real Soldiers?' (2012) 94 *International Review of the Red Cross* 711–37; Julie Allard, Olivier Corten, François Dubuisson, Vincent Lefebve and Julien Pieret (eds), *Arrêts sur images – Les représentations du juge au cinéma, Revue e-legal*, 1 (2018), http://e-legal.ulb.be/volume-n01, accessed 1 December 2019.
13 See, for example, David Ray Papke, 'Law, Cinema, and Ideology: Hollywood Legal Films of the 1950s' (2000) 48 *UCLA Law Review* 1473.
14 Stefan Engert and Alexander Spencer, 'International Relations at the Movies: Teaching and Learning International Politics Through Films' (2009) 17:1 *Perspectives* 83–104.
15 As attested by the following works: Michael Paul Rogin, *Ronald Reagan, the Movie: And Other Episodes in Political Demonology* (Berkeley: University of California Press, 1987); Sally Totman, *How Hollywood Projects Foreign Policy* (London: Palgrave Macmillan, 2009); Jean-Michel Valantin, *Hollywood, the Pentagon and Washington: The Movies and National Security from World War II to the Present Day* (London: Anthem Press, 2005); Barthélémy Courmont and Erwan Benezet, *Washington-Hollywood: Comment l'Amérique fait son cinéma* (Paris: Armand Colin, 2007); Matthew Alford, *Reel Power: Hollywood Cinema and American Supremacy* (London: Pluto Press, 2010); Sean Carter and Klaus Dodds, *International Politics and Film: Space, Vision, Power* (New York: Columbia University Press, 2014).
16 See however Robert W. Gregg, *International Relations on Film* (Colorado: Lynne Rienner, 1998), particularly the chapter 'Ethics and International Law'. This chapter was commented on by Anthony Chase, 'International Law on Films' (2000) 24 *Legal Studies* 559–72.

the fact that international law occupies a relatively limited place in films in general, especially compared to domestic law. As the contributions to this book illustrate, scenes such as the one described at the beginning of this chapter are fairly rare. While in courtroom movies, the legal argumentation is extensively reproduced as such (which viewer does not remember one or the other memorable pleading by a lawyer, dramatized by a score aimed at highlighting its importance?), this is highly exceptional when it comes to international law. *A priori*, this is undoubtedly understandable. For the ordinary audience, the international legal order is too abstract compared to domestic law, with which the viewer is confronted every day and which he/she perceives as directly applicable and binding.[17] In any case, while any quantitative evaluation remains a relative one, films scarcely feature international law, and when they do, they limit themselves to specific sets of rules such as international humanitarian law, human rights or diplomatic law.[18] Therefore, it is not surprising that those analysing cinematographic productions invoke rarely, if ever, international law, even when their theoretical approach would justify such an invocation. Indeed, there is a tendency to associate cinema with ideology,[19] and, in this context, to favour the analysis of representations, in parallel to the *Cultural Legal Studies* mentioned above. This applies even to specialists of international law who, when engaged in the study of films, abstain from developing a

---

17 Gregg, *International Relations*, 183; Chase, 'International Law on Films', 563.
18 A brief survey of the films commented on the aforementioned page of the ULB International Law Centre's website confirms this statement. Numerous commentaries bear on diplomatic law (*The Man Who Knew Too Much* (1956); *La valise* (1973); *Columbo* (season 5): *A Case of Immunity* (1975); *Lethal Weapon 2* (1989) and *The Interpreter* (2005)), on human rights and humanitarian law (*The Bridge on the River Kwai* (1957); *Paths of Glory* (1957); *Bridget Jones's Diary* (2001 and 2004); *Waltz with Bashir* (2008), *Inglourious Basterds* (2009); *Hatufim (Prisoners of War)* (2010–12); *The Ghost Writer* (2010), *Scandal* (2012); *Hannah Arendt* (2013); *American Sniper* (2014); *Good Kill* (2014); *Homeland* (season 5, 2015)), while others focus on the principle of non-intervention and the prohibition of the use of force (*The Sand Pebbles* (1967); *Bananas* (1971); *The Rescuers* (1977); *Air Force One* (1997); *Quai d'Orsay* (2013); *Game of Thrones* (2011–14)).
19 See, for example, Michael Ryan and Douglas Kellner, *Camera Politica: The Politics and Ideology of Contemporary Hollywood Film* (Bloomington and Indianapolis: Indiana University Press, 1988); Douglas Kellner, *Cinema Wars. Hollywood Film and Politics in the Bush-Cheney Era* (Chichester: Blackwell, 2010); Régis Dubois, *Hollywood, Cinéma et idéologie* (Paris: Editions Sulliver, 2008); Laurent Aknin, *Mythe et idéologie du cinéma américain* (Paris: Editions Vendemiaire, 2012); Anne-Marie Bidaud, *Hollywood et le rêve américain. Cinéma et idéologie aux Etats-Unis* (Paris: Armand Colin, 2nd edn, 2017). See also Shlomo Sand, *Le XXème siècle à l'écran* (Paris: Seuil, 2004).

specific legal analysis. This can be evidenced by the work of Serge Sur, a specialist of both international law and international relations, who has published extensively on the analysis of cinematographic productions. His book *Plaisirs du cinéma. Le monde et ses miroirs*, published in 2010, offers a highly specialised study on classical and recent films, without focusing on international law as such.[20]

Before concluding this general panoramic state of the art, we should mention two studies authored by members of the ULB International Law Centre that have inspired this book more or less directly. The first is Barbara Delcourt's article 'A propos du film *Bosna*. Analyse d'un discours idéal-type sur le conflit yougoslave', published in 1997, that deconstructs the discourse developed by its director Bernard-Henri Lévy on the conflict in the former Yugoslavia. The author reveals that Lévy's discourse is fraught with a number of representations obviously intended to foster support for the Bosnian government at the time in the context of the war.[21] Although the author grounds her analysis mainly in theoretical tools relating to political science and international relations, the article does have a legal dimension, which, while incidental, is not devoid of interest. Indeed, Barbara Delcourt argues that the conception of human rights emerging from the film is associated with a largely apolitical theory, that is characterised by justice or moral being conceived as 'natural', and, therefore, essentialist or absolutist in nature.[22] In other words, the promoted legal discourse is closely linked to *jus naturalism*, more specifically to a pre-modern understanding of the term, in that it distances itself from modern conceptions of reason. The second study on which this book draws is the article 'Cinéma et idéologie: représentation et fonction du terrorisme dans le film d'action hollywoodien', authored by François Dubuisson in 2004.[23] In this study, the author analyses how films depict terrorists as the incarnation of the 'opposite' of the United States and, consequently, how, through this projected image, films justify US hegemony

---

20 Serge Sur, *Plaisirs du cinéma. Le monde et ses miroirs* (Paris: France-Empire Monde, 2010). This book is composed of previously published articles, mainly in various *Mélanges*.
21 Barbara Delcourt, 'A propos du film *Bosna*. Analyse d'un discours idéal-type sur le conflit yougoslave', (1997) 207 *Cahiers marxistes* 97–9.
22 An analogous train of thought is developed, with respect to an entirely different production, by Jean-Baptiste Jeangène Vilmer, *24 heures chrono. Le choix du mal* (Paris: Presses Universitaires de France, 2012), 150–2.
23 The article is reproduced in Olivier Corten and Barbara Delcourt (eds), 'Les Guerres antiterroristes' (2004) 105 *Contradictions*, 53–79, available at: https://dipot.ulb.ac.be/dspace/bitstream/2013/133588/3/cinema_terrorisme.pdf, accessed 1 December 2019.

in international relations.[24] Again, the article does not analyse international law as such. Nevertheless, the study has undeniably inspired the Centre's project, mainly with respect to the method used. A particular mention should be made here of the high number of productions analysed. Moreover, it was decided to include mainstream productions which are generally considered as having little or no artistic cinematographic value, but which prove to be highly relevant as illustrations of a certain ideology. This is all the more so given that, in many cases, the impact of such productions goes beyond the small circle of cinephiles and reaches a wide audience.

Very recently, after the publication of the proceedings of the conference held by the International Law Centre,[25] several studies have been published, which specifically analyse the place of international law in films, mainly in the field of international criminal justice.[26]

24 See also Stephen Prince, *Firestorm: American Film in the Age of Terrorism* (New York: Columbia University Press, 2009).
25 Since then, the conference organizers have published several articles on international law and film: Olivier Corten, '"A la Maison-Blanche": le président des Etats-Unis se soucie-t-il du droit international lorsqu'il décide d'une intervention militaire?' European Society of International Law, 10th Anniversary Conference (4–6 September 2014, Vienna), http://dx.doi.org/10.2139/ssrn.2546414, accessed 1 December 2019; Olivier Corten, 'La mise en scène des doctrines interventionnistes dans les films étasuniens: Ronnie goes to Hollywood!' in Ninon Maillard, Stéphane Boiron and Nathalie Goedert (eds), *Les lois de la guerre. Guerre, droit et cinéma* (Clermont Ferrand: Institut Universitaire Varenne, 2015), 175–95; Olivier Corten, 'La banalisation de la torture comme un instrument de lutte contre le terrorisme: comme au cinéma?' (2017) 79:2 *Revue interdisciplinaire d'etudes juridiques* 229–51; Olivier Corten, 'Le droit d'intervention humanitaire: comme au cinéma', in Ivon Mingashang (ed.), *La responsabilité du juriste face aux manifestations de la crise dans la société contemporaine: Un regard croisé autour de la pratique du droit par le professeur Auguste Mampuya* (Bruxelles: Larcier, 2018), 247–70; Olivier Corten, 'La représentation des frontières dans les films d'action: la fin des territoires?' in Estelle Epinoux, Vincent Lefebve and Magalie Flores-Lonjou (eds), *Frontière(s) au cinéma* (Paris: Editions Mare et Martin, 2019) 363–80; François Dubuisson, 'Frontières et droit international dans les films concernant le conflit israélo-palestinien' in Estelle Epinoux, Vincent Lefebve and Magalie Flores-Lonjou (eds), *Frontière(s) au cinéma* (Paris: Editions Mare et Martin, 2019) 381–402; Anne Lagerwall, 'La répression des crimes internationaux à l'écran: l'apologie d'une justice sans frontières' in Estelle Epinoux, Vincent Lefebve and Magalie Flores-Lonjou (eds), *Frontière(s) au cinéma* (Paris: Editions Mare et Martin, 2019) 403–26.
26 See Kirsten Ainley, Stephen Humphreys and Immi Tallgren (eds), 'International Criminal Justice on/and Film', dossier published in (2018) 6:1 *London Review of International Law*; Immi Tallgren, 'Come and See? The Power of Images and International Criminal Justice' (2017) 17:2 *International Criminal Law Review* 259–80; Immi Tallgren, 'Watching *Tokyo Trial*' (2017) 5:2 *London Review of International Law* 291–316; Zahra Emamzadeh and Sabbar Shaho, 'How Can Cinema Justify Wars: A Qualitative Study on War Justification in American Cinema'

In the end, we find ourselves before a state of the art both rich, in the sense that it encompasses a great number of studies, and rather poor, in that international law as such comes up in these studies very rarely, or is subject to specific analysis only in a limited number of publications released a short time ago. As for methodology, the approaches followed vary greatly. Three main tendencies may be distinguished:

- a tendency to adopt a strict legal analysis when domestic law is examined in relation to films;
- the rising of studies of a critical character, focusing on the connection between cinema and ideology, both from legal scholars already associated with critical schools of legal thought and from specialists in international relations or political science;
- the taking into account of appreciations of a purely cinematographic character, integrating artistic or aesthetic considerations, more frequently found in studies authored by film specialists.[27]

This last aspect will not be taken up in this book, which is written by experts in law not in cinema. Therefore, the reader will not find in the following pages specific developments on narrative structures nor on the effects of specific techniques, such as travelling or framing.[28] Such aspects will only be addressed to the extent necessary to interpret the meaning of a film or scene, and to clarify the significance that can be given to the reference made to rules of international law. Thus, it is mainly the first two of the tendencies mentioned above that will be explored, and particularly the second one. That being said, it is important to give some indications of the approach followed by the contributions composing the book.

International law and films: a diversity of methods and approaches

The fact that the relationship between cinema and international law has not been studied yet – not in a book covering different aspects of international law in any case – is not an obstacle in defining a coherent methodology

---

(2017) 10 *Journal of Politics and Law* 18–24; Daniel Joyce and Gabrielle Simm, 'Zero Dark Thirty: International Law, Film and Representation' (2015) 3:2 *London Review of International Law* 295–318.

[27] See, for example, Jacques Aumont and Michel Marie, *L'analyse de film* (Paris: Armand Colin, 3rd edn, 2015); Diana Gonzalez-Duclert, *Le film événement* (Paris, Armand Colin, 2012); Laurent Jullier, *L'analyse de séquences* (Paris: Armand Colin, 4th edn, 2015); Anne Goliot-Lété and Francis Vanoye, *Précis d'analyse filmique* (Paris: Armand Colin, 4th edn, 2015).

[28] See, for example, Elie Yazbek, *Montage et idéologie dans le cinéma américain contemporain* (Riga: Editions Universitaires Européennes, 2010).

for such a study. The existing literature shows that there is no 'natural' choice of methodology for this subject. Thus, caution is needed in defining the approach to be followed. Moreover, this approach should be set out as clearly and in as much detail as possible. The aforementioned state of the art points to a pluralism of methods and interdisciplinarity. In this context, instead of embarking in a general theoretical and epistemological reflection, we thought it better to explore the different methodological possibilities through the example of *The Bridge on the River Kwai* mentioned above. In understanding this example, the starting point is a general theoretical framework that distinguishes between the various schools of legal thought such as legal dogmatics (in French *'technique juridique'* or *'dogmatique juridique'*), philosophy of law, theory of law and sociology of law.[29] We believe this distinction to be efficient and useful in analysing any subject, including new and original ones, from the perspective of legal science. In the following lines, we will apply this framework to *The Bridge on the River Kwai*, in order to better understand its implications and illustrate as concretely as possible the different methodological possibilities explored throughout this publication.

A first option would be to confront the cinematographic discourse to the generally accepted interpretation of current positive law. This approach is extensively illustrated by the studies analysing the relationship between cinema and domestic law, mentioned above. For example, in the scene from *The Bridge on the River Kwai* presented above, we could ask ourselves which of the two officers – Lieutenant Colonel Nicholson or Colonel Saito – is correct from a strictly legal point of view. Lieutenant Colonel Nicholson obviously grounds his arguments on conventional law, invoking the Geneva Convention relative to the treatment of prisoners of war adopted on 27 July 1929. However, at the time the film's action takes place, the convention had forty-two States parties, including the United Kingdom (which ratified the convention in 1931),[30] the United States and Germany, but ... not Japan, which, contrary to the UK, never signed nor adhered to the convention. It is thus difficult to consider that Japan, and consequently Colonel Saito, was bound by the convention as such. It remains to be seen whether article 27

---

29 Olivier Corten, *Méthodologie du droit international public* (Brussels: Editions de l'Université de Bruxelles, 2009), chapter 1, section 1. The cited publication distinguishes between the philosophy of law and theory of law. However, in the context of this contribution, such distinction will not be necessary since the theoretical and philosophical approaches are closely intertwined when applied to the relationship between international law and cinema.

30 The United Kingdom became party to the convention on 26 June 1931; see www.icrc.org/applic/ihl/dih.nsf/States.xsp?xp_viewStates=XPages_NORMStatesParties&xp_treatySelected=305, accessed 1 December 2019.

of the convention – according to which the work of officers is prohibited – could be binding on the Japanese authorities by another means. To this end, we can turn to article 6 of the 1907 Hague Regulations, which entered into force on 26 January 1910. This article provides that '[t]he State may utilize the labour of prisoners of war according to their rank and aptitude, *officers excepted*'.[31] This last instrument was ratified by both the United Kingdom, on 27 November 1909, and Japan, on 13 December 1911.[32] Japan had made a reservation concerning article 44 of the Regulations but not concerning article 6.[33] The emphasised words are all the more significant as they were introduced in 1907 and did not appear in article 6 of the 1899 Hague Regulations.[34] According to certain sources, in a directive dated 5 August 1937, Emperor Hirohito had decided that the constraints set out in international humanitarian law would not be applied to the treatment of Chinese prisoners of war.[35] Even if this directive is interpreted extensively as applying equally to British prisoners of war in Burma, it is difficult to see how this unilateral declaration could be sufficient to set aside the application of the aforementioned rule. In any case, in relation to the 1907 Hague Regulations, the Nuremberg Military Tribunal held that:

> [t]he rules on land warfare expressed in the Convention undoubtedly represented an advance over existing international law at the time of their adoption [...] [B]ut by 1939 these rules laid down in the Convention were recognized by all civilized nations, and were regarded as being declaratory of the laws and customs of war.[36]

In this context, if we look at the scene between Lieutenant Colonel Nicholson and Colonel Saito exclusively from the perspective of legal dogmatics, Lieutenant Colonel Nicholson is both wrong and right: he is wrong in invoking a treaty by which Japan is not bound, but he is right since the rule contained in the relevant article binds the Japanese authorities through the

---

31 Emphasis added. Regulations annexed to the Convention (IV) respecting the Laws and Customs of War on Land, The Hague, 18 October 1907.
32 www.icrc.org/applic/ihl/dih.nsf/States.xsp?xp_viewStates=XPages_ NORMStatesParties&xp_treatySelected=195, accessed 1 December 2019.
33 www.icrc.org/applic/ihl/dih.nsf/Article.xsp?action=openDocument&documentId=B6 A5BDD40E9ADA5BC12563BD002BA3FF, accessed 1 December 2019.
34 According to this article '[t]he State may utilize the labour of prisoners of war according to their rank and aptitude'. There is thus no exception for officers and assimilated military personnel.
35 http://fr.wikipedia.org/wiki/Crimes_de_guerre_du_Japon_Shōwa#Travail_forc. C3.A9.
36 *Trial of the Major War Criminals before the International Military Tribunal*, Nuremberg, 14 November 1945 – 1 October 1946, Nuremberg, 1947, vol. I, pp. 253–4.

application of another treaty, as well as under customary international law. In short, under the applicable legal framework, Lieutenant Colonel Nicholson was within his rights, even if it was for reasons that he undoubtedly ignored.

These technical developments provide an analysis related essentially to legal positivism. This approach could further be enlarged by integrating reflections relating to the philosophy of law or the theory of law. Such considerations would point to questions concerning whether the invoked legal rule is fundamentally just or unjust and to the different conceptions of justice animating the parties involved. Why does the invoked rule distinguish between, on the one hand, soldiers, which can be subjected to manual labour, and, on the other, officers and assimilated personnel, which cannot? Lieutenant Colonel Nicholson asserts this rule to be part of 'the laws of the civilised world' and does not consider it necessary to cite any supplementary source of legitimacy. Aside from that, the British officer seems to adopt a reasoning exuding a rigid, if not narrow-minded, legal formalism. This is evidenced by another scene of the film, where he explains to a group of amazed officers that the order of rendition formerly transmitted by the British hierarchy implies a formal obligation not to escape. This formalism will make him actively collaborate with the Japanese in order to ensure, as efficiently as possible, the construction of a bridge destined to improve the operational capacity of the Japanese army against the British. Lieutenant Colonel Nicholson follows his logic to the letter until the end of the film, trying to prevent soldiers sent by the British chief of staff with the mission to destroy the bridge from doing so. For Lieutenant Colonel Nicholson, the order implies obedience to the law, particularly to the letter of the law, as absurd as the consequences on the ground may be. As for Colonel Saito, he refers to the *bushido*, the Japanese code of honour. If we understand correctly the logic of that code, as the Colonel himself presents it before the previously discussed dialogue with Lieutenant Colonel Nicholson, surrender is inconceivable for a true soldier. If a soldier does surrender – and he accuses the British officers of having condoned or preferred this option – he can no longer pretend to be a soldier. He is nothing more than a simple prisoner totally submitted to the will of the enemy:

> English prisoners! Notice, I do not say 'English soldiers'. From the moment you surrendered you ceased to be soldiers [...] Your officers will work beside you. This is only just, for it is they who betrayed you by surrender. Your shame is their dishonour. It is they who told you: better to live like a coolie than to die like a hero [...] Therefore, they will join you in useful labour.

Aside from the *jus naturalist* connotations of this speech (the Japanese morals seem to be established as the only just ones, under the circumstances), Colonel Saito appears to be a 'realist', who does not preoccupy himself too much with legal considerations. The scene where he throws the Geneva Convention on the ground is emblematic in this respect. It is also not the only one. In another scene, when a British officer comes to plead the case for Lieutenant Colonel Nicholson and invokes again the force of the law, Saito replies: 'Do not speak to me of rules! This is war! This is not a game of cricket!' Thus, the two officers embody two conflicting visions of law: the British officer puts forth a conception of justice and law associating legal formalism with an incidental reference to a universal natural law (the laws of the civilized world); the Japanese officer personifies a view composed of particular morals (the Japanese code of honour) and realist considerations, insisting on the limits of law, especially in wartime. Under this approach, it is not the legal evaluation of whether the British position is in conformity with positive law or not (for example, are the British officers obliged by law to work?) that is of interest. The interesting part resides in exposing the diversity and confronting the conceptions about law and justice that are depicted in *The Bridge on the River Kwai*.

Aside from issues relating either to legal dogmatics or to a philosophical and theoretical dimension of the law, another possible approach would be a more sociological one, aiming at placing the discourse presented in the film into the social and political context of the film's production. Here, the main issue is not to determine what is formally legal or fundamentally legitimate and how the arguments are framed in this regard; it is to understand and explain how such a conception of legality or legitimacy imposes itself concretely. Thus, the analysis is centred on the legitimation process, that is on the process of constructing something as legitimate and of receiving the product of this construction. To come back to our example, *The Bridge on the River Kwai* shows how much the success of a discourse depends on power relations rather than on the inherent and abstract validity of the discourse as such. After having refused to comply with Saito's initial order, Lieutenant Colonel Nicholson agrees to cooperate with the construction of the bridge, provided that he is assigned to a task related to the conception and direction of the works and not to manual labour. This solution is more than satisfactory to Colonel Saito, who wishes to accomplish his mission irrespective of the means used. In the end, article 27 of the Geneva Convention was applied for reasons linked neither to legality nor to legitimacy. On a more prosaic level, its application was the result of a temporary – and thus relative and precarious – balance of powers. Consequently, no 'law of the civilised world', no abstract universality, be it of a legal norm or of a principle of justice, can be considered binding as such. In the final scene of the film, Lieutenant Colonel Nicholson tries in vain, and somewhat pathetically, to avoid the destruction of the bridge by soldiers from his own side. On a more general level, this undermining of

Lieutenant Colonel Nicholson could be interpreted as a denunciation of an obsolete discourse about the superiority of the British war culture. It should be reminded that the film was distributed in 1957, one year after the Suez crisis, which undoubtedly marks the inevitable decline of the British and French empires. In this context, Nicholson's conservative rhetoric may be pointing to the gap between the evolution of international relations and certain traditional political and legal colonial perceptions.[37]

Aside from the various hypotheses and reasonings to which they point, the three approaches sketched out above (strictly legal, philosophical/theoretical, and sociological) illustrate the diversity of the possible ways to understand the relationship between cinema and international law. In the following chapters, it was left to each contributor to articulate two or more of these approaches. The only constant is that the contributors do not limit themselves to one single approach. A strictly formalist analysis may certainly be interesting, especially in the context of the teaching of international law. Indeed, films offer a quasi-inexhaustible number of case studies, where one can either identify a legal argument, or – more frequently – find illustrations of possible violations of established rules.[38] Nevertheless, in this book, the main approach is a broader one: beyond the technical aspects, the book's focus is on the conceptions of the rule, or of law in general, that are conveyed by the analysed material. This approach does not exclude the development of a classical legal interpretation. It tends to complete such an interpretation with a perspective taking more into account the representations of a cinematographic production – and thus its ideological dimension.

Presenting a representation: taking ideology into account and its consequences

For the purposes of this book, we will rely on the following – regularly used in the literature[39] – definition of ideology: a system (having its own

---

37 For a similar perspective, see the debate on the ULB International Law Centre's website: http://cdi.ulb.ac.be/le-pont-de-la-riviere-kwai/#comments, accessed 1 December 2019.

38 For an example of the use of film extracts for illustrative and educational purposes, see: Olivier Corten, François Dubuisson, Vaios Koutroulis and Anne Lagerwall, *A Critical Introduction to International Law* (Bruxelles: Editions de l'Université de Bruxelles, 2019).

39 See Régis Dubois, *Hollywood, cinéma et idéologie* (Paris: Editions Sulliver, 2008); Barry Langford, *Post-Classical Hollywood: Film Industry, Style and Ideology Since 1945* (Edinburgh: Edinburgh University Press, 2010).

logic and rigour) of representations (images, myths, ideas or concepts, as the case may be) endowed with a historical existence and role within a given society.[40] Under this definition, ideology does not have a pejorative character and, therefore, highlighting its existence has no denunciatory aim.[41] In this perspective, this book has a double objective: first, to identify representations of international law in the cinematographic productions, and, second, to try to determine some of the functions fulfilled by these representations.

The first objective consists in detecting, behind the image and dialogue, the ways of thinking, especially of thinking about international law, which are present in the analysed works. In this regard, three main cases may arise. First, the rule of international law to which the film refers is presented in a way that can be considered (rather) faithful to the interpretation generally given to it. Then, conversely, the rule can be presented in a way that deviates more or less widely from that which is usually accepted. Finally, it is also possible to note the absence of any reference to a relevant rule of international law, in a narrative context where one would logically expect it to be mentioned (for example, in the case of a military attack likely to affect civilians). The mere identification of one of these three hypotheses does not in itself give any answer to the question of determining the representation of international law that is conveyed by the film. This will require an additional step of analysis, taking into consideration the place and function given to the reference (or absence of reference) to international law in the logic of the film narrative or in that of a particular scene.

This approach does not imply a belief in an unequivocal reality, in this case in the correct meaning of law, something that runs completely counter to the generally accepted relative character of legal interpretation.[42] This does not imply that the fundamental lack of determination of the law

---

40 Louis Althusser, *Pour Marx* (Paris: La Découverte-poche, 1996) 238. Translated by the authors. In the original French version, the definition is the following: 'système (possédant sa logique et sa rigueur propres) de représentations (images, mythes, idées ou concepts selon les cas) doué d'une existence et d'un rôle historiques au sein d'une société donnée'.

41 Raymond Boudon, *L'idéologie ou l'origine des idées reçues* (Paris: Fayard, 1986) 30ff. For applications in law, see Michel Troper, 'L'idéologie juridique' in G. Duprat (ed.), *Analyse de l'idéologie* (Paris: Galilée, 1980) 223ff.; Olivier Corten and Annemie Schaus, *Le droit comme idéologie. Introduction critique au droit belge* (Bruxelles: Editions de l'Université de Bruxelles, 2nd edn, 2009); Olivier Corten and Barbara Delcourt, *Ex-Yougoslavie: droit international, politique et idéologie* (Bruxelles: Bruylant, 2008).

42 See especially Richard Rorty, *The Linguistic Turn: Essays in Philosophical Method* (Chicago: University of Chicago Press, 1992).

precludes any scientific and rational analysis. It simply means that such an analysis will be nothing more than an interpretation, whose validity will depend not on its objective conformity with a set of unique rules and principles, but on its ability to convince an ideal 'community of lawyers' in a given time and place.[43] Therefore, this approach consists in comparing the interpretations and representations of law amongst lawyers to the ones depicted in cinematographic productions. It goes without saying that this inevitably involves a degree of subjectivity, since art works are particularly open to several meanings and interpretations.[44] In this respect, it will always be essential to correctly assess the scope and meaning of the scenes and dialogues, placed in the general context of the film. The comments made by a specific character, reflecting a particular conception of international law, will not inevitably reflect the vision conveyed by the film's authors. It will therefore be necessary to establish what is the general meaning of the movie, and how a particular scene or dialogue fits into it, which may be more or less easy, some productions offering a very binary message while others propose a more complex and dialectic reflection.

After having determined the type of filmic representation of the rule of international law, the next step is to examine the reasons for such representation. This is the object of the second aspect of the book's approach, which is dedicated to the roles and functions of the representation of international law. Identifying the relevant cinematographic representations of international law and highlighting possible matches, nuances and oppositions is an analysis essentially grounded on either legal dogmatics, or on the philosophy and theory of law. Inquiring about the functions of such representations has a more sociological connotation. This inquiry implies taking into account the political context of the production and reception of these representations, while integrating other factors linked to the strategy of the stakeholders and, when appropriate, to the mechanisms of reception

---

43 See Oscar Schachter, 'The Invisible College of International Lawyers' (1977–1978) 72 *Northwestern University Law Review* 217ff.; Jean d'Aspremont, *Epistemic Forces in International Law* (Cheltenham: Edward Elgar, 2015); Jean d'Aspremont, *International Law as a Belief System* (Cambridge: Cambridge University Press, 2017).

44 See Sand, *Le XXème siècle à l'écran*, 239; Michael Ryan and Melissa Lenos, *An Introduction to Film Analysis: Technique and Meaning in Narrative Film* (London: Bloomsbury Academic, 2012); John Gibbs and Doug Pye (eds), *Style and Meaning: Studies in the Detailed Analysis of Film* (Manchester: Manchester University Press, 2011); Harry Benshoff, *Film and Television Analysis: An Introduction to Methods, Theories, and Approaches* (London: Routledge, 2015); Sian Barber, *Using Film as a Source* (Manchester: Manchester University Press, 2015).

in order to evaluate the extent of such reception.⁴⁵ If this inquiry were to be comprehensively conducted, it would imply sophisticated empirical studies, including, for example, conducting interviews with directors or producers and taking into account surveys and opinion polls measuring the impact of the various representations. Such ambitions surpass, however, the scope of this book, composed of contributions of a general or transversal character and certainly not of comprehensive studies of one particular cinematographic work. Therefore, in most cases, the contributors will formulate certain hypotheses or point towards certain explanations, without pretending to reach definitive conclusions.

The approach has an explicative not an evaluative objective. For example, it does not aim at denouncing a manipulation, much less a conspiracy, in order to alter an authentic legal interpretation, nor at presenting cinema as a mere propaganda tool.⁴⁶ Furthermore, arguably, the efficiency of an ideology is based on its autonomy; it depends on representations being considered as evident or natural and becoming spontaneously widespread by stakeholders without any particular objective or political interest.⁴⁷ Our objective is to show how, and when appropriate why, cinematographic representations objectively (that is, outside or independently of their creators' intentions) depart from interpretations of rules generally accepted by lawyers. In this context, it should be mentioned that the whole approach relies on the conviction that films and TV series exercise a certain influence on viewers, even if this influence is hard to demonstrate with precision. In that sense, the book

> is based on the premise that hundreds of thousands of representations 'viewed' by masses of women and men since the creation of cinema [...] have modelled, through the years, part of their historical conscience and sensibility.⁴⁸

---

45 See Michel Condé, *Cinéma et fiction. Essai sur la réception filmique* (Paris: L'Harmattan, 2016).

46 Courmont and Benezet, *Washington-Hollywood*, 10. These authors claim that influence between Washington and Hollywood is reciprocal. See also Matthew Alford, *Reel Power: Hollywood Cinema and American Supremacy* (London: Pluto Press, 2010).

47 Bidaud, *Hollywood et le rêve américain*, 46. According to Sand, a large part of the population acquires more historical knowledge through 'historical' films than through the study on history books: *Le XXème siècle à l'écran*, 474–5.

48 Sand, *Le XXème siècle à l'écran*, 18. Translated by the authors. In the French original the text goes as follows: 'repose sur le présupposé que les centaines de milliers de représentations "visionnées" par des masses de femmes et d'hommes depuis la naissance du cinéma [...] ont modelé, au fil des ans, une part de leur conscience et de leur sensibilité historiques'.

From this point of view, cinema must be seen as an integral part of 'pop culture'. This notion covers several dimensions, depending on whether it is considered from the perspective of culture receptors or producers.[49] First, in terms of receptors, the concept is opposed to an elitist culture that would be the prerogative of the upper classes. It is then assimilated to a mass culture, largely transcending the demarcation lines drawn within our societies. In this context, another characteristic of pop culture is its transnationalization and the resulting globalization of the public, a phenomenon that has resulted both in a certain universality of dominant cultural codes (especially Anglo-Saxon) and an innovative combination of materials from a wide variety of origins. Then, on the producers' side, 'pop culture' covers the idea of reappropriating and mixing various elements of culture, history and daily life into new creations. In this respect, cinema appears to be a particularly emblematic and influential element of pop culture. Movies will contribute significantly to the public's perception of many sides of reality, and in particular, for what we're interested in, of various aspects of international law.

Pointing to the specificities of an interpretation or conception of law conveyed by a cinematographic production acquires an obvious interest on the basis of this premise. Moreover, this same premise explains why the material on which each of the subsequent analyses is based is mainly composed of films and TV series targeting a wide audience. Naturally, the material relevant to each contribution has its own specificities, which will be exposed in due course. As can be seen from the various filmographies, there has been an effort to ground the analysis on a large empirical basis, with an emphasis on widely distributed productions, which are more likely to 'model' a large number of viewers' perceptions of international law. From this perspective, priority was given to films and series from the United States, and to a lesser extent, from the rest of the Western world. This priority is explained by the fact that such productions constitute a material useful for revealing representations typical of a dominating ideology.

---

49 Richard Mèmeteau, *Pop culture. Réflexions sur les industries du rêve et l'invention des identites* (Paris: La découverte, 2019); Shirley A. Fedorak, *Pop Culture: The Culture of Everyday Life* (Toronto: University of Toronto Press, 2009); Henry Jenkins, Jane Shattuc and Tara McPherson, 'Defining Popular Culture' in Henry Jenkins, Jane Shattuc and Tara McPherson (eds), *Hop on Pop: The Politics and Pleasures of Popular Culture* (Durham, NC: Duke University Press, 2003), 26–42.

An individual approach within a collective framework: some clarifications on the elaboration and orientations of the project

Before moving on to the specific studies, one last methodological comment is necessary. The scarcity of studies focusing specifically on the relationship between international law and films has already been pointed out. This results in the absence of a generally accepted approach and methodology, which would allow the analysis of this subject in a scientifically defined way. Aside from that, this also implies a choice concerning the book's content: instead of concentrating on a specific theme, this book aims to present several possible research areas in the field of international law and cinema. Different workshops have thus been established, each one of which could have been the subject of a book on its own: 'International law, reality or (science) fiction?'; 'Wars, force and police operations: which law?'; 'Justice enters the scene'; and 'Human rights on the screen'. These titles attest to the diversity of analytical possibilities available. As it was suggested earlier, the objective here is not to (try to) exhaust the subject, but rather to attempt to explore what is still, to a very large extent, unchartered waters. In this sense, we have chosen to encourage the pluralism of analyses and inquiries rather than to impose an integrated and unified reasoning which might inhibit the contributors' analysis. In this perspective, each contributor has been chosen on the basis both of his/her specialisation in a particular branch of international law and his/her motivation to participate in this innovative project.

However, in view of ensuring a general coherence, each contributor has been asked to respect the few methodological guidelines presented above and to focus on the two aforementioned objectives: to identify the representations of law in cinema or TV productions and, from a critical standpoint, to indicate some possible explanations for these representations. A conference took place in February 2014, from which a number of theoretical models emerged that proved to be operational in understanding cinematographic representations focusing on several fields. These include:

- the opposition between one single law (constitutionalist pole) and multiple normative orders not (necessarily) articulated in a coherent and hierarchical way (pluralist pole); illustrations of this opposition were mainly found in the science fiction films;
- the opposition between, on the one hand, the idea that international law and institutions provide adequate means for resolution of conflicts (idealist pole) and, on the other, the conviction that power is the only relevant and legitimate factor on the international scene (realist pole); this opposition was more – but not exclusively – evident in action movies and films focusing on international justice;

- the opposition between, on the one hand, the tendency to preserve the rigour and integrity of legal norms ('utopian' pole), and the will to adapt these rules to the specificities and evolutions in State practice ('apologetic' pole); this opposition was particularly operational in understanding the cinematographic representations of law in war films.

As already mentioned, the 2014 conference resulted in the publication of a book in French.[50] This English edition includes most of the contributions, in substantially revised and updated versions, and is enriched by a series of new transversal comments, which deepen, discuss and extend the analyses proposed in the initial articles. Each contribution found in the following pages was drafted after – and is the outcome of – all the different steps described above, characterised by intense interaction and the desire to construct a collective project.

---

50 Corten and Dubuisson, *Du droit international au cinéma*.

2

International law, guardian of the galaxy?

Marco Benatar

Even in the far reaches of space, debates over international law rage on. Nowhere more so than on Third Earth, where the *ThunderCats*,[1] a motley crew of feline humanoids, engage in a heated argument over the prohibition of warp gas, a chemical weapon which toys with the emotional state of sentient beings. Having witnessed their foes, fearsome mutants, spray the outlawed gas on their victims, a conversation ensues amongst the *ThunderCats* (season 1, episode 4, 1985):

Tygra: So that's it! Warp gas!
Panthro: I thought the Interstellar Council ruled against warp gas?!
Cheetara: When did the mutants ever go by the rules?
Tygra: Rules are only meaningful if people agree to follow them, otherwise they're just words!

For over a century, the science fiction universe has excelled in diversity and creativity, telling tales of contact with extra-terrestrial life, dealings with diabolic artificial intelligence, journeys through black holes and cybernetic dystopias. But beyond the futuristic thrills, the genre has enabled us to reflect upon the major political questions of our era. This should not come as a surprise, for science fiction is replete with scenarios set in the future extrapolating from contemporary knowledge and experience – not only in the realm of science and technology but also in respect of societal structures.[2] Through the creation of alternative worlds,[3] in which humans

---

The author wishes to thank Olivier Corten, Mark Pollack, Lisa O'Leary, Sanjivi Krishnan and Robert Beta Arts for their valuable comments. The opinions expressed are those of the author and do not reflect the views of the International Tribunal for the Law of the Sea.

1 Tobin Wolf, USA, 1985–89.
2 Pierre-Jérôme Delage, 'Introduction' in Pierre-Jérôme Delage (ed.), *Science-fiction et science juridique* (Paris: IRJS Editions, 2013) 14. See also Brooks Landon, 'Extrapolation and Speculation' in Rob Latham (ed.), *The Oxford Handbook of Science Fiction* (New York: Oxford University Press, 2014).
3 On the relationship between counterfactual thought and international law, see Ingo Venzke, 'What If? Counterfactual (Hi)Stories of International Law' (2018) 8 *Asian J Intl L* 403.

International law, guardian of the galaxy? 21

(and non-humans) interact, establish institutions and govern, science fiction takes on a political dimension. The upshot is that a fair number of television series and movies address matters of a legal nature, thereby confirming that the legal maxim *ubi societas, ibi ius* ('wherever there is society, there is law') holds true even in galaxies far, far away.

Exploring the intersection of legal science and science fiction is hardly a novelty.[4] Many law review articles have used genre classics as a gateway to discuss topics as varied as the lawfulness of cloning and the impact of new technologies on individual freedoms. In contrast to their colleagues at international relations departments,[5] international lawyers seem less inclined to boldly go in this direction.[6] This is worth remedying, as major themes can fruitfully be debated through movies and television: the notion of a global or even 'intergalactic' order governing relations between sovereign actors, the law of treaties, human rights, environmental law ... The next few

---

4 See e.g. Mitchell Travis, 'Making Space: Law and Science Fiction' (2011) 23 *Law and Literature* 241; Cass R. Sunstein, 'How Star Wars Illuminates Constitutional Law' (2015) https://papers.ssrn.com/sol3/papers.cfm?abstract_id=2604998, accessed 1 December 2019; Fabrice Defferrard (ed.), *Le droit saisi par la science-fiction* (Paris: Mare et Martin, 2016).

5 See e.g. Daniel W. Drezner, *Theories of International Politics and Zombies* (Princeton and Oxford: Princeton University Press, 2011); Stefan Engert and Alexander Spencer, 'International Relations at the Movies: Teaching and Learning about International Politics through Film' (2009) 17 *Perspectives* 83; Nicholas J. Kiersey and Iver B. Neumann (eds), Battlestar Galactica *and International Relations* (New York: Routledge, 2013); Jutta Weldes (ed.), *To Seek Out New Worlds: Exploring Links between Science Fiction and World Politics* (Gordonsville: Palgrave Macmillan, 2003); Stephen Benedict Dyson, *Otherworldly Politics: The International Relations of Star Trek, Game of Thrones, and Battlestar Galactica* (Baltimore: Johns Hopkins University Press, 2015).

6 See however Roy Balleste, 'The Earth Alliance Constitution: International Human Rights Law and Babylon 5' (2008) 10 *Florida Coastal L Rev* 33; Orna Ben-Naftali and Zvi Triger, 'The Human Conditioning: International Law and Science-Fiction' (2018) 14 *Law, Culture and the Humanities* 6–44; Shai Lavi, 'Cloning International Law: The Science and Science Fiction of Human Cloning and Stem-Cell Patenting' (2018) 14 *Law, Culture and the Humanities* 83–99; Damien Roets, 'Le crime d'agression interplanétaire' in Pierre-Jérôme Delage (ed.), *Science-fiction et science juridique* (Paris: IRJS Editions, 2013) 349. The oeuvre of China Miéville deserves special mention. Having defended a PhD on international law earlier in his career (China Miéville, *Between Equal Rights: A Marxist Theory of International Law* (Leiden: Brill, 2005)), he has emerged as a leading author of speculative fiction. Academics have noted the influence of his scholarly work on his fictional writings and have used his novels to reflect on international legal themes (see e.g. Carl Freedman, 'Speculative Fiction and International Law: The Marxism of China Miéville' (2006) 20 *Socialism and Democracy* 25; Douglas Guilfoyle, 'Reading *The City and the City* as an International Lawyer: Reflections on Territoriality, Jurisdiction and Transnationality' (2016) 4 *London Rev Intl L* 195).

pages are strewn with examples of scenarios and scenes touching upon the fundamental or more technical aspects of international law.

This chapter examines the science fiction genre to the exclusion of works of fantasy. Whereas the first category takes leaps into the future informed by current knowledge, the latter conjures up imaginary worlds full of scientifically inexplicable elements – stories about magic, ghouls and ghosts would fit the bill admirably. Despite this exclusion, it would be remiss not to mention the influence of the fantastical on oral pleadings before international courts and tribunals, where works like *Alice in Wonderland*,[7] *Game of Thrones*[8] and *Pirates of the Caribbean*[9] have been quoted with varying rates of success.[10] Based on the viewing of many films, the following central thesis will be offered: future worlds portrayed in science fiction reproduce the tensions underlying contemporary theoretical approaches to the international legal order. This includes illustrations of constitutionalism, idealism and realism.[11] The basic tenets of each doctrine will be outlined, after which I will discuss a few movies and television series that best convey the approach in question. In the final part, I will seek to explain why contemporary approaches have come to be reproduced in science fiction and highlight some factors influencing the choice of certain theoretical approaches over others.

A constitutional dream: 'A sort of United Nations on the planetary level …'

A popular understanding of constitutionalism is that of an order built around an (un)written constitution establishing and/or regulating political

---

7 See e.g. *Legality of Use of Force (Serbia and Montenegro v United Kingdom)* (Provisional Measures) [1999] CR 1999/34 (Greenwood) 11; *Maritime Delimitation and Territorial Questions between Qatar and Bahrain (Qatar v Bahrain)* (Merits) [2000] CR 2000/9 (David) 25; *Territorial and Maritime Dispute (Nicaragua v Colombia)* (Application by Costa Rica for Permission to Intervene) [2010] CR 2010/13 (Reichler) 32.

8 *Arctic Sunrise Case (Kingdom of the Netherlands v Russian Federation)* (Provisional Measures) [2013] ITLOS/PV.13/A22/1/Rev.1 (Lefeber) 27 ('Winter is coming').

9 *Territorial and Maritime Dispute (Nicaragua v Colombia)* (Merits) [2012] CR 2012/14 (Reichler) 43.

10 References to works of science fiction have also found their way into case law. See e.g. *Territorial and Maritime Dispute (Nicaragua v Colombia)* (Application by Honduras for Permission to Intervene) [2010] CR 2010/22 (Pellet) 14 (mentioning *Back to the Future*); *Questions relating to the Seizure and Detention of Certain Documents and Data (Timor-Leste v Australia)* (Provisional Measures) (Separate Opinion of Judge Cançado Trindade) [2014] ICJ Rep 147, 187 (quoting *Nineteen Eighty-Four*).

11 A presentation of these approaches can be found in the introduction to this book.

institutions. Alongside the attribution of powers to these public bodies and the granting of fundamental rights to individuals, a system of checks and balances is put in place to keep the exercise of power within accepted bounds.[12] Two major schools of thought can be discerned, the first being the so-called 'classic' school. According to its adherents, a constitution encapsulates transcendent, invariable values. Conversely, the 'functional' school views constitutions as undergoing constant evolution in tandem with societal changes and opts for a flexible approach more suited to meet the needs of daily governance.[13]

As a model for individual States, constitutionalism does not have a true counterpart at the international level. After all, the international legal order is essentially a decentralized structure, lacking a constitution in the strict sense, while its principal subjects, States, have (at least formally) retained a considerable part of their sovereignty. Yet this seeming incompatibility has not stopped constitutional thought from leaving a lasting impression on international law.[14] By way of example, it would hardly be a stretch to acknowledge the impact of 'classic' constitutionalism on the emergence of *jus cogens*, the peremptory norms of international law, whereas 'functional' thinking has influenced the more recent notion of 'accountability' in the law of international organizations.[15] Amongst international lawyers, the pull of constitutionalism is apparent throughout the decades. Reference can be made, *inter alia*, to Henri La Fontaine's *magnissima charta*, a vision for a global constitution aimed at averting war,[16] the UN Charter reforms advocated by Louis B. Sohn in *World Peace Through World Law*[17] or, in

---

12 Philippe Raynaud, 'Constitutionnalisme' in Denis Alland and Stéphane Rials (eds), *Dictionnaire de la culture juridique* (Paris: Presses Universitaires de France, 2003) 266.

13 Jan Klabbers, 'Setting the Scene' in Jan Klabbers, Anne Peters and Geir Ulfstein (eds), *The Constitutionalization of International Law* (Oxford: Oxford University Press, 2009) 9.

14 On the developments that have led to greater demand for international constitutionalization, see Jeffrey L. Dunoff and Joel P. Trachtman, 'A Functional Approach to International Constitutionalization' in Jeffrey L. Dunoff and Joel P. Trachtman (eds), *Ruling the World? Constitutionalism, International Law, and Global Governance* (Cambridge: Cambridge University Press, 2009) 5–9.

15 Dunoff and Trachtman, 'A Functional Approach', 10–11.

16 Henri La Fontaine, *The Great Solution. Magnissima Charta. Essay on Evolutionary and Constructive Pacifism* (Boston: World Peace Foundation, 1916). See also Henri La Fontaine, *International Judicature* (Baltimore: American Society for Judicial Settlement of International Disputes, 1915) (outlining his proposal to establish a world supreme court).

17 Grenville Clark and Louis B. Sohn, *World Peace through World Law* (Cambridge, MA: Harvard University Press, 1958).

more recent times, the works of Richard A. Falk[18] and Bardo Fassbender.[19] Irrespective of the approach, the constitutionalist mindset conceives of a unique international order, as opposed to the pluralist model with its emphasis on multiple political and legal orders operating in a parallel, fragmented or even contradictory fashion.

Constitutionalist ideas come to the fore in science fiction, at times in extreme portrayals. An excellent example of the latter is the 'world government' trope, a sole political authority around which the remnants of humanity have coalesced:[20] the nations of earth or a collection of planets inhabited by humans come together to form a single government bent on facing existential threats, most often an alien invasion. The resulting political entity is akin to a federal State. International law of yesteryear is replaced with a quasi-national legal system of planetary proportions. Legal pluralism grounded on the coexistence of sovereign States, each with legal orders of their own, has given way to the unity of the global legal order.

This motif is evident in the movie *Starship Troopers*,[21] based on the eponymous novel by Robert A. Heinlein. In the distant future, humanity is locked in an interminable war with giant insectoids, the 'Arachnids'. In a significant scene, we witness the Federal Council in session. During that gathering, the sky marshal informs his audience of plans to attack Klendathu, the star system home to the Arachnids. The architecture of the hall bears a striking resemblance to the United Nations General Assembly; its seat, Geneva, is the host city *par excellence* of international institutions. The parallels with the contemporary era, however, stop here, as States are no longer equal and sovereign subjects, rather they are subordinate to the 'Federation'. As the plot unfolds, it becomes apparent that the Federation can rely on an impressive bureaucracy and holds considerable sway over human activity.

Yet another illustration can be gleaned from *Battlestar Galactica*,[22] which chronicles humanity's struggle against the 'Cylons', robotic humanoids

---

18 Richard A. Falk, Robert C. Johansen and Samuel S. Kim, *The Constitutional Foundations of World Peace* (Albany: State University of New York Press, 1993).
19 Bardo Fassbender, *The United Nations Charter as the Constitution of the International Community* (Leiden and Boston: Martinus Nijhoff, 2009).
20 Catherine Lu, 'World Government', *The Stanford Encyclopedia of Philosophy* (2012) http://plato.stanford.edu/archives/fall2012/entries/world-government/, accessed 1 July 2018.
21 Paul Verhoeven, USA, 1997.
22 Ronald D. Moore and Glen A. Larson, USA, 2004–9.

with genocidal intentions[23] towards their creators. A revolt launched by the oppressed Cylons ends in a truce, following which they disappear into space. After four decades, the Cylons resurface more formidable than ever. It is noteworthy that in the period preceding the return of their robotic foes, the human colonies, spread out over twelve planets, signed a treaty known as the 'Articles of Colonization', through which sovereignty was transferred to a centralized government. Such is the significance of the treaty that it is commemorated each year during a national holiday (season 1, episode 11, 2005). Thus, political unity firmly takes root to the detriment of distinct legal orders.

Pertinent examples of constitutionalism can also be found in animation. Amongst Japanese productions, the 'mecha' subgenre – depicting giant robots commanded by pilots battling it out with one another – is striking for the importance it assigns to the United Nations, either as government or supreme commander of powerful armies. The series *Gundam Wing*,[24] *Macross*[25] and *Neon Genesis Evangelion*[26] all share this storyline. The world government theme is portrayed – with a touch of sarcasm – in the series *Futurama*.[27] In the thirty-first century, the United States of Earth is ruled by the head of Richard Nixon preserved in a container. Earth is a member of the Democratic Order of Planets (D.O.O.P.), an ill-conceived interplanetary organization openly compared to the United Nations of our era (season 2, episode 6, 1999). Despite its inefficacy, D.O.O.P. constitutes a centralized power, the likes of which is hard to find in the contemporary international legal order. Once more, screenwriters have presented a vision of the future where political and legal unification has put an end to the prevailing pluralism of our age.

So far all illustrations have exhibited human resolve to attain political integration on a global scale. It would be wrong to believe that such an accomplishment lies beyond the ability of extra-terrestrial societies. *The Day the Earth Stood Still*[28] tells the tale of a visitation to earth by an alien, Klaatu, and his invincible robot, Gort. Klaatu has come to convey a message to humanity. Their achievements in nuclear energy research and

23 See Jon D. Bohland, ' "And They Have a Plan": Critical Reflections on *Battlestar Galactica* and the Hyperreal Genocide' in Nicholas J. Kiersey and Iver B. Neumann (eds), Battlestar Galactica *and International Relations* (New York: Routledge, 2013) 98.
24 Masashi Mukaeda, Japan, 1995–96.
25 Shōji Kawamori, Japan, 1982–83.
26 Hideaki Anno, Japan, 1995–96.
27 Matt Groening, USA, 1999–2003, 2008–13.
28 Robert Wise, USA, 1951.

space exploration coupled with their penchant for violence are a cause of concern for extra-terrestrials. In the final scene, our alien herald delivers a remarkable speech:

> We of the other planets have long accepted this principle. We have an organization for the mutual protection of all planets – and for the complete elimination of aggression. A sort of United Nations on the Planetary level ... The test of any such higher authority, of course, is the police force that supports it. For our policemen, we created a race of robots – (indicating Gort). Their function is to patrol the planets – in space ships like this one – and preserve the peace. In matters of aggression we have given them absolute power over us.[29]

Klaatu does not shed light on the competences of the organization. Nonetheless, this extract is strongly reminiscent of Articles 43 *et seq.* of the UN Charter, which stipulate that armed forces are to be made available to the Security Council, an obligation yet to be fulfilled by UN Member States.[30] On viewing *The Day the Earth Stood Still*, one is under the impression that in establishing a robust international constabulary force, aliens have succeeded where we have failed.[31]

More generally, these movies and television series point to the constitutionalization of international relations through the integration of legal subjects in a supreme body empowered to govern their interactions. In doing so, and to the extent that law and institutions are deemed a path to peace, such works also fall under the 'idealist' category. This qualification can also be assigned to other examples, as will be discussed in the ensuing paragraphs.

The idealist temptation: 'The law is paramount!'

Idealism is premised on a collection of concepts about international relations some of which have left an indelible mark on contemporary IR theories such as liberalism. In broad terms, idealism is characterized *inter*

---

29 The entire movie script may be consulted at: Edmund H. North, 'The Day the Earth Stood Still. Revised Final Draft' (*Sci Fi Scripts*) www.scifiscripts.com/scripts/TheDayTheEarthStoodSTill.html, accessed 1 July 2018.
30 See Thomas M. Franck, *Recourse to Force: State Action Against Threats and Armed Attacks* (Cambridge: Cambridge University Press, 2002) 21–4.
31 See also Barbara Delcourt, 'Le Jour où la terre s'arrêta (Robert Wise, 1951): la souveraineté est-elle un concept intergalactique?' (Centre de droit international – Université libre de Bruxelles, 2013) http://cdi.ulb.ac.be/le-jour-ou-la-terre-sarreta-robert-wise-1951-la-souveraninete-est-elle-un-concept-intergalactique-une-analyse-de-barbara-delcourt/, accessed 1 July 2018.

alia by the key role played by norms, law and institutions in the settlement and prevention of international disputes. Amongst the core ideas, mention should be made of a sincere belief in progress and humanity, the spread of democracy and the centrality of individuals and their fundamental rights.[32] Being the embodiment of norms, international law takes pride of place in idealist thought. The legal system enjoys 'normative legitimacy',[33] making compliance with its rules and procedures an essential goal. Functioning as a common form of discourse, international law contributes in large measure to inter-State co-operation and stability. Legal developments can even lead to the establishment and strengthening of institutions, which can coincide with constitutionalist thinking, as discussed in the previous chapter. But idealism can also find expression in the more modest view that treaty-making and dispute settlement through adjudication may keep or usher in the return of peace, without States having to achieve full-fledged integration through supranational organizations. In this contribution, idealism is understood in the latter sense.

One of the finest representations of the idealist model in science fiction is surely the *Star Trek* franchise. Since the 1960s, *Star Trek* has recounted the exploits of Starfleet, entrusted with the heavy task of exploring the galaxy whilst defending the United Federation of Planets, a seasoned interplanetary organization. *Star Trek* sets itself apart from its peers when it comes to the treatment of legal topics.[34] Various episodes touch upon questions of international humanitarian law, human rights, diplomatic law, recourse to force and even international criminal law.[35]

The universe of *Star Trek* makes a fairly neat distinction between two legal orders.[36] The first is the law of the United Federation of Planets, a *corpus juris* composed of rules applicable to Federation citizens and institutions. More relevant to our discussion is the second legal order,

---

32 Olivier Corten, *Méthodologie du droit international public* (Brussels: Editions de l'Université de Bruxelles, 2009) 69–70.
33 Daniel Bodansky, 'Legitimacy in International Law and International Relations' in Jeffrey L. Dunoff and Mark A. Pollack (eds), *Interdisciplinary Perspectives on International Law and International Relations: The State of the Art* (Cambridge: Cambridge University Press, 2013) 327.
34 See Robert Chaires and Bradley Chilton, *Star Trek Visions of Law and Justice* (Dallas: Adios Press, 2003); Sylvie Rozenfeld, 'Fabrice Defferrard. Science-fiction: quand l'imaginaire devient source de droit' (2018) 437 *Expertises: droit, technologie et prospectives* 248, 251–2.
35 Michael P. Scharf and Lawrence D. Roberts, 'The Interstellar Relations of the Federation: International Law and "Star Trek. The Next Generation"' (1994) 25 *U Toledo L Rev* 578.
36 Scharf and Roberts, 'The Interstellar Relations of the Federation', 581–2.

the aptly designated 'interstellar law', which governs relations between the Federation and non-Federation alien races. The most notable legal rule, the 'Prime Directive',[37] prohibits *Starfleet* from intervening in the internal affairs of lesser developed civilizations outside of the Federation. Parallels with the contemporary principle of non-intervention are readily drawn and much like its counterpart in international law, the Prime Directive is violated in the name of higher values. A good example of unauthorized intervention is shown in the opening scene of *Star Trek Into Darkness*[38] when Captain Kirk of the *USS Enterprise* (Federation vessel) takes a bold decision to come to the aid of the inhabitants of Nibiru by stopping a volcanic eruption in its tracks. Given that the illegal nature of this action is openly acknowledged, the Prime Directive retains its status as a fundamental principle underpinning Starfleet's activities. Despite its circumvention or even breach in specific instances, the law itself is not called into question.[39] Its observance is valued for its essential contribution to peace and stability.

The idealist image emerges in other episodes centred on disputes involving the interpretation and application of interstellar law. The law features as a suitable and effective tool for controlling power relations. Three examples will be considered in this regard.

In the first such dispute, pitting the Federation against the Klingon Empire (*Star Trek: The Original Series*[40] (season 2, episode 15, 1967)), the stakes are high: both parties lay claim to sovereignty over the planet Sherman, located in the neutral zone. In light of the parties' antagonistic history and the lure of territorial expansion, predictions of inevitable military confrontation would not be overly pessimistic. Overcoming their disagreements, however, the crisis is resolved through recourse to the law. The Treaty of Organia, concluded between both parties, stipulates that a contested celestial body situated in the neutral zone shall be given to the party which best develops

---

37 On the Prime Directive, see Richard J. Peltz, 'On a Wagon Train to Afghanistan: Limitations on *Star Trek*'s Prime Directive' (2003) 25 *U Arkansas Little Rock L Rev* 635–64; Thomas C. Wingfield, 'Lillich on Interstellar Law: U.S. Naval Regulations, *Star Trek*, and the Use of Force in Space' (2001) 46 *South Dakota L Rev* 95–6; Fabrice Defferrard, *Le droit selon Star Trek* (Paris: Mare et Martin, 2015) 33–86.
38 J.J. Abrams, USA, 2013.
39 See *Military and Paramilitary Activities in and against Nicaragua (Nicaragua v United States of America)* (Merits) [1986] ICJ Rep 14, para 186: 'If a State acts in a way prima facie incompatible with a recognized rule, but defends its conduct by appealing to exceptions or justifications contained within the rule itself, then whether or not the State's conduct is in fact justifiable on that basis, the significance of that attitude is to confirm rather than to weaken the rule.'
40 Gene Roddenberry, USA, 1966–69.

its resources. Acting in the spirit of the treaty, the Federation adopts an agronomic policy favouring the cultivation of a superior grain, enabling them to have the better claim.

Star Trek: The Next Generation[41] (season 3, episode 2, 1989) delves into a dispute between the Federation and the Sheliak, an aloof alien race. The Treaty of Armens brought an end to the state of war between these belligerents. In accordance with the agreement, the Federation ceded certain territories to the Sheliak, i.e. a collection of 'H' category planets, generally inhospitable to human life. The terms of the treaty granted the Sheliak the right to unilaterally remove any unauthorized colony established on one of these planets. In this episode, Captain Jean-Luc Picard of the *USS Enterprise* receives an automated transmission from the Sheliak, announcing the discovery of a human settlement on Tau Cygna V (a planet ceded by virtue of the Treaty of Armens) and demanding its dismantlement within three earth days. The settlers descend from the crew of the *SS Artemis*, a Federation ship that had crash-landed on Tau Cygna V almost a century ago. Unable to organize a speedy evacuation of the colonists and fearful of what might happen to them, Captain Picard tries to convince the Sheliak to extend the deadline. He calls for negotiations and pragmatism in order to avoid an abrupt uprooting of a population that has lived on the land for so long. He invokes the spirit of the treaty, which was 'designed to smooth relations', in support of his requested respite. The representative of the Sheliak remains unswayed by this line of argument: 'Negotiate to what purpose? The treaty is signed [...] The law is paramount.' Complicity in an illegal colonization is unthinkable, the sole acceptable course of action being the removal of the settlers within three days in strict observance of the terms of the treaty. Having come to grips with the intransigence of his interlocutors, Picard accepts to play it by the rules. He thus pores over the Treaty of Armens, an astounding feat given its length of some 500,000 words – the Sheliak are a legalistic, fastidious alien race. Becoming well-versed in the treaty, the Starfleet Captain cobbles together a brilliant legal strategy hinged on the threat to invoke a compromissory clause opening the path to arbitration of their dispute. Worried about the amount of time needed to constitute the arbitral tribunal, the Sheliak yield to Picard's demand, granting three weeks to carry out the evacuation of Tau Cygna V.

A pacific solution is achieved in conformity with interstellar law. Rather than seek confrontation on the battlefield, the parties find a way out of their quagmire through legal reasoning. The scene juxtaposes two wholly dissimilar groupings, humans on the one hand, and metallic creatures on

---

41 Gene Roddenberry, USA, 1987–94.

the other hand. In order to communicate, the opposing sides must rely on computer-guided translation, resulting in a type of automatized dialogue. Despite the many practical challenges, the law provides a common language and frame of reference amenable to peaceful coexistence.[42]

The final dispute hails from *Star Trek: Deep Space Nine*[43] (season 1, episode 14, 1993). Dignitaries of two rival factions are invited on board the Starfleet space station Deep Space Nine for a summit hosted by the captain of the station, Benjamin Sisko. The aim of the meeting is to resolve a territorial disagreement, which could trigger armed hostilities. The Paqu and the Navot are neighbouring tribes on planet Bajor. The river Glyrhond forms the border separating the respective territories of the parties, as stipulated in the Paqu-Navot Treaty. It is revealed that the Cardassians, a third power, militarily occupied the planet Bajor for five decades. During the occupation, the Cardassians diverted the flow of the Glyrhond from its natural course on account of their mining operations. The shift of the river caused the Navot to lose swathes of land, which the Paqu refuse to return. Once more, a legal instrument forms the way out of the impasse: as in the prior example, brute force must yield to nuanced legal argumentation. Another similarity is the clash of grammatical and teleological treaty interpretations. Pursuing their own interests, the Paqu support a literal reading of the convention: the border 'shall forever be' the river Glyrhond, irrespective of subsequent modifications. The Navot make the case for an interpretation in harmony with the spirit of the law, taking into consideration the military occupation as the cause of fluvial changes. They believe that these changes, which are unrelated to erosion or other natural causes, cannot affect the trajectory of the boundary. The latter, they argue, should be delimited with reference to the initial location of the river at the time of signing the treaty and thus prior to the illegal occupation. The negotiated outcome of the dispute is consolidated in a new agreement, which returns the lost territories to the Navot and gives free trade access to both sides of the river to the Paqu. An agreement was reached through mediation, one of the recognized methods of peaceful dispute settlement,[44] thanks to the active participation of a neutral third party, Captain Sisko of Starfleet. Law and dispute settlement guide the actions of the involved actors and contribute to the maintenance of peace.

---

42 Olivier Corten, 'Le positivisme juridique aujourd'hui: science ou science-fiction?' (2016) *Quebec J Intl L* 19, 34 and 38.
43 Rick Berman and Michael Piller, USA, 1993–99.
44 United Nations, *Handbook on the Peaceful Settlement of Disputes between States* (New York: United Nations, 1992) 40–5.

The interstellar law of the *Star Trek* universe finds some resonance in the galactic law of *Doctor Who*,[45] which chronicles the adventures of an extra-terrestrial humanoid who travels through time. It would appear that galactic law has the trappings of an international criminal justice system. The Shadow Proclamation, a tribunal of sorts headquartered on a group of asteroids, is determined to enforce galactic law throughout the Milky Way. To carry out its mission, the Proclamation has tapped the Judoon, alien rhinoceroses, to serve as their galactic police force. The ungainly rhinos are famed for their small brains and strict adherence to the law, including local traffic regulations. Notwithstanding their limited intelligence, they know full well that their enforcement jurisdiction does not extend to Earth (primitive planets, ours being one of them, enjoy certain protections under galactic law). The Judoon overcome this legal hurdle by teleporting a hospital from Earth to the Moon, a neutral territory, so they may apprehend a suspected galactic war criminal who has been hiding in the building all along (season 3, episode 1, 2007). Yet again, the approach adopted by the protagonists relies on legal thinking and rule application. The idealist model of international relations is most suited to describe the scenario.

Examples abound, but idealism is hardly a predominant trend in science fiction cinema and television. We will now turn to illustrations of 'realism', which have more to do with cold power calculations and State interests than any perceived requirement to respect the law.

Realism strikes back: we must all respect the law. 'Is that a fact?'

Realism is a foremost school of the international relations discipline harking back to a long tradition. Its adherents view the international system as essentially anarchic. The relations between the main actors, sovereign States, are subject to the vicissitudes of the balance of power – military, economic and diplomatic coercion. Realist thought is founded on a set of assumptions: all States strive to survive; rationality informs State behaviour; each State has a certain military capacity and is not always aware of its neighbours' intentions; and the great powers set the pace.[46] Given these suppositions, the pessimistic outlook reserved for international law and global institutions is unsurprising.[47] This is not to say that realists necessarily

---

45 Sydney Newman, C.E. Webber and Donald Wilson, UK, 1963–89, 2005–present.
46 Anne-Marie Slaughter and Thomas Hale, 'International Relations, Principal Theories', *Max Planck Encyclopedia of Public International Law* (2013), paras 2–4, http://opil.ouplaw.com/home/epil, accessed 1 July 2018.
47 Slaughter and Hale, 'International Relations', para 6.

deny the existence of international law. It would be hard to explain away States' involvement in the development of legal rules and their systematic calls for compliance and implementation. Key to realist thought is that international law is generally deemed an 'epiphenomenon'. These norms are born out of power relations, but statecraft is hardly conditioned by concern for questions of international law.[48] Hence, international law can only work when important national interests are not in the balance. At times the law serves other purposes, namely as a useful form of discourse to justify State conduct.[49]

In *Ghost in the Shell*,[50] the realist vision transpires through the transgression of a rule as sacrosanct as diplomatic immunity. Agents of the anti-terrorist cell Section 9 (Japanese Ministry of the Interior) are hot on the trail of an elusive hacker who goes by the name 'Puppet Master'. In an early scene of the animated movie the viewer is privy to an altercation between a diplomat from a third State and Japanese police officers who have entered his premises:

> **Diplomat:** I have diplomatic immunity! Let me see who's in charge!
> **Police officer:** Transporting a listed programmer out of the country violates our arms export treaty. I could also have you charged with kidnapping. Give the man up.
> **Diplomat:** I'm afraid not. He's applied for political asylum with us and he's already signed a statement to that effect!
> **Police officer:** When?!
> **Diplomat:** I don't have to tell you! By right of international law, my country can offer him protection and right of safe passage. The document is on file at our embassy. I'll transfer a copy to you in a few days.
> **Police officer:** Are you sure about this? They won't take you back alive.
> **Diplomat:** I must ask that you watch what you say. Our country is a peace-loving democracy.[51]

---

48 Barbara Delcourt, 'Le droit' in Thierry Balzacq and Frédéric Ramel (eds), *Traité de relations internationales* (Paris: Presses de Sciences Po, 2013) 279.
49 Frédéric Mégret, 'International Law as Law' in James Crawford and Martti Koskenniemi (eds), *The Cambridge Companion to International Law* (Cambridge: Cambridge University Press, 2012) 74.
50 Mamoru Oshii, Japan, 1995.
51 The entire movie script may be consulted at: 'Ghost in the Shell Script – Dialogue Transcript' (*Drew's Script-O-Rama*) www.script-o-rama.com/movie_scripts/g/ghost-in-the-shell-script.html, accessed 1 July 2018.

Upon uttering these words, we hear a woman's voice originating from an unknown location: 'Is that a fact?' The diplomat is struck by bullets, which, on impact, cause his body to explode. The assassin, a Section 9 agent, makes a spectacular escape, activating her thermal-optic camouflage. Even diplomatic law – often portrayed as robust in productions intended to reflect reality[52] – offers scant protection in the science fiction realm.

The Animatrix,[53] an American-Japanese collaboration, exemplifies the potential for abuse of international law and intergovernmental fora. Comprised of several animated short films, *The Animatrix* explores the universe of the *Matrix* movies in greater detail. The *Matrix* trilogy follows the trials and tribulations of Neo, a young hacker who comes to learn that the world around him is but a virtual reality, the Matrix, put in place by machines to – spoiler alert – subjugate mankind and feed off its bioelectricity. *The Animatrix* reveals how this simulated existence came to be in the first place. Intelligent machines were created to lighten the load of daily human life. Over time, human–robot relations soured, as it became increasingly evident that the latter group would never be granted rights and citizenship in human-run society. The governments of Earth, predicting an uprising of their computerized servants, greenlit a wide scale programme of robot destruction. The surviving machines join forces to found a new State in the Middle East, Zero One, which enjoys spectacular economic growth despite human efforts to strangle the nascent robot nation. It is worth noting that the strategy of the homo sapiens States is partly implemented through the manipulation of international law and the UN Security Council. Zero One is made the target of economic sanctions and a naval blockade even though its innocuous actions do not threaten the peace.[54] Zero One's bid to join the United Nations is met with a resounding rejection. The Security Council's negative vote was not, however, based on an examination of the legal criteria that an aspiring Member State must satisfy.[55] Quite to the contrary, the outcome was predicated on *Realpolitik*. Following the rejection, a war sweeps the globe from which the robots emerge victorious. Their triumph is facilitated by the substitution of cynicism for faith in international law. In the decisive scene, a summit is held at UN Headquarters, New York, to

---

52 See also Marco Benatar, ' "L'Arme fatale 2" et le droit des immunités diplomatiques (Richard Donner, 1989)' (Centre de droit international – Université libre de Bruxelles, 2013) http://cdi.ulb.ac.be/larme-fatale/, accessed 1 July 2018.
53 Kôji Morimoto et al., USA/Japan, 2003.
54 See Charter of the United Nations (signed 26 June 1945, entered into force 24 October 1945) 1 UNTS XVI art 39.
55 See Charter of the United Nations (signed 26 June 1945, entered into force 24 October 1945) 1 UNTS XVI, art 4 para 1.

sign a peace treaty between robots and humans. Against all expectations, the representative of the machines detonates a nuclear bomb wiping out the dignitaries. The momentous gathering of diplomacy was a ruse – even a perfidious act – devised to annihilate the last high officials of humanity, who were foolish to think the long-harboured enmity could be put to rest through peaceful dispute settlement.

Realism is equally patent in the *Stargate SG-1*[56] series, where the principle of *pacta sunt servanda* fares poorly against geopolitical interests. Under the bilateral Protected Planets Treaty, the Goa'uld and the Asgard are bound by reciprocal obligations: the Goa'uld must refrain from attacking certain listed planets (including Earth), whereas the Asgard may not come to the aid of these planets in the event of an (imminent) natural catastrophe nor may they transfer their superior technology. A commission of inquiry is set up to investigate any alleged treaty breach (season 5, episode 17, 2002). The ample legal framework does not prevent the Asgard from giving the humans faster-than-light modes of transport and shields (season 6, episode 17, 2003; season 8, episode 8, 2004). In a similar vein, the treaty notwithstanding, the Goa'uld launch attacks against Earth on several occasions (season 7, episode 22, 2004). In sum, the rules do not suffice to limit, let alone contain, the power of the actors involved.

The Sokovia Accords, a treaty featured in several movies of the Marvel Cinematic Universe, serve as a reminder that international law can stand in the way of international peace and security. Alarmed by the consequences of superheroes' actions, the international community decided to regulate their activities through the so-called Sokovia Accords (*Captain America: Civil War*[57]). The accountability framework put in place by the agreement lays down many requirements, including the duty for enhanced individuals to provide their biometric data as part of a centralized registration system and subjecting their participation in enforcement operations to prior governmental or UN approval. In the recent instalment *Avengers: Infinity War*,[58] it became painfully apparent that the Accords had considerably weakened the Avengers and thus Earth's ability to fend off an alien menace.[59]

Finally, on a more general note, the anthropomorphism of sovereignty[60] crops up in a good deal of productions. Often the 'Other', whether the

---

56 Brad Wright and Jonathan Glassner, Canada/USA, 1997–2007.
57 Anthony Russo and Joe Russo, USA, 2016.
58 Anthony Russo and Joe Russo, USA, 2018.
59 'Sokovia Accords' (*Marvel Cinematic Universe Wiki*) http://marvelcinematicuniverse.wikia.com/wiki/Sokovia_Accords, accessed 1 July 2018.
60 See Alexander Wendt and Raymond Duvall, 'Sovereignty and the UFO' (2008) 36 *Political Theory* 607.

ruthless robot, sinister android or bug-eyed alien, does not receive recognition because it is so dissimilar to the human form. Lacking recognition, any prospect of building up relations sustained by norms is remote. The Cylons of *Battlestar Galactica* are denigrated as 'toasters' while the extra-terrestrials in *Starship Troopers* are derogatorily called 'bugs'. The transformation of the machines in *The Animatrix* speaks volumes. At first, the robots took on a humanoid shape (even wearing hats and clothes to looks more like human beings) and were keen on joining the family of nations. Once their hopes were irrevocably dashed, the robots morphed into ghastly molluscs.

Numerous productions appear to attribute little or no significance to international law. Even the decidedly idealistic *Star Trek* franchise has occasionally lapsed into an anguished sense of realism.[61] Any belief in the preponderance of constitutionalist and idealist models in science fiction would therefore be misguided. The genre appears to replicate today's tensions between the various approaches, reimagined in an alternative universe by screenwriters.

Is international law lost in space?

If the selected scenes are anything to go by, the future of international law – or other legal systems[62] – does not bode particularly well. While it is occasionally presented as a valued system for the orderly conduct of politics, other times international law is nothing more than a fig leaf for the naked force of (extra-)terrestrial powers. The general panorama points to divergence and at times contradiction between constitutionalist, idealist and realist representations, even within one and the same production. It seems

---

61 Kevin Jon Heller, 'Apparently Perfidy Is Not Prohibited in 2256' (*Opinio Juris*, 2 October 2017) http://opiniojuris.org/2017/10/02/apparently-there-is-no-prohibition-of-perfidy-in-2256/, accessed 1 July 2018 (decrying a blatantly perfidious act committed by the Federation against the Klingons in *Star Trek: Discovery* (Bryan Fuller and Alex Kurtzman, USA, 2017–present) (season 1, episode 2, 2017)).

62 See e.g. Francis Lyall and Paul B. Larsen, *Space Law: A Treatise* (London: Routledge, 2nd edn, 2018) 505–7 (on the concept of 'metalaw', a natural law system conceived for the purpose of governing interactions between human beings and intelligent extra-terrestrial life); Robert Kolb, *Theory of International Law* (Oxford: Hart Publishing, 2016) 61 (on 'inter-celestial international law') and Haroldo Valladão, 'Droit interplanétaire et droit "inter gentes" planétaires' in Erik Brüel, Dimitri Constantopoulos, Rudolf Laun, Josef Soder and Hans Wehberg (eds), *Internationalrechtliche und Staatsrechtliche Abhandlungen: Festschrift für Walter Schätzel zu seinem 70. Geburtstag* (Düsseldorf: Hermes, 1960) (on 'planetary *inter gentes* law').

taxing for screenwriters to envisage a novel analytic framework allowing them to think outside of the approaches we have today or agree on the prevalence of one of said approaches for framing international/intergalactic relations. How can this state of affairs be explained? Without claiming to extensively answer the question, I will offer a few musings on the influence of Kantianism, historical context and cinematographic specificities.

The influence of Kantian thought as the vector of constitutionalist and idealist representations

The popularity of the world government theme, which I presented as an extreme form of constitutionalism, is undoubtedly linked to its venerable place in political philosophy. Amongst the eminent thinkers who have contemplated this theme, Immanuel Kant is arguably the most famous.[63] I won't venture to guess whether Kant being one of the earlier philosophers to ruminate on intelligent extra-terrestrial life is a pure coincidence.[64] Whatever the case may be, judging by the academic literature of the past few years, the concept of world government (and its attenuated form of global governance) still manages to capture the imagination of IR theorists.[65] For some of them, the world State is the result of a teleological transition in the way humanity organizes itself politically.[66] The import of these ideas to science fiction is manifest since the early days of the genre, in the writings of giants such as H.G. Wells (*The Open Conspiracy*) and Aldous Huxley (*Brave New World*). The idealist representation is connected to the notion of 'progress' and the liberal spirit, aspects that mainly had an impact on classic works of science fiction. Increased human dominion over nature is perceived in a positive light. Analogously, technology is considered a means to greater freedom.[67] *Star Trek* fits neatly within this mindset, a show created at a time when the advent of space exploration generated a culture of optimism. This enthusiasm translated into hope on the political terrain.

---

63 Immanuel Kant, *Perpetual Peace: A Philosophical Sketch* (trans. Ted Humphrey, Indianapolis: Hackett, 1983).
64 See Peter Szendy, *Kant in the Land of Extraterrestrials: Cosmopolitical Philosofictions* (New York: Fordham University Press, 2013).
65 Campbell Craig, 'The Resurgent Idea of World Government' (2008) 22 *Ethics and Intl Affairs* 133.
66 Alexander Wendt, 'Why a World State is Inevitable' (2003) 9 *European J Intl Relations* 491.
67 Ken Macleod, 'Politics and Science Fiction' in Edward James and Farah Mendlesohn (eds), *The Cambridge Companion to Science Fiction* (Cambridge: Cambridge University Press, 2003) 231.

The United Nations, depicted as a sovereign actor in numerous productions, remains a hobby horse amongst supporters of global federalism. The attitude of the organization vis-à-vis science fiction is somewhat ambivalent. The UN sent a letter to the makers of *Doctor Who* to express their dissatisfaction with the use of their name to designate the 'United Nations Intelligence Taskforce' (UNIT), a *Men in Black* of sorts.[68] The name of the fictitious taskforce was subsequently changed to the more anodyne 'Unified Intelligence Taskforce'. Taking a different tack, *Battlestar Galactica* received a warm welcome from the UN: the producers and cast attended a panel hosted in the hall of the UN Economic and Social Council (ECOSOC) to discuss the relationship between the subjects broached in the television series and the current challenges faced by the organization.[69] The UN, eager to preserve its image, will continue to inspire screenwriters attracted to constitutionalist or idealist approaches.

War as an appropriate context for realist representations

Depictions of the realist model go hand in hand with Manichean portrayals of zero-sum and intractable interspecies conflicts.[70] To this we can add the influence of the bipolar structure inherited from the Cold War. This perspective is noticeable in the *Star Wars*[71] franchise, in which the malignant plans of the Galactic Empire are uncovered. The Empire's ideology, derived from the dark side of the Force, is fostered by passion and violence. Their nemeses, the Jedi, call upon the bright side of that same Force, associated with virtues of preservation, benevolence and assistance. The rift between the Galactic Empire, malevolence incarnate, and their righteous rivals could not be greater. Similarly, one can refer in passing to Skynet, the artificial intelligence keen on eradicating humans in *The Terminator*.[72] In settings such as these, any concern for normativity would seem non-existent.[73] The list of examples is long and continues to grow in the post-Cold War era.

---

68 *Doctor Who Magazine* (August 2005) no. 360.
69 Nicholas J. Kiersey and Iver B. Neumann, 'Introduction: Circulating on Board the Battlestar' in Nicholas J. Kiersey and Iver B. Neumann (eds), Battlestar Galactica *and International Relations* (New York: Routledge, 2013) 4.
70 Barry Buzan, 'America in Space: The International Relations of *Star Trek* and *Battlestar Galactica*' (2010) 39 *Millennium: J Intl Studies* 176.
71 George Lucas, USA, 1977.
72 James Cameron, USA, 1984.
73 See however Timothy D. Peters, '"The Force" as Law: Mythology, Ideology and Order in George Lucas's *Star Wars*' (2012) 36 *Australian Feminist LJ* 125 (exploring the relationship between 'the force' and law).

The 'war against terror' has reproduced and even intensified the image of a sharp, inescapable distinction between good and evil. The robot wars in *Transformers*,[74] the Martian invasion in *War of the Worlds*[75] and the battles at land and sea in *Pacific Rim*[76] are all apt illustrations of this trend.

The specifics of cinematography: sci-fi subgenres and personal influences

An important factor influencing the representation of international law is the subgenre in question. Take, for example, the difference between military sci-fi and cyberpunk. The former subgenre is known for its epic adventures set in a complex geopolitical environment. Extensive space exploration, hefty bureaucracies, administration of far-flung empires and diplomacy are staples of military sci-fi. Such traits provide fertile ground for plots incorporating leitmotifs of international law and dispute settlement. Cyberpunk fiction takes place in technologically sophisticated societies stricken with violence and gloom. On the political stage, States are often eclipsed by mega-corporations and crime syndicates.[77] They show contempt for the law, occasionally possess their own armies, or even control large tracts of land. In such a situation, it would be difficult to imagine a system of international law as we understand it.

To be sure, other factors should equally be borne in mind. The identity of the producer, director or screenwriter, for instance, can be a strong determinant. Japanese history casts a long shadow over *The Animatrix*. Zooming in on the image of the peace treaty concluded between the machines and humans reveals that the text is none other than a replica of the Instrument of Surrender signed by Japan at the end of the Second World War,[78] with modifications as to the names of the parties: 'Allied Powers' and 'Emperor [and] the Japanese Government' are replaced by 'Machine Powers' and 'United Nations of the Human Race' respectively. It is fair to assume that the nationality of the makers played no small part in inspiring this plotline.

---

74 Michael Bay, USA, 2007.
75 Steven Spielberg, USA, 2005.
76 Guillermo del Toro, USA, 2013.
77 James Kneale, 'Space' in Mark Bould, Andrew M. Butler, Adam Roberts and Sherryl Vint (eds), *The Routledge Companion to Science Fiction* (London and New York: Routledge, 2009) 424; Jutta Weldes, 'Popular Culture, Science Fiction, and World Politics: Exploring Intertextual Relations' in Jutta Weldes (ed.), *To Seek Out New Worlds: Exploring Links between Science Fiction and World Politics* (Gordonsville: Palgrave Macmillan, 2003) 10.
78 Instrument of Surrender by Japan (signed 2 September 1945) 139 UNTS 387.

From apology to utopia?

It would be fitting to revisit Martti Koskenniemi's thesis, which holds that assessing the existence or interpretation of an international legal rule gives rise to two clashing predispositions. On the one hand, the need is felt to ground a rule in State practice, which runs the risk of bestowing legitimacy (an 'apology' to use his terminology) upon such practice and reducing the law to the sum of what States do. On the other hand, if one evades this obstacle by defending the integrity of the rule defined in isolation from the actions and desires of States, the peril of succumbing to a gentle but dangerous utopia is tangible.[79] Makers of science fiction cannot escape this dilemma. Therefore it is understandable that sometimes the utopian pole prevails, in the form of constitutionalist and idealist representations, whereas in other instances the apologetic pole takes centre stage, with its straightforward portrayal of law being the reproduction of the balance of power. If certain productions come across as naive, others appear exceedingly cynical. The sci-fi genre redefines the terms of the debate, but cannot do away with them.

---

79 See Martti Koskenniemi, *From Apology to Utopia: The Structure of International Legal Argument* (Cambridge: Cambridge University Press, 2006).

3

Interspecies relations in science fiction movies and human international law

Vincent Chapaux

'This isn't a war', said the artilleryman. 'It never was a war, any more than there's war between man and ants'.

H.G. Wells, The War of the Worlds

In *Avatar*,[1] James Cameron presents the story of a mining company trying to exploit the resources of a distant moon: Pandora. To get access to its mining resources (*the unobtanium*), the company must destroy majestic trees inhabited by the local anthropoid species: the Na'vi. The movie is centred on the following moral dilemma: 'Do human beings have the right to subdue other species for the sole reason of fulfilling their needs?' The movie offers three archetypal answers to this question. The first is embodied by Giovanni Ribisi, in charge of the mining company. According to him, the domination of the humans is legitimate. The exploitation must be carried on in negotiation with the indigenous species – if possible – or by force – if necessary:

> Killing the indigenous looks bad, but there's one thing shareholders hate more than bad press – and that's a bad quarterly statement. Find me a carrot to get them to move, or it's going to have to be *all stick*.

Dr Grace Augustine (Sigourney Weaver) is a scientist. She is in charge of the botanical mission and does not share the vision of the previous character. According to her, each species has a right to live and grow in its own way. She develops a systemic and interdependent vision of interspecies relations. In the movie, this interdependence is quite literal. The roots of the trees are actually an information network at the scale of the moon itself:

> Alright, look – I don't have the answers yet, I'm just now starting to even frame the questions. What we think we know – is that there's some kind of electrochemical communication between the roots of the trees. Like the synapses between neurons [...] It's a network – a global network. And the

---

1 James Cameron, USA, 2009.

Na'vi can access it – they can upload and download data – memories – at sites like the one you destroyed. The Na'vi know that, and they're fighting to defend it. If you want to share this world with them, you need to understand them.

The third and final vision comes from the Na'vi themselves. The indigenous species defends a relational model to other species, not only based on the idea of cohabitation and communication but on the respect of each individual life. This welfare vision appears clear when a Na'vi is forced to kill wolflike predators in order to save the life of a human, who was recklessly wandering in the forest. The human thanks the Na'vi for her rescue and here is what she answers:

> Don't thank! You don't thank for this! This is sad. Very sad, only [...] All this is your fault! They did not need to die! [...] You are like a baby, making noise, don't know what to do. You should not come here [...].

The movie tells the story of the battle and, ultimately, the victory of the last two visions. To that extent, it is fairly in line with the majority of contemporary science fiction movies in which characters preaching for the right of the strongest species to subdue the less powerful are usually presented in a negative fashion.

This trait of science fiction movies might seem surprising for anyone familiar with the (international) legal organization of modern societies, which is mainly speciesist and anthropocentric.[2] It is speciesist in that the right to have rights is usually granted to the individual, first and foremost, on the ground of his or her species. The right to not be subjected to torture or to inhuman or degrading treatment, for instance, is universally granted to human beings but usually denied to rats or plants.[3] In addition to being speciesist, legal systems are largely anthropocentric. Not only do they usually rely on species belonging to organize themselves, they also use species differentiation to favour humans over other species and institutionalize their domination. International trade law, for example, allows for the general and global exploitation of other planetary species by categorizing these living creatures as 'products'.[4]

---

2 A very thorough list of international norms showing strong anthropocentric tendencies can be found in François Roch, *Vers un nouveau paradigme en matière de développement?* (Paris: Presses académiques francophones, Vol. I, 2013) 448.

3 Legal norms prohibiting torture or degrading treatment is limited *rationae personae* to the human beings, or, in the words of the United Nations General Assembly (UNGA) to the 'members of the human family'. UNGA Res 217 A (III) (10 December 1948, Preamble).

4 GATT for instance refers to animals or plants as fisheries products, agricultural products or animal products. General Agreement on Tariffs and Trade (adopted 30 October 1947 entered into force 1 January 1948) 55 UNTS 187 art XI.

This author is not of the opinion that current international law is entirely anthropocentric. As the botanist in the above-mentioned movie, international law can sometimes be characterized as biocentric, which means that some of its rules embrace the vision according to which each species has an equal right to live on the planet. It is the case of numerous conventions protecting whales or other species from commercial predation, for instance.[5] Other rules of international law aim at protecting not only the existence, but the general welfare of non-humans, following a logic that would be closer to what the Na'vi would defend. One can think of the rules designed to protect farmed animals, such as chickens or cows.[6] But all these rules are designed as exceptions to the core of the legal system, which stays mainly speciesist and anthropocentric.

The goal of this chapter is to understand the extent to which mainstream science fiction movies promote an alternative vision of the world, one in which (unlike international law) speciesism or anthropocentrism would not be legitimate.

'Science fiction' as a category is both quite obvious and uneasy to fully grasp. Science fiction was originally a literary genre and can be included in what can be broadly referred to as speculative fiction,[7] i.e. fictions unfolding in worlds that never existed or are still unknown. Books, novels or movies describing what happens in the future (which is unknown by definition), in a past that contradicts History or in worlds other than the Earth belong to speculative fiction. Two main subgenres have to be distinguished: science fiction and fantasy. Even though numerous overlaps exist, speculative fiction unfolding in worlds following the (supposed or demonstrated) law of nature can be considered as science fiction. In the opposite case, the term fantasy will be preferred.[8] In short, science fiction tells stories

---

5 *Convention on International Trade in Endangered Species of Wild Fauna and Flora* (adopted 3 March 1973 entered into force 1 July 1975) 993 UNTS 243.
6 We mainly refer here to EU rules. For a comprehensive vision of EU rules on that matter, see Communication from the Commission to the European Parliament, the Council and the European Economic and Social Committee on the European Union Strategy for the Protection and Welfare of Animals 2012–2015, COM/2012/06. Read also: Vincent Bouhier, 'Le difficile développement des compétences de l'Union européenne dans le domaine du bien être des animaux' (2013) *Revue semestrielle de Droit Animalier* 357. At the time of writing, four years after the end of the first EU strategy on Animal Welfare, the EU process seems to be on hold. See Council of the European Union on animal welfare – an integral part of sustainable animal production, Brussels, 16 December 2019, ST 14975 2019 INIT, p. 7, § 4.
7 On the looseness of that category, see R.B. Gill, 'The Uses of Genre and the Classification of Speculative Fiction' (2013) 46:2 *Mosaic: A Journal for the Interdisciplinary Study of Literature* 71–85.
8 Orson Scott Card, *How to Write Science Fiction and Fantasy* (Cincinnati: Writers Digest Book, 1990) 17–24.

about what could be (but is not), whereas fantasy tells stories about what could never be.[9] This definition confirms the common understanding of the term. *Star Trek*[10] will be considered as a science fiction movie because its universe follows the (supposed or demonstrated) law of nature. *The Lord of the Rings*,[11] on the other hand, will be categorized as a fantasy work. It is set in in a world where the laws of nature are different and where the use of magic is, for instance, possible.

Science fiction movies are numerous and watching them all to answer the above-mentioned question is not a realistic option. The production of science fiction movies is quite ancient. 1902 is the date usually chosen as the year of production of the first science fiction movie (*Le Voyage dans la lune*).[12,13] More than 115 years later, the genre is alive and well and is part of a sharply increasing number of movies.[14]

Two criteria were used to limit the scope of the selection of movies analysed in this study. First, was the centrality of the interspecies relations. Conceptually, any production featuring extra-terrestrial life or sophisticated machines and robots could be integrated in the study, but we only selected those where the relations between species were central.[15] We used our own experience as a viewer and consulted science fiction reference books to help us isolate the works in which that theme was central. This criterion alone was still not sufficient to decrease the number of movies in a way that would become manageable. Interspecies relations have been one of the central subjects of science fiction since its inception. *The War of the Worlds*, released in 1898 as a book,[16] is already centred on the encounter of the human race with a species from outer space.[17] That is why we decided to focus, amongst the remaining movies, on the ones that were the most popular, what we could call 'mainstream science fiction movies'.

---

9 Card, *How to Write Science Fiction and Fantasy*, 50.
10 *Star Trek: The Motion Picture* (Robert Wise, USA, 1979).
11 Peter Jackson, USA/New Zealand, 2001.
12 Georges Méliès, France, 1902.
13 Michel Chion, *Les films de science-fiction* (Paris: Éditions de l'étoile/Cahiers du cinéma, 2009) 31.
14 In Northern America for instance, the numbers of movies kept growing (36 per cent) between 2009 and 2018. Motion Pictures Association of America, *A Comprehensive Analysis and Survey of the Theatrical and Home Entertainment Market Environment (THEME) for 2018*, www.motionpictures.org/wp-content/uploads/2019/03/MPAA-THEME-Report-2018.pdf, accessed 1 December 2019.
15 *Stars Wars* (George Lucas, USA, 1977) or *Men in Black* (Barry Sonnenfeld, USA, 1997) for instance will not be analysed in this study as interspecies relations are not amongst the central issues of the plot.
16 H.G. Wells, *The War of the Worlds* (London: William Heinemann, 1898).
17 Chion, *Les films de science-fiction*, 31.

After careful consideration of this sample, it appears that science fiction movies, in a large majority, follow the example of the above-mentioned *Avatar*, in that they usually promote inclusive visions of alterity, in which species belonging alone is not considered as a valid ground for inter-individual domination and exploitation. We did not find examples of normative logics promoting the right of a species to dominate another one for the sole reason of its ability to do so. Some movies, such as science fiction survival films, do not oppose speciesist logic and present humans as being forced to use violence against non-humans, in a perspective of preservation or self-defence, but without really tackling the general issue of the form that an interspecies relations model should take. But lots deal with this question very directly. And when they do, they usually plead quite vigorously against the speciesist model. Ideal interspecies models are, for instance, depicted from a biocentric perspective. Humans, extra-terrestrial life and sentient machines are considered to have an equal right to live and a duty to peacefully coexist. Other movies tend to embrace a welfare logic and plead for the well treatment of any individual, regardless of his or her species. In short, in one way or another, these movies challenge the speciesist logic that is at the core of human (international) legal organisation. At the end of this chapter, we will discuss a few elements that could explain this peculiar trait of science fiction movies.

Reflecting upon interspecies relations is irrelevant: 'We're fighting for our right to live'

Survival movies are interested in situations where an individual, or a group of persons, face a danger so imminent that their survival is immediately at stake. This kind of movies usually do not take a lot of time to expose what could be an ideal interspecies relations model, nor do they explain the origins of the danger or the motivations of the assailants. Rather, they focus on the moment during which the attackee tries to defend his or herself. In science fiction movies, the attackee is usually the human and the assailant a non-human entity, such as a robot, a mutant animal or some form of extra-terrestrial life.

Numerous movies are built on that model. Sometimes, the survival of the entire human species is at stake, such as in the various adaptations of *The War of the Worlds*[18] or *Independence Day*.[19] As mentioned above, these

---

18 *The War of the Worlds* (Byron Haskin, USA, 1953); *War of the Worlds* (Steven Spielberg, USA, 2005).
19 Roland Emmerich, USA, 1996.

movies focus on the attack itself. What is central is how humans organize themselves to counter the immediate extra-terrestrial aggression. *Why* the attack is taking place or how humans could coexist with the attacker is not immediately relevant. Humankind is in grave danger. As the President of the United States famously stated in *Independence Day*:

> Mankind. The word has new meaning for all of us now. We are reminded not of our petty differences but of our common interests. Perhaps it's fate that today, July the Fourth, we will once again fight for our freedom. Not from tyranny, persecution or oppression. But from annihilation. We're fighting for our right to live, to exit. From this day on, the fourth day of July will no longer be remembered as an American holiday but as the day that all of mankind declared we will not go quietly into the night. We will not vanish without a fight. We will live on. We will survive.

Sometimes, the danger only concerns one or a few humans but the core logic of the movie stays the same, as demonstrated by a movie like *Pitch Black*.[20] The movie depicts the arrival of a group of humans on a desert planet. The group soon realizes that fierce animals lie underground, only waiting for the suns (three of them) to set before launching their attack. *Screamers*[21] is built on the same logic, even though the danger come from robots instead of organic life.

Some horror movies are also built as sci-fi survival movies. They are most often set on Earth, where animals start to behave aggressively or mutate into a more dangerous species, be they piranhas (*Piranhas*;[22] *Piranha 3D*[23]), anacondas (*Anaconda*),[24] spiders (*Arachnophobia*)[25] or ants (*Empire of the Ants*).[26]

It is undeniable that some of these sci-fi survival movies reinforce the idea that human beings are inherently entitled to subdue other species. This quote from *Them!*[27] in which the United States are threatened by a colony of giant ants, shows that the confrontation between humans and monstrous animals is conceived in terms of domination:

> I am telling you gentlemen, science has agreed, that unless something is done, and done quickly, man as the dominant species of life on earth would be extinct, within the year.

20 David Twohy, USA, 2000.
21 Christian Duguay, Canada/Japan/USA, 1995.
22 Joe Dante, USA, 1978.
23 Alexandre Aja, USA, 2010.
24 Luis Llosa, USA/Brazil/Peru, 1997.
25 Frank Marshall, USA, 1990.
26 Bert I. Gordon, USA, 1977.
27 Gordon Douglas, USA, 1954.

The use of military means will therefore be regarded as legitimate to destroy all ants, just as napalm bombardments will have to be used to exterminate the giant spider in *Tarantula*.[28]

However, in other cases, these sci-fi survival movies offer a more nuanced discourse, questioning human responsibility in the preservation of nature and questioning interspecies relations. When they do so, it is interesting to notice that they usually embrace the vision that will be described in the two following sections, dedicated to biocentrism and welfarism.

Jurassic Park,[29] for instance, is clearly a survival movie. A group of humans is trapped on an island, which is in fact a zoo full of the dinosaurs that an eccentric billionaire managed to clone. The movie is centred on the survival of the humans, but a tale is told about the relations humans should entertain with other species. Two statements are particularly obvious. First, it is natural for animals in captivity to try and escape, which seems to imply that humans do not have a natural right to lock them up. Second, humans are *part* of nature and not above it. The nature–culture divide is questioned, and humans are invited to recognize that they cannot, and should not, control all living beings. When they do (when they clone dinosaurs for example) they are heading for a fall. The recent reboot of the series (*Jurassic World*[30] and *Jurassic World: Fallen Kingdom*[31]) is in fact taking the argument a step further. The first *Jurassic World* movie tackles the issue of animal welfare as illustrated in this argument between a velociraptor trainer and a man wanting to use them as a weapon for armed combat:

> **Owen:** I don't know. You come here and you don't learn anything about these animals except what you want to know. You made them, and now you think you own them.
> **Hoskins:** We do own them. Extinct animals have no rights.
> **Owen:** They're not extinct anymore, Hoskins.

The second *Jurassic World* movie is a plea for human beings' involvement in the fight against species extinction.

Other survival movies take the time to explain the motivation underlining the confrontation between species. In *Predator*,[32] soldiers face an extremely violent creature in the jungle. The movie goes beyond what survival movies usually offer in terms of motivation. It underlines for instance that the predator never attacks unarmed humans, questioning their respective status.

---

28 Jack Arnold, USA, 1955.
29 Steven Spielberg, USA, 1993.
30 Colin Trevorrow, USA, 2015.
31 Juan Antonio Bayona, USA, 2018.
32 John McTiernan, USA, 1987.

Who is attacking who? Over time, the audience also realizes that the extra-terrestrial entity is in fact conducting a safari to bring human heads home. Aside from the horror that this hunting practice triggers for the viewer it also serves as an implicit denunciation of the right to hunt for pleasure or interior decoration.

Finally, a movie like *Alien*[33] also offers some sort of explanation for the aggressive behaviour of its title character. Her goal is not to destroy the humans for pleasure but instead to use them as a necessary incubator in her reproduction cycle. The Alien is finally also in a survival situation, and while it does not preclude humans from defending themselves, it certainly does not justify the domination of humans over other species.

That said, in all these movies, emphasis is placed on action and survival. Elements of rationalization or questions regarding the ideal model of interspecies relations are largely at the periphery. Biocentric movies, on the other end, follow an entirely different logic.

Biocentric logic in science fiction movies: 'It's a network!'

Biocentric movies tend to mock the confrontational logic usually present in survival movies. Instead, they tend to praise openness and collaboration between species. In science fiction, this tendency is often materialized by scripts in which heroes resist the oppositional or militaristic tendencies that human groups develop towards extra-terrestrial or machine alterity.

This benevolent attitude can be found in *Abyss*,[34] which tells the story of a group of humans confined in an underwater facility. The camera observes the reaction of these humans when confronted with the discovery of an intelligent species living on the ocean floor. Some humans want to launch a preventive strike against what is clearly a more evolved species. Another faction is fascinated by the discovery and will try to learn to communicate with it. The story proves that the pacifist faction was right.

The same opposition between confrontation and dialogue can be found in *E.T. the Extra-Terrestrial*.[35] E.T. is an extra-terrestrial who lands on Earth with a few members of his (her?) species to conduct a quiet botanical mission. Spooked by governmental agents, E.T. is set apart from his (her) colleagues and finally left behind on Earth. It appears quite quickly that E.T. doesn't pose any threat and only wants to return home, as the young boy sheltering E.T. soon realises. The American government, on the other

---

33 Ridley Scott, USA, 1979.
34 James Cameron, USA, 1989.
35 Steven Spielberg, USA, 1982.

hand, will pursue in its confrontational logic. The movie clearly takes the side of the boy and pleads in favour of an interspecies dialogue.

Biocentric values are clearly detailed in the movie. E.T. and the boy are for instance mentally connected and the respect the boy shows for E.T. is soon extended to other earthly species such as the frog that he refuses to dissect at school. The more time E.T. and the boy spend together, the more their connection seems to deepen, to the point where physical symptoms of one of them are felt by the other as well. The pair soon become an allegory of the unavoidable interconnexion in which all living entities are evolving. It can be pointed out that Steven Spielberg already praised the virtues of communication over brute force in *Close Encounters of the Third Kind*.[36]

More recently, *Monsters*[37] displayed the same kind of argument. *Monsters* takes place in a future in which an extra-terrestrial form of life (looking like thirty-metre-high cephalopods) end up occupying most of Mexico. Soldiers from the United States and Mexico have been bombing them for years. Unsuccessfully. The movie follows a young couple, forced to cross the occupied territory on foot. They will slowly realize – and the viewer through them – that these forms of life (whose seeds landed on Earth through an asteroid fall) are not invaders but mere creatures, with their reproduction system, their language and customs.

Other movies like the above-mentioned *Avatar* are also centred on the importance of dialogue and interspecies communication. In that case, living beings of the planet are actually physically connected through the communication system grounded in the roots of the plants ('It's a network!'). The planet is in reality envisioned at the end as a single organism, able to rise against the aggressions of the humans. In *Arrival*,[38] learning how to communicate between humans and an alien species is absolutely essential, both to prevent an unnecessary war that China wants to unleash against what it misinterprets as a threat of aggression and to share essential knowledge for the benefit of human and alien civilizations.

A final and very striking example of this non-confrontational logic is *Starship Troopers*.[39] In that movie, the main characters are part of the army. They are young earthly recruits enrolled in the army to fight a war against extra-terrestrial insectoids called 'the bugs'. The film starts with a military tone. The confrontation with 'the bugs' seems unavoidable and victory the only option, as defeat would mean the end of humankind. But as the movie

---

36 Steven Spielberg, USA, 1977.
37 Gareth Edwards, UK, 2010.
38 Denis Villeneuve, USA, 2016.
39 Paul Verhoeven, USA, 1997.

unfolds, it becomes clear that the situation is not that simple. First, the so-called 'attacks of the bugs' seem to have been carried out as a simple response to an anterior human strike. Second, and more importantly, it becomes plainly obvious that these 'bugs' are in fact mere animals, repulsive by human standards, but not more aggressive than any attacked animal. These 'bugs' are furthermore able to communicate (through telepathy) and have developed a very sophisticated social hierarchy. All these elements will be ignored by the heroes, prisoners of their warmonger mindset, noble at the inception of the movie, tragicomic at the end.

All these productions can be qualified as biocentric for a simple reason. They plead in favour of the main rule of biocentrism according to which every species has a right to exist and a duty to let the others live. They plead for a logic of cooperation rather than confrontation. Movies centred on welfare issues mainly share this view but go a step further in the interspecies protection they demand.

Welfare issues in science fiction movies: 'What are they doing to these prawns?'

Welfare-centred movies ask the question of the standards that a dominant species has to follow in its daily interaction with other species. Is it justifiable to kill, confine or force another individual to work for the sole reason of its belonging to another species? These moral and ethical questions are raised in numerous movies and the standards they present as legitimate are quite high. When based on species belonging, most of the following behaviours are deemed unacceptable: the right to breed living beings; to force them to work; to conduct experiments on them; or to use them as disposable pets.

Against the right to breed other species

The question of the right of the dominant species to breed other species is raised in numerous movies in which humans are alternately breeder or cattle.

In Bernard Werber's *Nos amis les terriens*,[40] humans are the breeders. The movie is presented as a documentary made on Earth by extra-terrestrials. Using a clinical tone, the narrator explains how humans treat the species with whom they share the planet. Here is how he describes the relations humans entertain with chickens. Images show a slaughterhouse in which thousands of chickens are killed, hanged upside down, plucked and eviscerated.

---

40 Bernard Werber, France, 2006.

> Earthlings have a peculiar relation to the species feeding them. They set them up in dimly lit halls, regroup them, circulate them from room to room. Layer by layer, earthling will strip off what could still render their identification possible. They remove their singularities, their differences. They want all of them to look alike in order to forget that these beings once were, like them, full-blown tribes with their own social life, culture, idiom and ways to educate their offspring.[41]

The violence of the images combined with the implicit belief of the narrator that humans and non-human animals are, in the end, quite similar inevitably raises the question of the right of the humans to proceed to the confinement and breeding (particularly through intensive farming) of other species of the planet.

An analogous denunciation of intensive livestock production is depicted in *Cloud Atlas*.[42] The movie is set in a futuristic Korea in which human clones are locked up in basements and work without any kind of compensation. To ensure their obedience, humans promise the clones that they will be freed after twelve years of labour. In reality, clones are brought to a slaughterhouse where they are treated exactly like the chickens above. This treatment is justified, according to the humans, by some sort of natural law: 'There's a natural order to this world, fabricant. And the truth is this order must be protected.' This 'natural law' is contested in the movie by the heroes and the clones. Their argument is that any kind of rule is a social construct waiting to be modified:

> I understand now, that boundaries between noise and sound are conventions. All boundaries are conventions, waiting to be transcended. One may transcend any convention, if only one can first conceive of doing so.[43]

In *The Matrix*,[44] the message is similar, but the roles are reversed. Humans are the cattle. Machines are the breeders, penning human up in endless fields in order to harvest the energy they produce. Machines offer a Darwinian explanation of their behaviour (there are the fittest) but the whole movie is centred on the right of the cattle to overturn their farmers.

As a final example, the film *Okja*[45] denounces the practices of the food industry, telling a disenchanted dystopic tale. A multinational company, Mirando Corporation, plans to exploit genetically modified 'super pigs' on

---

41 Author's translation.
42 Tom Tykwer, Andy Wachowski and Lana Wachowski, Germany/USA, 2012.
43 The question of the right of the clones is also raised incidentally in *Oblivion* (Joseph Kosinski, USA, 2013).
44 The Wachowskis, USA, 1999.
45 Bong Joon Ho, South Korea/USA, 2017.

an industrial scale, and disguises this project as a pig breeding competition, supposed to promote natural and eco-responsible farming. Okja, one of the super pigs, raised in the mountains by Mija, a young Korean girl, is recovered by Mirando Corporation for marketing purposes. It is released by the Animal Liberation Front (ALF) with the help of Mija, to publicly denounce the animal exploitation and the abuses Okja suffered in a laboratory, recorded on video. The pig will be captured once again and taken to the slaughterhouse, where Mija will be able to save its life by buying it with gold, Mirando's director declaring that she is only doing business. In its defence of the animal cause, the film humanizes the pig Okja, applying to it (explicitly and implicitly) legal rules normally provided for the human person, the cruelties it suffers being qualified as 'crimes against humanity' by the ALF, and the slaughterhouse to which it is led visually referring to the extermination camps and thus to the notion of genocide.

Against the exploitation of other species for forced labour

If forced labour is defined as the situation in which an individual is not free to choose his or her occupation and is not compensated for his or her labour, there is no doubt that human beings resort extensively to forced labour in their relation to the other species of the planet. Science fiction movies usually reject this type of behaviour, especially when they are justified on species belonging.

One classic example is *Planet of the Apes*.[46] The movie is about a group of humans who accidently land on a planet where the relations between humans and apes are reversed. Apes rule and humans are enslaved. Amongst other things, the movie jeers at the interspecies dominations and show how they are based on illogical and biased representations of the world. The scene representing a hearing at a simian tribunal is particularly eloquent in that regard. The prosecutor, incapable of justifying human inferiority on empirical grounds, is forced to fall back on religious logic:

> Learned Judges: My case is simple. It is based on our first Article of Faith: that the Almighty created the ape in his own image; that He gave him a soul and a mind; that He set him apart from the beasts of the jungle, and made him the lord of the planet. These sacred truths are self-evident.

By putting the human in the position of the dominee and the animal in the shoes of the dominant, as well as by revealing the arbitrary nature of

---

46 Franklin J. Schaffner, USA, 1968.

this social organization, the movie openly questions the right to subdue the weakest species and subject them to forced labour.[47]

A similar question lies at the core of *X-Men*[48] and of most of the *X-Men* saga.[49] *X-Men* revolves around the tense relation between two groups: the humans and the mutants. Mutants are human beings who evolved, through genetic mutation, into a new species with various spectacular abilities: tremendous muscular strength, telekinesis, cellular modification, ability to master fire or ice … But mutants are divided when it comes to the relation they should entertain with the human species. Should they, in a sort of twisted Darwinian logic, embrace the 'evolution' and subdue the lesser beings? Or should they treat these mutations as a simple 'difference' and peacefully collaborate with the human species? The heroes (and the moral of the story) unconditionally embrace the second option.

A similar logic can be found in *I, Robot*.[50] In the movie, a police detective will slowly understand that the robots forced to work for the human race can feel certain emotions and are capable of exercising free choice. Once this realization occurs, the hero will feel an acute moral obligation to stop treating them as slaves.

Finally, *Blade Runner*[51] can also be read as a plea against interspecies slavery. The movie tells the story of a hero in charge of 'retiring' (killing) bioengineered humans called replicants who escape their condition of slavery. The movie quickly moves from an anthropocentric point of view (in which both the hero and the viewers feel that the capture of the escapees is legitimate) to a position of empathy towards the replicants who express deep existential suffering. As this quote from one of the replicants illustrates, slavery is at the core of the replicants' motivation for escape: 'Quite an

---

47 Numerous movie adaptations have been made afterwards: *Beneath the Planet of the Apes* (Ted Post, USA, 1970), *Escape from the Planet of the Apes* (Don Taylor, USA, 1971), *Conquest of the Planet of the Apes* (J. Lee Thompson, USA, 1972), *Battle for the Planet of the Apes* (J. Lee Thompson, USA, 1973), *Planet of the Apes* (Tim Burton, USA, 2001), *Rise of the Planet of the Apes* (Rupert Wyatt, USA, 2011), *Dawn of the Planet of the Apes* (Matt Reeves, USA, 2014), *War for the Planet of the Apes* (Matt Reeves, USA, 2017).
48 Bryan Singer, USA, 2000.
49 *X-Men* (Bryan Singer, USA, 2000); *X-Men 2* (Bryan Singer, USA, 2003); *X-Men: The Last Stand* (Brett Ratner, USA, 2006); *X-Men Origins: Wolverine* (Gavin Hood, USA, 2009); *X-Men: First Class* (Matthew Vaughn, USA, 2011); *The Wolverine* (James Mangold, USA, 2013); *X-Men: Days of Future Past* (Bryan Singer, USA, 2014); *X-Men: Apocalypse* (Bryan Singer, USA, 2016); *X-Men: Dark Phoenix* (Simon Kinberg, USA, 2019).
50 Alex Proyas, USA, 2004.
51 Ridley Scott, USA, 1982.

experience to live in fear, isn't it? That's what it is to be a slave.' The question of forced labour and slavery stays central in the 2017 sequel (*Blade Runner 2049*)[52] in which the replicants oppose Niander Wallace, CEO of Wallace Corporation, who sees himself as a slave provider for humanity: 'Every leap of civilization was built off the back of a disposable workforce. We lost our stomach for slaves. Unless ... engineered.' Once again, the moral of the tale is on the side of those who fight interspecies slavery.

Against experimentation on other species

Some movies, like *District 9*,[53] stand up against the claim of the dominant species to use other species as experimentation material. The movie unfolds in Johannesburg, where extra-terrestrials have been contained in camps for years. The movie follows the destiny of a human who will slowly turn into an alien. This biological mutation will go together with a change in his social status and the revocation of his most fundamental rights. Captured by humans, the hero will be submitted to a long and painful experimentation process. He will also develop a sort of empathy for his new biological species (pejoratively called 'prawns'), who are similarly abused ('What are they doing to these prawns?'). Playing with the empathy the audience has for the human during the first part of the movie, the director of *District 9* forces us to follow the slow demotion of rights caused by the change of species belonging.

Numerous other movies touch on the question of experimentation on living beings, such as the above-mentioned *The Planet of the Apes* (1968) where it is found that human beings are laboratory animals for apes' experimentation. Other denunciations of these behaviours can be found in *Starship Troopers*, *Twelve Monkeys*[54] or *Rise of the Planet of the Apes*.[55] In that last instance, we learn that it is actually the physical abuse inflicted on the apes that triggered the apes' revolution which will eventually lead to the apes' domination depicted in *Planet of the Apes*. In any case, the abuse of sensitive living beings for experimentation purposes is, in all these instances, clearly regarded as unjustifiable.

---

52 Denis Villeneuve, USA/UK, 2017.
53 Neill Blomkamp, USA/New Zealand/South Africa/Canada, 2009.
54 Terry Gilliam, USA, 1995. In the movie, human activists pleading for the liberation of the animals from the zoo and the laboratories are first considered to be responsible for the mysterious near extinction of the human race before being rehabilitated at the end of the film.
55 Rupert Wyatt, USA, 2011.

Against the use of other species as disposable pets

The question of interspecies relations can also question the rights and duties of an individual towards his or her companion animals. One movie was centred on that topic: *Artificial Intelligence: A.I.*[56] Set in a future in which a company managed to create companion robots who can feel subjective emotions, *A.I.* follows the life of David, one of those robots (called *Mechas*), shaped as a boy and programmed to give unconditional love to its adoptive parents (who will nevertheless abandon him in the forest). The movie raises the question of the duties that should be assigned to an individual who seeks and obtains the affection of a member of another species with less capabilities. This question is asked to the creator of the *Mechas* by one of his collaborators at the start of the movie:

> **Collaborator:** If a robot could genuinely love a person, what responsibility does that person hold toward that mecha in return? It's a moral question, isn't it?
>
> **Creator:** The oldest one of all. But in the beginning, didn't God create Adam to love him?

The movie will not treat that question lightly and will plead in favour of the adoptive species' responsibility in that matter. According to the movie, seeking and creating an emotional bond with a member of another species creates a moral duty to respect it in the long run.[57]

Defence of the weakest species in science fiction movies: between activism and metaphor

Science fiction movies usually offer models of interspecies relations grounded in a deep acceptation of the alterity and a rejection of situational or structural violence when that violence is justified on a speciesist ground. By doing so, they deeply question our current relations to other species, which are profoundly structured by an anthropocentric logic, as exemplified by the current state of international law. Science fiction movies seem to be willing to go beyond the rule according to which 'humans have rights, but non-humans don't'.[58]

---

56 Steven Spielberg, USA, 2001.
57 On the current existing legal obligation to prevent the distress of pet animals, see *European Convention for the Protection of Pet Animals* (adopted 13 November 1987 entry into force 1 May 1992) art 3.
58 Pierre-Jérôme Delage, *Science-fiction et science juridique* (Paris: Institut de Recherche Juridique de la Sorbonne Éditions, 2013) 20.

How can we account for this major difference between the macro-social organisation of our societies and this dissonant discourse emanating from our analysis of the (mainstream) science fiction movies? Science fiction has of course always been the lair of those wanting to question our reality. By creating utopian or dystopian worlds, it inevitably produces certain assertions on the ideal city.[59] Yet the scope of the agreement on the way interspecies relations should look like is a surprise. Is the movie industry, and Hollywood in particular, infiltrated by a group of individuals determined to promote a more horizontal model of interspecies relations on Earth?

The answer to this question is partly positive. James Cameron, for instance, in most cases screenwriter and director of his movies (e.g. *The Terminator*,[60] *Aliens*,[61] *The Abyss*, *Terminator 2: Judgment Day*,[62] *Avatar* (2009)), is a vegan and justifies his (relatively recent choice) by a political will to change the relations humans entertain with nature: 'By changing what you eat, you will change the entire contract between the human species and the natural world.'[63] Lana Wachowski (who directed *Matrix* and *Cloud Atlas*) is vegetarian as well.[64] E.T. is vegetarian, but Steven Spielberg is not. That being said, he showed the extent of his compassion to the animal kingdom in a movie centred on the eight million horses slaughtered during the Second World War (*War Horse*):[65] 'This was the horse as an instrument of warfare. I hope the film raises awareness of the contribution animals make.'[66] Colin Trevorrow, director of *Jurassic World* (2015) and producer of *Jurassic World: Fallen Kindgom* (2018), said about the latter:

> We have a relationship with animals on this planet that is tenuous and is strained. They suffer from abuse and trafficking and the consequences of

---

59 Raymond williams, 'Utopia and Science Fiction' (1978) 5 *Science Fiction Studies* 203–14.
60 James Cameron, USA, 1984.
61 James Cameron, USA, 1986.
62 James Cameron, USA, 1991.
63 'James Cameron Advocates Vegan Diet During National Geographic Society Gala Speech', Huffington Post (18 June 2013) www.huffingtonpost.com/2013/06/18/james-cameron-vegan-diet_n_3459199.html, accessed 16 July 2018.
64 See the interview 'DP/30: Cloud Atlas, screenwriter/directors Lana Wachowski, Tom Tykwer, Andy Wachowski' www.youtube.com/watch?v=3MXR4MCuA0o, accessed 16 July 2018.
65 Steven Spielberg, USA, 2011.
66 Anita Singh, 'Steven Spielberg on War Horse: America Has Less Regard for History', *Telegraph* (9 January 2012), www.telegraph.co.uk/culture/film/film-news/9003454/Steven-Spielberg-on-War-Horse-America-has-less-regard-for-history.html, accessed 16 July 2018.

our environmental choices [...] To find a way to build essentially a children's franchise about how we have a responsibility to the creatures that we share the planet with felt like a worthwhile thing to do.[67]

That being said, numerous filmmakers didn't make any statement on the well-being or the preservation of non-human species and it is likely that the tolerant macro-social model they depict in their movie must be explained in other ways.

One of the most obvious is to consider that the interspecies tolerance praised in these movies is in fact a metaphor for the *intraspecies* model directors favour. Interspecies movies would not mainly be about *them* than they would be about *us*, the human species. Machines and extra-terrestrial forms of life would simply be an allegory of the cultural or physical differences existing amongst human themselves.

X-Men (2000), for example, can be read as a tale of tolerance between species or as a simple plea against those are trying to pretend that some human 'races' are superior to others. The fact that the opening scene of the movie is taking place in Nazi Germany during a round-up of the Polish Jews strongly suggest that this intraspecies argument is certainly present in the director's mind.

Similarly, *District 9* certainly invites interspecies tolerance but is based on real events and in particular the story of a district of Cape Town (District 6), from which non-white humans were deported between 1966 and 1982 on the basis of the apartheid politics of the time.[68] The author recognizes that the movie is the result of two intentions: writing a movie about apartheid and a science fiction movie.

> I felt like half of my mind wanted to make some serious film about these topics [segregation and apartheid] and the other half wanted to make a bloody genre film. And then I thought maybe I'll be able to do both.[69]

In fact, a lot of the above-mentioned movies suggest a message that is more centred on intra- than interspecies relations because the dominated species is often quite similar to the human being. Sometimes the dominated species

---

67 Jake Coyle, 'In "Jurassic World", a Dino-Sized Animal-Rights Parable', Associated Press (18 June 2018) www.apnews.com/efa105ac66bc480b8da4ebab6d705fd4, accessed 17 July 2018.
68 A history of the District 6 events can be found on the website of the museum dedicated to them: www.districtsix.co.za, accessed 1 December 2019.
69 A quote from the director, Neill Blomkamp, from Brad Balfour, 'Q&A: Sci-Fi Director Neill Blomkamp Describes Life in District 9 As No Picnic', The Huffington Post (21 September 2009) www.huffingtonpost.com/brad-balfour/qa-sci-fi-director-neill_b_265672.html, accessed 16 July 2018.

is the human being (as in *Matrix*, *X-Men* or *Planet of the Apes*). Sometimes they are physically close (*A.I.*, *Blade Runner*, *Cloud Atlas*, *Avatar*). And if not, they often display an articulated language (*I, Robot*, *District 9*).[70]

But in the end, the intention of the directors and screenwriters is not unequivocally fundamental. Their work unquestionably advocates for a macro-social organization in which physical attributes cannot be used to subdue any individual. Whatever the original intention of the plea was, however, it still contributes, with the same strength, to the denunciation of racism, sexism or, as we have shown in the previous pages, speciesism.

---

70 That is not to say that alterity is never represented through animal-like creatures as it is the case in the above-mentioned *Monsters* (speechless giant octopi), *Jurassic Park* (dinosaurs), *Pitch Black* (unidentified predators close to dinosaurs) or *Starship Troopers* (giant insects and arachnids).

4

The UN Charter in action movies

Olivier Corten

An episode of the TV series *JAG*, aired at the end of 2003,[1] pictures a debate before the International Criminal Court about the war launched in Iraq by the United States:

> **Prosecutor:** *Monsieur le Secrétaire général*, in September 2003 you made a speech to the United Nations regarding US military intervention in Iraq. Do you recall what you said?
>
> **Secretary General:** I stated such intervention could set a dangerous precedent.
>
> **Prosecutor:** ... resulting in proliferation of unilateral and lawless use of force not sanctioned by the UN ... Was the United States armed invasion of Iraq in 2003 supported by any provisions of the United Nations' Charter?
>
> **Secretary General:** No [...].
>
> **Defence:** Sir, in your speech, you have also stated that the UN Charter allows for military actions for the purpose of self-defence?
>
> **Secretary General:** Under limited circumstances. But the United States was not attacked by Iraq.
>
> **Defence:** Not yet ... But we know here is a man with a record of using weapons of mass destruction. Is it not reasonable to anticipate that he would not hesitate to use them again?
>
> **Secretary General:** No weapons of mass destruction were found.
>
> **Defence:** Not yet ...
>
> **Secretary General:** Also, preventive war is not a legitimate reason for armed violence. When conflict arises between nations, peace must always be the ultimate goal [...].
>
> **Prosecutor:** Did the world ask you to be its saviour?
>
> **Defence:** In 1917, in 1941 and throughout the forty years of the cold war, the world asked us for help. And we gave it. But now the war on

---

1 *Judge, Advocate General* (Donald B. Bellisario, NBC, USA, season 9, 2003, episode 14).

terrorism has begun and we can't wait to be asked. We must do what has to be done.

Prosecutor: So, you feel free to attack every nation of which you disapprove?

Defence: If that nation causes an imminent threat we reserve the right to use military force to protect us.

As we can see, the defence counsel who is the main hero of the series supports a rather flexible interpretation of the Charter. At the same time, it is the only scene in *JAG*'s ten seasons that deals directly with the lawfulness of a military intervention.

This example is quite illustrative of the pattern that emerges from the viewing, for the purposes of the present contribution, of cinematographic artwork and TV series: even though we are dealing with 'action movies', that is movies that deal with the use of armed force, particularly in international relations, the rules of the Charter are only very rarely and stealthily cited. And when these rules are evoked, a broad interpretation favouring the use of force is put forth. The reference to the rules on the use of force thus depicts international law as playing a merely marginal role and bowing to the imperatives of politics or ethics. Very far from the perspective that permeates many legal writings with regard to the importance of the United Nations Charter for the maintenance of international peace and security, cinema and television convey a conception in which the law appears as a lure, or even a detrimental obstacle for the achievement of the objectives legitimately pursued by the actors involved on the ground. Beyond the variety of films and the nuances that characterize them – the different movies being far from conveying the same vision – this conception seems obvious, even natural, which testifies to its pronounced ideological character.

Before further developing this idea, it should be noted that the movies were selected in the following way: relying both on personal memories and intuitions, on exchanges with other colleagues and on several books dedicated to the relations between cinema and war which will be mentioned throughout the contribution, I have identified a number of films and series relating to the prohibition of the use of force. Even if, in practice, most of them turned out to be US productions, my research was not *a priori* limited by any type of considerations and was meant to encompass a broad selection of films. The identified film assortment is not intended to be exhaustive – supposing that exhaustiveness is possible for a topic like this one – but it can certainly provide a basis for formulating a number of questions that I will successively address in this piece. First, how are the rules on the use of force legally interpreted in the exceptional cases in which they are mentioned? Second, can we detect a certain criticism or assessment of the existing legal rules, even when they are not expressly mentioned? More generally, what is the conception of law that emerges from representations offered to the public? Finally, how can one explain the predominant place of some of these conceptions of law and international relations, taking into account the historical context of production of the selected films and series? The treatment of all these questions will involve combining technical legal analysis, mainly in the first stage, with a more critical perspective associating cinema, law and ideology, in the following ones.[2]

The prevalence of flexible legal arguments justifying action

A scene from *House of Cards* briefly alludes to the circumvention of the Russian veto through the adoption of a UN General Assembly resolution based on the precedent of the 'Uniting for Peace' resolution.[3] However, in general, legal debates remain rather rare, and when they are portrayed, they do not deter an action in the name of the UN Charter.

Self-defence in response to a terrorist attack: 'It's like being invaded … we have to fight back'

A first example in which this debate is evoked is the cinematographic account of the Israeli operation in Entebbe in 1976. In *Raid on Entebbe*,[4] the Israeli Cabinet meets to assess the situation and consider the appropriate response. The main problem lies in the technical difficulties of carrying out a rescue operation several thousand kilometres from the national territory, without unduly endangering the lives of the soldiers but especially the hostages held by the hijackers at the Entebbe airport with the obvious complicity of the local authorities. From the legal perspective, however, an adviser indirectly refers to a broad conception of self-defence: 'This hijacking, it's like being invaded. That's why we have to fight back.' A similar representation can be found in *Entebbe*,[5] *Operation Thunderbolt*[6] and in *Victory at Entebbe*[7] where the Israeli prime minister boldly dismisses the contingency that 'of course, we'll be accused of violating the sovereignty of Uganda'. In this perspective, international law should not be a hindrance to action, which

---

2 See the introductory remarks to the present book, Chapter 1.
3 *House of Cards* (Beau Willimon, Netflix, USA, season 3, episode 3, 2015).
4 Irvin Kershner, USA, 1977.
5 José Padilha, USA, 2018.
6 Menahem Golan, Israel, 1977.
7 Marvin J. Chomsky, USA, 1976.

probably explains why the legal debate is cut short. It is, however, clear that a broad concept of self-defence is conveyed, quite similar to that defended at a certain point by Israel that invoked Article 51 of the UN Charter to respond to a terrorist attack. By contrast, there is no mention in the films devoted to this episode of the lively debates that took place within the UN in this context, and of the condemnation by a large majority of States of the Israeli operation in Entebbe.[8]

Another example comes from *The West Wing*, a popular and successful TV series.[9] On several occasions, military interventions are justified by a broad interpretation of the concept of self-defence, in the name of the fight against terrorism, as shown in this statement by President Bartlet: 'terrorists aren't nations ... International law has no prohibition against any government, superpower or otherwise, targeting terrorist command and control centers'.[10]

In short, when self-defence is evoked and interpreted, it is often in a rather extensive sense. The same pattern can be detected when one refers to another argument conventionally used to justify the use of force: the consent of the State in whose territory an intervention takes place.

An intervention based on the sole consent of the rebels provisionally recognized as representing a sovereign State? 'Let's do it!'

International law has long been divided on the conditions under which military action may be validly justified based on the consent of the State in whose territory it takes place.[11] One of the most contentious issues is whether intervention in a civil war – which is clearly prohibited in favour of the rebels – would be allowed at the request of the government authorities, and if so, for what purpose. Consensus, by contrast, seems to exist on one point: in any event, State consent, in order to be valid, must come from the officially recognized government of the State concerned, and not from the subordinate authorities or irregular forces.

In this context, the scene from *The Sum of All Fears*[12] conveys a particularly extensive interpretation of existing international law. Debating

---

8 Olivier Corten, *The Law against War* (Oxford: Hart, 2010), chapters 3 and 7.
9 *The West Wing* (Aaron Sorkin, NBC, USA, 7 seasons, 1999–2006); Olivier Corten, 'A la Maison-Blanche: le président des Etats-Unis se soucie-t-il du droit international lorsqu'il décide d'une intervention militaire?', in *Select Proceedings of the European Society of International Law*, Vol. 5, 2014 (Oxford: Hart, 2016), 505–8.
10 *The West Wing*, Aaron Sorkin, USA, season 5, episode 1, 2003–4; see also: season 3, episode 22, 2001–2, season 4, episode 6, 2002–3.
11 Corten, *The Law against War*, chapter 5.
12 Phil Alden Robinson, USA, 2002.

the possibilities of responding to a chemical attack led by Moscow against Grozny, advisers to the US president believe that sending 'NATO peacekeeping' soldiers would constitute the best option. One of them points out, however, that Chechnya 'is not a sovereign state' to which one of his colleagues replies: 'He wants to be recognized, so let's recognize him; not totally, provisionally; the Chechens will ask for international help, and we will send soldiers' – followed by – 'Let's do it', coming from the president. This proposed interpretation of the rule cannot but draw the attention of an international lawyer: it would be sufficient to recognize (even provisionally) an authority to be able to validly rely on its request and send troops on the territory of a sovereign State. To my knowledge, lawyers and politicians have never proposed to go this far. In this sense, this scene relays a particularly extensive interpretation in favour of military intervention. Beyond the question of substance, international law itself appears only as a body of rules particularly flexible and malleable, likely to give rise to the most imaginative reasoning justifying unbridled interventionism.

The overall impression that prevails is therefore both the scarcity of legal considerations and, in cases where they are conveyed, the emphasis on flexible interpretations tending to justify rather than to prevent military action. From the same perspective, when legal rules are at stake, they are often presented – without being subject to interpretation from a strictly legal angle – as unsuitable for international realities and the need for an intervention.

Legal constraints unsuited to international realities

Many films, without giving rise to strictly legal debates on its interpretation, depict situations in which the legal rule seems to be challenged as such. This can be illustrated using two examples: the principle of non-intervention, on the one hand, and self-defence in its classical conception, on the other. In both cases, cinematographic productions tend to challenge the restrictive character of the existing legal rule in the name of the imperative nature of the military intervention.

The limitations of the principle of non-intervention: 'I broke my own rule. I started to give a fuck'

The classical debate opposing the respect of the sovereignty of each State to the universal guarantee of human rights has focused, in recent years, on notions such as the 'right of humanitarian intervention' and the 'responsibility to protect'. From the UN perspective, a rather restrictive conception, very attached to the principle of non-intervention, prevails: while the powers of the Security Council to take action have been extensively recognized since the end of the Cold War, the possibility for States to act without its authorization has never been enshrined in the texts, nor in practice for that matter.[13] For some, however, the formal obligation to stick to the rule sometimes bows to some kind of a higher moral imperative. We will recall such an approach from the war against Yugoslavia in 1999, which was mainly justified by the need to put an end to the repression of the Albanian population in Kosovo, a war sometimes referred to as 'illegal but legitimate'.[14] This perspective undoubtedly prevails in the cinema and TV productions that have caught our attention, as illustrated by several examples.

In *Tears of the Sun*,[15] the United States decides to evacuate its nationals following the overthrow of the democratically elected government in Nigeria by dangerous Muslim extremists. The commander of the intervention force, Lieutenant Waters (Bruce Willis), is responsible for the exfiltration of an American woman, Dr Lena Kendricks (Monica Bellucci), a doctor in a bush clinic where she cares for the victims (mostly Christian) of the repression by the new authorities. The rules of engagement are clear: the United States must fulfil its mission without taking sides in the conflict, scrupulously respecting the principle of neutrality. The reality of the field and the confrontation with the horrors of the repression will however put these rules to a harsh test. As US soldiers arrive at the clinic in the middle of an emergency medical procedure, Lena Kendricks refuses to leave her patients at the mercy of the approaching hordes of Nigerian army. After having tricked Kendricks into being evacuated against her will, Lieutenant Waters discovers the horrifying massacre of Christians perpetrated by the ruthless Islamists. Moved, he turns around and decides, against the orders of his hierarchy, to save the remaining Christians by escorting them to the Cameroon border. During a decisive scene, Waters gathers his men as he wants to make sure that he has their full support. In this context, the respect of the rules appears not only as an obstacle to an objectively necessary action, but also as a deeply immoral act. In turn, their violation represents a real act of contrition: 'I broke my own rule. I started to give a fuck', says Lieutenant Waters in a low voice. Heartened by such a leap of faith, his men follow him, and successfully carry out their mission, at the price of fierce fighting with the Nigerian forces sent to track them down. In the final scene, the rescued Africans thank the brave American soldiers, while tearful music combining percussion and panpipes

---

13 GA/Res 60/1, paras 138–9 and Corten, *The Law against War*, chapter 8.
14 The Independent International Commission on Kosovo, *The Kosovo Report* (Oxford: Oxford University Press, 2000) 372pp.
15 Antoine Fuqua, USA, 2003.

plays in the background. As for Waters, exhausted and wounded, he literally falls into the arms of benevolent Lena, in an almost Christ-like posture that seems to symbolize the triumph of the heart over reason. The film ends with a quote from Edmund Burke reproduced on full screen: 'The only thing necessary for the triumph of evil is for good men to do nothing.' It is difficult to find a better example depicting the questioning of the principle of non-intervention at least in certain exceptional situations where a duty (moral or even religious) of interference prevails.[16]

This shift towards the overcoming of the principle of non-intervention, associated with indifference, cowardice and even cruelty, is portrayed in other productions. In *Air Force One*,[17] President Marshall is committed to 'change American policy', before stating: 'Never again will I allow our political self-interest to deter us from doing what we know is morally right.' In *The West Wing*, President Bartlet declares: 'No country has ever a had a doctrine of intervention when only humanitarian interests were at stake. That streak's going to end Sunday at noon.' In the presence of his staff, he then proceeds on a self-congratulatory note: 'Congratulations, folks. We've got ourselves a doctrine.'[18] We spotted similar scenes in *Three Kings*,[19] *Rambo: The Fight Continues*[20] and in *JAG*.[21]

This overview of the existing filmography should not leave the impression that there are no productions subject to a different interpretation. *The Rescuers*,[22] a film produced by the Disney studios, tells the story of a 'humanitarian intervention' conducted, not unilaterally, but under the auspices of a collective security organization, which holds a vote in the cellars of its New York City headquarters. In this 'mouse version' of the UN (renamed 'Rescue Aid Society'), there is no veto, but rather a vote by consensus that could be compared to a General Assembly decision-making process. It is noteworthy that this Rescue Aid Society version of the assembly is composed in accordance with a Western-centric world vision: 'Africa' has only one seat, just like 'Arabia', while 'Austria' and 'Vienna', for example,

---

16 Jean-Michel Valantin, *Hollywood, le Pentagone et le monde. Les trois acteurs de la stratégie mondiale* (Paris: Autrement, 2010) 177–82; Sean Carter and Klaus Dodds, *International Politics and Film* (New York: Columbia University Press, Wallflower Press, 2014) 73–5.
17 Wolfgang Petersen, USA, 1997.
18 Season 4, episode 15, 2003.
19 David O. Russell, USA, 1999.
20 Sylvester Stallone, USA, 2008.
21 Season 3, episode 3, 1997–8; Valantin, *Hollywood, le Pentagone et le monde*, 178. See also: *24: Redemption* (Jon Cassar, USA, 2008); Jean-Baptiste Jeangène Vilmer, *24 heures chrono. Le choix du mal* (Paris: Presses universitaires de France, 2012) 150–2.
22 Wolfgang Reitherman, John Lounsbery, Art Stevens, USA, 1977.

also have one seat each. It appears that, in principle, the intervention is decided in a multilateral and institutional framework, after reflection and debate. We are far from the pattern showcased by movies and episodes mentioned above, that of an impulsive indignation that pushes a maverick into action. However, within the selected material, these movies and episodes embody the dominant vision conveyed on large and small screens. Let us now see if a similar pattern can be found with regard to criticisms directed against another principle of international law, that of self-defence within the framework of Article 51 of the Charter?

The limits of the legal framework of self-defence: a 'right to live, to exist'

As mentioned above, by staging legal debates, some productions depict a broad interpretation of Article 51 of the Charter. In addition to these rare occurrences, other cases seem to call into question the legal framework of self-defence as such. We no longer follow a dialogue articulated around the interpretation of the rule. Rather, for the most part, these productions tend to contest its existence, at least in its classical conception.

In this category, one can place a number of productions insisting on the dangers of an external military aggression and on the necessity to take all measures to repel it, without any consideration of the limits put forth in the UN Charter. In *Invasion USA*,[23] the United States suffers a massive air strike launched from Alaska by forces that are not explicitly identified but whose identity leaves little room for doubt (their goal supposedly being to spread Marxism under the aegis of a single party). The authorities, with the support of a massively mobilized population, are attempting to retort: 'we have returned blow for blow', states a senior military official. However, there is never a mention of the United Nations, self-defence or international law. The response appears 'natural', especially because it opposes the 'evil forces' to the 'united strength of the free peoples of the world'. The same pattern emerges from *Battle Beneath the Earth*[24] where a Chinese general orders the digging of thousands of kilometres of tunnels under the Pacific to invade the United States 'from beneath'. Fortunately, the plan is thwarted and the enemy is pushed back. This is also the case in *Red Dawn*[25] (with a similar remake, where the invader is North Korean[26]). The Soviet, Cuban and Nicaraguan troops invade the United States across the border of

---

23 Joseph Zito, USA, 1952.
24 Montgomery Tully, UK, 1967.
25 John Milius, USA, 1984.
26 Dan Bradley, USA, 2012.

Mexico, a country that has just undergone a revolution. With disturbing music playing in the background, the viewer learns that NATO had been dissolved, with only Great Britain remaining a faithful ally. The driving forces of the North American population will of course resist and eventually triumph over evil.[27] A close comparison can be drawn with *Invasion USA*[28] where the Soviet attack on Miami is almost singlehandedly repelled by the valiant Matt Hunter (Chuck Norris).[29] Shifting from the Cold War theme but in the same vein, we can evoke some productions on the 'war on terror'. *Delta Force*[30] sets the tone: the United States sends an intervention force to Lebanon to put an end to the activities of Palestinian terrorists, without any legal argument ever being evoked. The fight against terrorism naturally allows for a military response in foreign territory, especially when the State concerned is a 'failed state' or a 'rogue state' whose consent would have no meaning in any case.[31] More generally, the territories subject to the military intervention resemble more a wild zone or even a *terra nullius*, rather than places under the sovereignty of a State.[32]

Beyond the diversity of these productions, there seems to be a certain particular pattern. The rule vanishes when vital interests, or even existence, are at stake, and the need for a right to self-defence and survival naturally or even intuitively prevails.[33] In this respect, it is not surprising that a parallelism has been considered between this type of movie and other productions, even if they diverge in their form.[34] We can evoke the productions depicting the

---

27 Michael Ryan and Douglas Kellner, *Camera Politica: The Politics and Ideology of Contemporary Hollywood Film* (Bloomington and Indianapolis: Indiana University Press, 1988) 213–14.
28 Joseph Zito, USA, 1985.
29 Ryan and Kellner, *Camera Politica*, 227–8. See also: *Olympus Has Fallen* (Antoine Fuqua, USA, 2013).
30 Menahem Golan, USA/Israel, 1986.
31 Valantin, *Hollywood, le Pentagone et le monde*, 121–2. See also: *Navy Seals* (Lewis Teague, USA, 1990).
32 Olivier Corten, 'La représentation des frontières dans les films d'action: la fin des territoires?' in Esrelle Epinoux, Vincent Lefebve and Magalie Flores-Lonjou (eds), *Frontière(s) au cinéma* (Paris: Mare & Martin, Droit & Cinéma, 2019) 363–80; Anne-Marie Bidaud, *Hollywood et le rêve américain. Cinéma et idéologie aux Etats-Unis* (Paris: Armand Colin, 2nd edn, 2012) 19; Régis Dubois, *Hollywood, Cinéma et idéologie* (Paris: ed. Sulliver, 2008) 49.
33 Valantin, *Hollywood, le Pentagone et le monde*, 12.
34 Dubois, *Hollywood, Cinéma et idéologie*, 125–6; Valantin, *Hollywood, le Pentagone et le monde*, 27–32; Laurent Aknin, *Mythe et idéologie du cinéma américain* (Paris: éd. Vendemiaire, 2012) 23ff.; Shlomo Sand, *Le XXème siècle à l'écran* (Paris: Seuil, 2004) 354ff.; François Dubuisson, 'Cinéma et idéologie: représentation et fonction du terrorisme dans le film d'action hollywoodien' (2004) 105 *Contradictions* 57.

defeat of extra-terrestrial invaders, such as *Independence Day*.[35] The United States is obviously destined to defend the world against hordes of invaders, and their 'right to live, to exist' (to use the words of the US president in a famous speech) is exercised naturally, without any apparent legal or institutional limitation (the UN is, for instance, never mentioned).[36] In this context, the enemy, devoid of humanity, no longer enjoys a legal personality. Rather, he represents an outside malignant force or a threatening otherness,[37] legitimate to fight by all means, whether it he is 'red', a 'terrorist', an extra-terrestrial, a zombie[38] or even an evil insect or beast.[39] In this perspective, it has been noted that, even though, in reality, the 'other' rather incarnates the victim, these cinematographic productions put forth a reversed representation where the humans, in general, and (often) the United States in particular, find themselves in a situation of self-defence.[40]

Does this mean that the existing productions never depict self-defence as a legal concept with absolute limits?

Certainly not. In a series of movies, there is a reflection on the need to ensure that the State against which one wishes to exercise self-defence is indeed responsible for a prior armed attack. The risks – with potential or actual devastating consequences – generated by an impulsive reaction are thus highlighted. This is evidenced by productions like *Fail-Safe*[41] (and its almost identical remake[42]), *Doctor Strangelove*[43] or *24*.[44] All these scenarios, whether with a dramatic or a comical undertone, push to a reflection on the war, especially the nuclear war.[45] Contrary to the legal writings or political doctrines insisting on the need to respond immediately and from the very outset – and even before the launch – of an attack, these representations seem to prescribe caution and the exhaustion of all peaceful

---

35 Roland Emmerich, USA, 1996.
36 Barthélémy Courmont and Erwan Benezet, *Washington-Hollywood: Comment l'Amérique fait son cinéma* (Paris: Armand Colin, 2007) 145.
37 Valantin, *Hollywood, le Pentagone et le monde*, 16; Dubuisson, 'Cinéma et idéologie', 60–7.
38 Jean-Baptiste Thoret (ed.), *Politique des zombies: l'Amérique de Georges A. Romero* (Paris: Ellipses, 2007).
39 Valantin, *Hollywood, le Pentagone et le monde*, 122–3; Dubois, *Hollywood, Cinéma et idéologie*, 125–6.
40 Dubois, *Hollywood, Cinéma et idéologie*, 126; Bidaud, *Hollywood et le rêve américain*, 171.
41 Sidney Lumet, USA, 1964.
42 Stephen Frears, USA, 2000.
43 Stanley Kubrick, UK/USA, 1964.
44 Joel Surnow and Robert Cochran, Fox, USA, season 2, episodes 16–24, 2002–3.
45 Valantin, *Hollywood, le Pentagone et le monde*, 30–2; Serge Sur, *Plaisirs du cinéma. Le monde et ses miroirs* (Paris: France-Empire Monde, 2010) 84–94.

means before triggering something that may well lead to irreparable harm. At the same time, one should not get the false impression that the examples just mentioned are defences of the classic conception of self-defence within the meaning of international law, since the rule, as such, is not considered as a binding legal limit. Only considerations of political expediency dictating the decision to enter into war are taken into account.

Once more, beyond the diversity of the above-mentioned scenes, the selected filmography seems to confront international legal rules on the use of force to practice and, by doing so, it puts forth two marked trends. The first one criticizes the restrictiveness of the rules of the Charter, both on non-intervention and on self-defence, by a clear incitement to ignoring them in the name of humanitarian values, in the first case, and of requirements of national security, in the second. A second (minority) trend, especially with regard to the 'right of humanitarian intervention', favours the maintenance of existing rules while denouncing the potential consequences of their rejection. Be that as it may, and beyond the contemplation of specific rules of international law, there are ultimately two competing conceptions of law: the first and dominant one, with a rather realistic connotation, and a second one, more idealistic or pacifist. The third section of this chapter will explore this divide and highlight the dominating assimilation of international law to an arbitrary frame of reference.

Is there any international legal order?

As we know, the role of law in international relations is often considered through the prism of the opposition between a realistic pole and an idealistic pole.[46] If we follow the logic of the first one, the protagonists of the international scene – especially the States – act according to their own interests, the only limits being the constraints translated into the balance of power with other States. The idealistic pole, on the other hand, refers to the role of law as a factor of pacification and integration of the international community, which should lead jurists to codify and propose new rules embodying a certain universal legitimacy, rules that effectively influence the behaviour of the protagonists (States, but also international organizations, NGOs or individuals) in their behaviour. From this perspective, if we evaluate the productions relevant for the present study, the result can be hardly questioned: the general trend that emerges is resolutely realistic.

---

46 Olivier Corten, *Méthodologie du droit international public* (Brussels: Editions de l'Université de Bruxelles, 2009) 68–80.

International law: ineffective and very often ignored

The dozens of films and series viewed for the purpose of this chapter contain no reference to issues of lawfulness of military interventions in Iraq (1991 and 2003, with the exception of *W*[47] and *Vice*[48]), Yugoslavia (1999), Georgia (2008), Libya (2011), Ukraine (2014–) or Syria (2014–), to name but the particularly iconic examples.[49] To the extent of our knowledge, cinema does not enquire either about the responsibility, under international law, for triggering older conflicts like the Korean War,[50] the Vietnam War,[51] the US interventions in Cuba (1961), in the Dominican Republic (1965) or in Panama (1989), or the USSR's in Hungary (1956), Czechoslovakia (1968) or Afghanistan (1979).

Interestingly enough, this silence also prevails in productions obviously intended to criticize a given war, even though one might have expected that the argument pertaining to the compliance with the rules of the Charter would be mentioned. *Fahrenheit 9/11*[52] offers an emblematic example. This is indeed a particularly biting critique against President Bush, presented as an incompetent, lazy, cheating and corrupt character.[53] In this context, the decision to launch the war against Iraq is vigorously denounced. Michael Moore, the director, emphasizes the lack of legitimacy of this war: it is based on a lie (the alleged possession of weapons of mass destruction by Saddam Hussein's regime and his supposed links with Al-Qaeda) and it leads to death and desolation in the families of US soldiers sent to the front. All this is depicted in the context of a coalition whose partners are ridiculed

---

47 Oliver Stone, USA, 2008.
48 Adam McKay, USA, 2018.
49 Olivier Corten, 'La mise en scène des doctrines interventionnistes dans les films étatsuniens: *Ronnie goes to Hollywood*!' in Stéphane Boiron, Nathalie Goedert and Ninon Maillard (eds), *Les lois de la guerre* (Clermont-Ferrand: Institut universitaire Varenne, 2015) 175–95.
50 See for example: *The Steel Helmet* (Samuel Fuller, USA, 1951), *This is Korea!* (John Ford, USA, 1951), *War Hunt* (Denis Sanders, USA, 1962), *The Manchurian Candidate* (John Frankenheimer, USA, 1962), *The Bridges at Toko-Ri* (Mark Robson, 1954).
51 Laurent Tessier, *Le Vietnam, un cinéma de l'apocalypse* (Paris: éd. du Cerf/éd. Corlet, 2009); Michel Jacquet, *Nuit américaine sur le Viet-Nam. Le cinéma U.S. et la 'sale guerre'* (Paris: éd. Anovi, 2009), Pierre-Emmanuel Barral, 'La guerre du Viet-nam au cinéma' in Philippe d'Hugues and Hervé Coutau-Bégarie (eds), *Le cinéma et la guerre* (Paris: Economica, 2006) 157–75; Thomas Doherty, *Projections of War: Hollywood, American Culture and Word War II* (New York: Columbia University Press, 1993) 282–92.
52 Michael Moore, USA, 2004.
53 Douglas Kellner, *Cinema Wars: Hollywood Films and Politics in the Bush-Cheney Era* (Oxford: Wiley-Blackwell, 2010) 148–50; Carter and Dodds, *International Politics and Film*, 11; Stephen Prince, *Firestorm: American Film in the Age of Terrorism* (New York: Columbia University Press, 2009) 51–159.

(for example, the island country of Palau is mentioned while images of naked men dancing on a beach with spears are shown in the background, generating the idea of a primitive and wild people). As for international law, which was frequently mentioned at the time, namely during the pacifist demonstrations in Europe, it is absolutely overlooked by the production, just like the UN. While the director's voice tells us that Iraq as a nation has not attacked the United States, nor has it threatened, or murdered a single American citizen, no legal argument is ever raised, even indirectly. The criticism rather points out the lack of a political opportunity to attack Iraq in the context of that time. The war is not denounced as such, Michael Moore expressing substantial depiction of compassion towards the families of the soldiers of the US army without ever mentioning the Iraqi victims of the conflict.[54] This is thus not a pacifist production and this is confirmed by the belief expressed by Michael Moore that US military engagement in Afghanistan is clearly insufficient. In any event, the lack of reference to the UN Charter is certainly significant.

Other rather critical productions about the war in Iraq, from 2003 (*Battle for Haditha*,[55] *Redacted*,[56] *The Mark of Cain*,[57] *Generation Kill*[58]) or 1991 (*Jarhead*[59]) can be interpreted in the same way: the denunciation concerns the difficulty of understanding the meaning or the appropriateness of the intervention or the occupation, and sometimes the crimes possibly committed by the soldiers who become disillusioned and disoriented by a situation of armed conflict.[60] In these cases the reference frame comes from human rights law,[61] humanitarian law or *jus in bello* rather than from the question of the legality of the conflict under the Charter, the *jus contra bellum*. The same trend can be observed in films on the Vietnam War, such as *Apocalypse Now*,[62] *Platoon*,[63] *Full Metal Jacket*[64] and *Casualties of War*.[65] Although they undoubtedly embody a different sensibility, films like

---

54 Prince, *Firestorm*, 157; Kellner, *Cinema Wars*, 151.
55 Nick Broomfield, UK, 2007.
56 Brian de Palma, USA/Canada, 2007.
57 Mark Munden, UK, 2007.
58 David Simon and Ed Burns, HBO, USA, 2008.
59 Sam Mendes, USA/Germany, 2005.
60 See for example Kellner, *Cinema Wars*, 222–3; Prince, *Firestorm*, 302.
61 Prince, *Firestorm*, 61, 213 and 247.
62 Francis Ford Coppola, USA, 1979.
63 Oliver Stone, USA, 1986.
64 Stanley Kubrick, USA/UK, 1987.
65 Brian de Palma, USA, 1989.

Rambo III[66] or *The Beast*[67] can be interpreted in the same way: while the war waged by the Soviet Union on Afghanistan is violently criticized, the criticism is never based on an argument pertaining to the UN Charter.

Thus, the main representation is that of an action decided on without any questioning of its compliance with the rules of law prohibiting the use of force. This does not mean that the law as such is totally absent but, when it is staged, it is usually through a reference to the domestic legal order which, in turn, seems to constitute both a legitimate and a binding framework.[68] In *The West Wing*,[69] the president is essentially concerned by his dealings with Congress when it comes to deciding on a military response to an attack in Gaza against US citizens. Never, however, are any limits drawn from the UN Charter, at most an adviser scornfully points out that Syria might make a fuss in order to obtain a UN resolution condemning the strikes.

Finally, the international legal order appears as non-binding, especially in comparison with domestic law. The latter is characterized by its multiple rules and precision, and can above all rely on a centralized institutional structure capable of enforcing it, as well as a judicial system that can be staged by writers. By comparison, international law could at most, as we have seen, be equated with morality. Even then it is often presented as lacking not only the effectiveness but also the legitimacy necessary to incarnate a framework of reference likely to guide the action of the protagonists of the international scene.

International law as illegitimate or even ridiculous: 'a cultural misunderstanding'?

Various productions insist on the illegitimacy of any legal order that does not sufficiently take into account the requirements of the battlefield from a military perspective.[70] Indeed, who can claim to regulate and judge the behaviour of a soldier 'in the heat of the moment', without having himself experienced such a situation? Thus, according to these productions, it is

---

66 Peter MacDonald, USA, 1988.
67 Kevin Reynolds, USA, 1988.
68 Valantin, *Hollywood, le Pentagone et le monde*, 166.
69 Aaron Sorkin, NBC, USA, season 5, episodes 21–22, 2003–4 and season 6, episodes 1–2, 2004–5.
70 See Chapter 7 by Martyna Fałkowska-Clarys and Vaios Koutroulis in the present volume.

important to factor in the military ethics or a certain 'code of honour' as an essential criteria of legitimacy. This however remains unachievable for public international law developed by diplomats entirely removed from the theatre of operations. Several episodes of *JAG* thus contrast, on the one hand, the relevance of a soldier's decision-making process, forced to act without always having time for reflection, with the rigid and arbitrary nature of legal rules enacted in the name of peace, on the other.

In other productions, international law is (admittedly indirectly) presented as a trap used by the enemy, a trap that must be avoided if one wants to survive. In *Mars Attacks!*[71] the Martians' landing on Earth is accompanied by broadcasts of reassuring messages: 'we come in peace, we come in peace, we come in peace [...]'. The purpose here is to take advantage of the naivety of the earthlings and trigger a massive attack against the United States, sparing neither civilians nor fighters who surrender, let alone the pacifists. At first, several senior officials deny the obvious, and evoke a 'cultural misunderstanding' in their attempt to justify the action of the Martians. For the rest, the film conveys the belief that international law is radically ridiculous: while the president of the United States despairs of finding a solution to curb the Martian invasion, he receives a phone call from his French counterpart. The result is the following dialogue:

Amercian president: Hello Maurice, ça va?
French president: Très bien, I have some good news for you; the Martian ambassador is here and we've negotiated a settlement.
Amercian president: Maurice, get out of the room, get out now!'.

The conversation is then interrupted by the Martians suddenly slaughtering the French leaders while, at the same time, launching a massive attack against the City of Lights and the Eiffel Tower collapsing under the blaze of laser weapons of mass destruction. The idealistic belief in a treaty solution is absurd and is used by the enemy to fool our vigilance.

All these productions obviously reproduce representations associating international law with a frame of reference at best detached from the realities on the ground, at worst as a decoy to which only the naive or fools can yield. In this perspective, one is undoubtedly presented with a manifestation of a realistic conception of international relations. This does not mean, however, that no trace of a more idealistic conception can be detected in the existing productions, as will be briefly shown below.

---

71 Tim Burton, USA, 1996.

International law as a pacifying ideal? 'Peace is our profession'

In *Doctor Strangelove*,[72] the inscription 'peace is our profession' is featured in the military buildings where General Jack Ripper prepares to launch a nuclear attack. Beyond the irony that this contrast highlights,[73] the film is deeply pacifistic. Just like in *Fail-Safe*,[74] the solution to the threat is to be found in negotiation, in cooperation with the adversary, and ultimately in the conclusion of peace agreements. *Fail-Safe* pictures the ultra-realistic opinion of a consultant professor of political science, who proposes to take advantage of the situation to launch a massive nuclear attack against the Soviet Union, stating that the latter will not fight back for ideological reasons (in the Marxist and determinist logic it would be better to avoid a nuclear war, even at the cost of a temporary surrender which could not hinder the inevitable advent of communism in the long run). Paradoxically, the US military denounce the absurdity of this option by ensuring that the Soviet armed forces would react in the same way any armed forces would in such a situation. The path of the law is therefore the most reasonable, the realistic and hawkish option only paving the way towards the world sinking into destructive madness.[75] Albeit in a lighter tone, other films like *The Russians are Coming, the Russians are Coming*[76] or *Spies Like Us*[77] seem to convey a similar logic, as they praise the cooperation between men and women of good will.[78] Finally, *The Hour*[79] and *The Crown*[80] picture a protest against the invasion of Suez by the French and British forces. The protesters hold banners reading 'Law, not War' and international law is also mobilized by the opposition as well as by a journalist who is one of the series' heroes.

This overview clearly shows that the idealistic productions are rare and that, if we stick to the selected material, they bow before the strength and number of films and series that convey, explicitly or implicitly, a resolutely realistic conception denying, minimizing or criticizing the place of international law in relations between States. At this stage, we have thus observed a certain consistency, regardless of the diversity of the possible scenarios. The last part of this chapter will be an occasion to highlight and question the factors that may explain this state of affairs.

72 Stanley Kubrick, USA, 1964.
73 Sur, *Plaisirs du cinéma*, 85.
74 Sidney Lumet, USA, 1964.
75 See Sand, *Le XXème siècle à l'écran*, 384–5.
76 Norman Jewison, USA, 1966.
77 John Landis, USA, 1985.
78 Ryan and Kellner, *Camera Politica*, 216.
79 Abi Morgan, BBC, UK, 2011–12.
80 Peter Morgan, Netflix, USA/UK, season 2, 2017.

A 'military-cinematographic complex'?

How can we explain the tendency to interpret extensively, to minimize or to ignore the role of the United Nations Charter in international relations? First, one can simply recall the tendency of the political authorities to utilize films to justify military interventions, sometimes in defiance of existing international law. This explanation, which refers to the possible association between cinema and political propaganda, is as such explored in *Wag the Dog*.[81] In this clairvoyant comedy, the US president sees the prospect of a second term compromised because of a sex scandal that is revealed in the news.[82] A team of communications advisers decides to divert media attention to the outbreak of an imaginary war against Albania, a State supposedly supporting the growth of international terrorism. They turn to a movie producer who will go so far as to shoot studio scenes supposed to show a mother with her cat fleeing the armed hostilities (in reality, all the scenery is entirely digital). A popular song is then used in an advertisement spot supporting the military campaign. Thus, cinema makes it possible to shape and configure the public opinion in a particularly effective way, in particular when it comes to conflicts in little known regions.[83] In this context, it seems logical that the law of the Charter is far from being highlighted.

Beyond this cinematic illustration, several scholars have pointed out the links that have historically and on several occasions bound the Pentagon and Hollywood.[84] During the Second World War, a close cooperation established with the film studios resulted in a cinematographic production closely associated with Washington's foreign policy.[85] One can also recall a meeting that took place a few weeks after the 9/11 attacks, between major cinema producers and the Bush administration officials, to establish a common strategy for the 'war on terror'.[86] More specifically, certain films are sometimes identified as having been the result of an explicit desire to support the US armed forces, as part of what has been termed a 'military-cinematographic

---

81 Barry Lenvinson, USA, 1997.
82 Kellner, *Cinema Wars*, 113; Prince, *Firestorm*, 259–60.
83 Courmont and Benezet, *Washington-Hollywood*, 172; Sand, *Le XXème siècle à l'écran*, 69–70.
84 Matthew Alford, *Reel Power: Hollywood Cinema and American Supremacy* (New York: Plutopress, 2010) 3ff.
85 Régis Dubois, *Une histoire politique du cinéma. Etats-Unis, Europe, U.R.S.S.* (Paris: éd. Sulliver, 2007) 64–70.
86 Courmont and Benezet, *Washington-Hollywood*, 65; Valantin, *Hollywood, le Pentagone et le monde*, 137; Bidaud, *Hollywood et le rêve américain*, 180.

complex'.[87] It is the case of *The Green Berets*,[88] a film openly presented by John Wayne as a defence of the military engagement in Vietnam,[89] or *Top Gun*,[90] which was produced with the support of the Pentagon and sparked a wave of enlistment campaigns carried out by the recruitment offices located near the cinemas where the movie was screened.[91] Beyond these few particularly enlightening examples, one can note a close concordance between the ideology conveyed by certain productions and by the doctrines defended by the political authorities of the moment. The classic example is the resurgence of films such as those of the *Rambo* franchise[92] during the two Reagan administrations.[93] The comparison between the abundance of productions narrating – and incidentally justifying – the victorious Israeli raid on Entebbe (four films) and the absence of any portrayal of the fiasco of the rescue operation of the American hostages in Tehran is also characteristic.[94] With regard to this last point, it seems difficult not to notice that Hollywood preferred glorifying the exfiltration of the employees of a private company (*On Wings of Eagles*, 1986) or of a few diplomats who managed to leave the country thanks to the cooperation of the Canadian authorities (*Argo*, 2012).

More recently, in *24* (2001–10, 2014)[95] and *Homeland* (2011–20),[96] we could detect two versions of the war on terror that are, more or less ostensibly, justified. A common thread featured in many of the analysed productions refers to the representation and the construction of a threat likely to justify the use of force by the political power.[97] In *24*, violence is more directly

---

87 Ryan and Kellner, *Camera Politica*, 194ff.
88 John Wayne and Ray Kellogg, USA, 1968.
89 Valantin, *Hollywood, le Pentagone et le monde*, 33; Tessier, *Le Vietnam, un cinéma de l'apocalypse*, 48–58.
90 Tony Scott, USA, 1986.
91 Courmont and Benezet, *Washington-Hollywood*, 55–6; Valantin, *Hollywood, le Pentagone et le monde*, 19. We can also notice that some movies, such as *Behind Enemy Lines* (John Moore, USA, 2001) were used in advertisements for military recruitment campaigns; Kellner, *Cinema Wars*, 25.
92 *First Blood* (Ted Kotcheff, USA, 1982), *Rambo: First Blood Part II* (George Pan Cosmatos, 1985), *Rambo III* (Peter MacDonald, 1988).
93 Valantin, *Hollywood, le Pentagone et le monde*, 37–41 and 46–7; Dubois, *Une histoire politique du cinéma*, 139–40; Kellner, *Cinema Wars*, 2; Ryan and Kellner, *Camera Politica*, 227; Dubuisson, 'Cinéma et idéologie', 58.
94 Sally Totman, *How Hollywood Projects Foreign Policy* (New York: Palgrave Macmillan, 2009) 154.
95 Joel Surnow and Robert Cochran, Fox, USA, 2001–10, 2014.
96 Howard Gordon, Alex Gansa, Gideon Raff, Showtime, USA, 2012–20.
97 Valantin, *Hollywood, le Pentagone et le monde*, 8.

represented, and Jack Bauer (Kiefer Sutherland) appears as the archetype of 'the man for the job', who does not hesitate to get his hands dirty in the name of the need to protect the country against the terrorist threat, even if this means violating legal rules (including international law).[98] In *Homeland*, the struggle seems less radical at first sight. The main character, Claire Mathison (Claire Danes) uses little or no torture or violence and constantly discloses her problems of conscience. Obviously, these two very popular series cannot be reduced to propaganda and contain a subtlety that would be sought for in vain in many other aforementioned productions: we have already mentioned the hollow criticism of the war against Iraq in the second season of *24*, and we can add that *Homeland* undeniably forces the viewers to reflect, especially as they observe another central character, Nicholas Brody (Damian Lewis), strongly disturbed by the excessive interventionism of his own government. The justification of the fight against terrorism is nonetheless generally present, in particular through the representations of a particularly daunting enemy, who benefits from relays, complicities and ramifications at the very heart of the national territory. And, as regards international law, and especially the rules prohibiting the use of force in relations between States, it must be noted that their representation does not differ from all the productions analysed for this study.

On the whole, the representation of the law of the Charter that lacks both efficiency and legitimacy seems to transcend political and artistic divides. At the national level, courtroom movies and legal series have met with great success, featuring trials, lawyers, judges, and even developing legal arguments.[99] The predilection of the cinematographic productions for the action or the destinies and the individual experiences[100] does not therefore exclude that law play a certain role. Still on the national scene, this success of the 'legal film' was explained by the desire to portray the American society as being governed by the rule of law, where disputes can be settled peacefully and efficiently through a particularly well-developed legal and institutional apparatus.[101] By contrast, the international political and legal order seems (even more?) akin to a state of nature than to a State governed by the rule of law, a state of nature whose effects will be more easily contained by the use of national legal frameworks rather than of the illusory

---

98 Vilmer, *24 heures chrono*, 97.
99 Paul Bergman and Michael Asimow, *Reel Justice: The Courtoom goes to the Movies* (Kansas City: Andews McMeel, 2006).
100 Sand, *Le XXème siècle à l'écran*, 59; Sur, *Plaisirs du cinéma*, 62–3.
101 David Ray Papke, 'Law, Cinema, and Ideology: Hollywood Legal Films of the 1950s', *Marquette University Law School. Faculty Publications*, 2001, Paper 275 (2001) 48 *UCLA Law Review*; see also Bidaud, *Hollywood et le rêve américain*, 93.

standards of the international community.[102] And it should be emphasized that, apart from the few almost caricatural examples mentioned above, this perception does not stem from a propaganda coherently orchestrated from within the premises of the White House. The strength of these examples is precisely to assert themselves as obvious, thus constituting an ideology effectively impregnating people's minds.

This undoubtedly raises the question of the potentially widening gap between the conceptions shared by the specialists of the law of the Charter, on the one hand, and those conveyed to the public opinion, on the other hand. One way to reconcile them could aim at promoting a modification of the rules in order to bring them closer to 'popular' representations, a path that can be detected in certain legal proposals that are more inclined to justify the war on terror. Another way would tend, on the contrary, to change or qualify these representations by trying to bring them closer to the generally shared legal interpretations. This last path could lead to the development of new scenarios, with the prospect of productions explaining – even legitimizing – the logic and scope of the existing rules. Of course, this process requires artistic and creative skills that we do not claim to possess. Less ambitious, but hopefully, equally effective, the purpose of the present chapter is rather to raise awareness of the ideological character of the concepts enshrined in the UN Charter and conveyed by action movies. An awareness that can foster a more vigilant and critical vision of these films and series.

---

102 Valantin, *Hollywood, le Pentagone et le monde*, 86.

5

The Israeli–Palestinian conflict: a cinematic saga

François Dubuisson

The famous 1960 film *Exodus*,[1] by Otto Preminger, is a particularly emblematic example of the way in which cinema portrays the conflict and forges a certain representation thereof in the eyes of the general public. It relates a key moment in the genesis of the dispute, describing a series of events surrounding the end of British Mandate over Palestine and the Partition Plan adopted by the United Nations General Assembly in November 1947.[2] A scene from this film allows us to illustrate two conceptions of international law that can be conveyed by the cinema about this conflict, and which will serve as points of reference in our analysis. While kibbutz residents welcome the radio announcement of the adoption of the UN Partition Plan, which provides for the creation of a Jewish State and an Arab State, Ari Ben Canaan (Paul Newman), commander of the Haganah (Zionist army), and his childhood friend Taha (John Derek), head of the neighbouring Palestinian village, begin a discussion about the consequences of this adoption:

> **Ben Canaan:** Taha, What's wrong?
> **Taha:** You won your freedom, I have lost mine.
> **Ben Canaan:** But we never had freedom. You or I. All of our lives we have been under British rule. Now, we'll be equal citizens in the free state of Israel. The resolution (of the UN) guarantees it.
> **Taha:** Guarantees are one thing, reality is another. Now it makes my lands part of Israel.
> **Ben Canaan:** These are still your lands.
> **Taha:** I'm a minority.
> **Ben Canaan:** We have always been friends. Minority, majority, we prove it makes no difference.

1 Otto Preminger, USA, 1960.
2 General Assembly of the United Nations, Resolution 181 (II), Future government of Palestine, 29 November 1947.

Taha: If it makes no difference, why did you fight so hard to bring this about?

Ben Canaan: Because we had hundreds of thousands of people with no other place to go.

Taha: And now where shall my people go?

Ben Canaan: Why should they go anywhere? This is their home as well as ours. Taha, don't you see we are going to prove to the world that we can get along together. If we don't, the British will claim that we can't govern ourselves without their help.

The dialogue opposes two conceptions of the role that international law can play in the settlement of the Israeli–Palestinian question (or here, of one of its particular aspects, the equality between Jewish and Arab citizens). On the one hand, Ben Canaan develops an idealistic vision of international law[3] which considers that conflicts will be effectively settled by the provisions of the UN resolution. International law is thus presented as an efficient and effective tool for resolving disputes, ensuring respect for rights, in this case those of the Palestinian population destined to live in the State of Israel. On the other hand, Taha believes that these guarantees will be insufficient in the light of realities and the existing relations of domination. In this perspective, international law will be considered as a tool whose effective application depends largely on the realities of the international society, which favours power relations. The implementation of international law thus depends on the contradictions that exist between States. This is what we will call the 'critical' conception.[4]

Beyond this renowned production, the Israeli–Palestinian conflict has inspired a very abundant filmography, which retraces its main events and deals with many aspects of it. From a material composed of a hundred fiction movies and TV series, we will study the conceptions of international law in the context of the Israeli–Palestinian conflict that are conveyed on the screen. Three main themes emerge in this respect, which correspond to three main chronological stages of the conflict. First, that of the creation of the State of Israel (1948) and its consequences on the Palestinian population. Then, the question of the conception of the conflict as it developed after the 1967 Arab-Israeli war, seen as either a war against Palestinian terrorism or a struggle against the Israeli occupation. Finally, the peace process in the Middle East as it unfolded after the conclusion of the Oslo Accords (1993). For each of these stages, we will examine the opposition or the articulation of the 'idealistic' and the 'critical' conceptions that we have just presented

---

3 See Olivier Corten, *Méthodologie du droit international public* (Brussels: Editions de l'Université de Bruxelles, 2009) 69–73.

4 Corten, *Méthodologie du droit international public*, 59–62.

based on the example of *Exodus*. In the last part, we will elaborate some explanations concerning the types of conception of international law that emerge from the film material analysed and formulate some reflections on the place of cinema in the conflict.

The creation of the State of Israel and the expulsion of the Palestinian population

These events have been depicted in a significant number of movies, portraying the conflict in a way that has evolved over time. At first, Israeli and American cinema presented the conflict as largely settled by the United Nations, the only remaining contestation resulting from the intransigence of the Arab States. Israeli and Palestinian filmmakers who developed a critical approach then challenged this idealized vision. They thus endeavoured to show the discrepancy between the UN texts and the practical realities, in particular concerning the status of the Palestinian population remaining in Israel and the question of refugees.

A 'heroic-nationalist' vision of the creation of Israel: 'Gentlemen, Hill 24 is attributed to Israel'

For a long time, the vision of the history of the conflict and the context of the creation of the State of Israel has been the one conveyed by Hollywood and a movement within the Israeli cinema that has been labelled as 'heroic-nationalist'.[5] A vision of history that largely follows the traditional Israeli narrative emerges from these movies[6] as well as a very formalistic and idealistic reading of international law based on the texts adopted by the United Nations. The movie *Exodus* is very emblematic in this respect. It narrates, in a way that rather freely interprets the historical reality, the story of the ship 'Exodus', which tries to bring from Europe to Palestine the Jewish immigrants, survivors of the Holocaust. It also describes the actions carried out in Palestine by the various Zionist organizations (Haganah, Irgun) against the British authorities, then the beginning of the confrontation with the Arabs following the vote of the UN Partition Plan. The Zionist movement

---

5 See Ella Shohat, *Israeli Cinema: East/West and the Politics of Representation* (New York and London: I.B. Tauris, 2010) 53–104; Ariel Schweitzer, *Le cinéma israélien de la modernité* (Paris: L'Harmattan, 1997) 58–69.
6 Rachel Weissbrod, '*Exodus* as a Zionist Melodrama' (1999) 4 *Israel Studies* 129–52; Yosefa Loshitzky, 'National Rebirth as a Movie: Otto Preminger's *Exodus*' (2002) 4 *National Identities* 119–31; Schweitzer, *Le cinéma israélien*, 61.

is portrayed as a national liberation movement fighting mainly against the British Mandate, seen as a regime of occupation.[7] The film insists on the ancestral links existing between the Land of Palestine and the Jews, and the resulting foundation for the establishment of their State. The Partition Plan voted by the United Nations is thus presented as consecrating this link and as awarding a direct legal title to the creation of the State of Israel.[8] The Zionist authorities aspire to live peacefully, in full equality, with the Arab inhabitants of Palestine, and it is only because of the radicalism of certain Arab leaders, likened to Nazis,[9] that this cohabitation is difficult to achieve. In a scene that immediately follows the announcement of the vote on the Partition Plan, Barak Ben Canaan reads a statement of the National Zionist Committee in the presence of the inhabitants of the kibbutz:

> To the Arab population of Jewish Palestine, we make the following appeal: the Grand Mufti [of Jerusalem] has asked you either to annihilate the Jewish population or to abandon your homes and your lands and to seek the weary path of exile. We implore you: remain in your homes and in your shops and we shall work together as equals in the Free State of Israel.

While the above-mentioned dialogue between Ari Ben Canaan and Taha confronts two positions as to the possibility of achieving this vow of equality, the film will later validate Ari's point of view: Taha will refuse to associate with the Arab fighters to attack Gan Dafna and will pay for this decision with his life. In the final scene of the film, he will be symbolically buried in the kibbutz, alongside Karen, a young Jewish victim.

According to the film's depiction, the creation of the State of Israel is based on the UN Parititon Plan resolution rejected by the Arabs, and a complete equality of rights was recognized, within the new State, for the Palestinians who wished to remain on their land, guaranteed both by the resolution and by the commitments of the Zionist authorities. Law thus settles all questions, and the Arab States maintain the existence of a conflict by their very refusal of this international legal setting.

The consecration of the creation of the State of Israel and its borders by international law is also particularly highlighted in another film: *Hill 24*

---

7 This theme is also at the centre of the first Hollywood production dedicated to the events that led to the birth of the State of Israel: *Sword in the Desert* (George Sherman, USA, 1949).

8 The question of the legal basis for the creation of the State of Israel has given rise to intense doctrinal debates. See James Crawford, *The Creation of States in International Law* (Oxford: Oxford University Press, 2006) 421–48; Victor Kattan, *From Coexistence to Conquest: International Law and the Origins of the Arab-Israeli Conflict, 1891–1946* (London and New York: Pluto Press, 2009) 232ff.

9 In the film, the position of the Arab nationalists is expressed by a German former Nazi leader, acting as an emissary of the Grand Mufti of Jerusalem.

Doesn't Answer.[10] This movie constitutes the archetype of the 'heroic-nationalist' Israeli cinema. A map is presented in the introductory scene and its outlines are explained by a voiceover narration in the following way:

> On the eastern shore of the Mediterranean, Palestine. On May 14, 1948, the State of Israel, sanctioned by the United Nations, was declared and the British mandate ended on that day. Seven Arab countries challenged the borders set by the United Nations. Thus began the War of Liberation, during which Israel fought for survival.

The movie recounts the fate of four Israeli soldiers, called to sacrifice their lives to conquer 'Hill 24', in the context of the fight against the Arab Legion, just before the implementation of a truce established by the UN on 18 July 1948.[11] The goal of the mission is to take control over hills overlooking the main road to Jerusalem, thus improving Israeli positions before the entry into force of the truce. As stated by Captain Berger during the briefing to his soldiers: 'there must be no dispute about our right to claim them'. In the final scene, a delegation from the Truce Commission of the UN goes to Hill 24. It is composed of two 'neutral' French and American soldiers, and two observers, an Israeli and a Transjordan officer. At the top of the hill, the delegation discovers the lifeless bodies of the four Israeli fighters. The Transjordan officer comments: 'It is clear that the hill belongs to us, the defender did not survive to claim it.' The French delegate then discovers the flag of the State of Israel folded in the hand of a dead soldier and proclaims: 'Gentlemen, Hill 24 is attributed to Israel.' By the end of the movie, the borders of the State of Israel thus appear to be legally founded and validated by UN decisions,[12] including territories acquired by armed operations during the war, located beyond the limits set by the Partition Plan.[13] The territories defined by what are in reality only armistice lines[14] appear to be officially recognized as definitely belonging to Israel.

---

10 Thorold Dickinson, Israel, 1955.
11 See Resolution 54, UN Security Council, 15 July 1948.
12 The same type of presentation of facts can be found in the Holywood movie *Cast a Giant Shadow* (Melville Shavelson, USA, 1966), which insists that the proclamation of the State of Israel is legally based on the UN Partition Plan, which David Ben Gurion (appearing in the movie under the name of Jacob Zion) sees as a 'decision granting us independence', of an 'irrevocable' character.
13 See Uri S. Cohen, 'From Hill to Hill: A Brief History of the Representation of War in Israeli Cinema' in Miri Talmon and Yaron Peleg (eds), *Israeli Cinema: Identities in Motion* (Austin: University of Texas Press, 2011) 44–8.
14 Israel-Jordan Armistice Agreement, 3 April 1949, text available at: www.mfa.gov.il/mfa/foreignpolicy/mfadocuments/yearbook1/pages/israel-jordan%20armistice%20agreement.aspx, accessed 1 December 2019.

In the end, these films convey a rather idealistic vision of the law: the question of the State and its borders is entirely regulated by the decisions of the United Nations and the equality between Jewish and Palestinian inhabitants within the State of Israel is fully guaranteed by the text of Resolution 181 and the Declaration of Independence.[15] Such depiction of the situation is achieved at the cost of a very selective reading of the content of these texts – for example, Resolution 194 (II) concerning the Right of return of refugees is never mentioned – and evacuating a large part of the factual reality. The reference to international law actually fulfils a function of occultation. What matters is (part of) the law as it was proclaimed, and not the reality on the ground which is not consistent with the said law and must thus be concealed.

The vision of history and international law conveyed by all these films will be widely questioned as from the 1970 and 1980s, when an activist Palestinian *cinema d'auteur*[16] and a wave of critical Israeli filmmakers will emerge.[17] Movies showing the hidden aspects of the creation of the State of Israel become numerous and varied. They evoke the extension by armed force of the 'borders' of the State of Israel, the consequent expulsion of a large part of the Palestinian population and the discrimination against the remaining Arab minority in the State of Israel.

An equality of facade: 'Israel recognizes the civil rights of Nazarenes without distinction of race, language or religion. Sign here, please'

The 1948 war is at the centre of the film *The Time that Remains* (2009), directed by Elia Suleiman, an Israeli filmmaker of Palestinian origin. The film narrates the destiny of the Palestinian city of Nazareth. Allocated to the Arab State in the UN Partition Plan, the city was eventually incorporated into the 'borders' of the State of Israel after its conquest in July 1948 and subjected,

---

15 See François Dubuisson, 'Frontières et droit international dans les films concernant le conflit israélo-palestinien' in Estelle Epinoux, Magalie Flores-Lonjou and Vincent Lefebve (eds), *Frontière(s) au cinéma* (Paris: Mare & Martin, 2019) 381–402.
16 See Nurith Gertz and George Khleifi, *Palestinian Cinema: Landscape, Trauma and Memory* (Edinburgh: Edinburgh University Press, 2008) 20–53; Joseph Massad, 'The Weapon of Culture: Cinema in the Palestinian Liberation Struggle' in Hamid Dabashi (ed.), *Dreams of a Nation: On Palestinian Cinema* (London and New York: Verso, 2006) 32–44; Livia Alexander, 'Is There a Palestinian Cinema? The National and Transnational in Palestinian Film Production' in Rebecca L. Stein and Ted Swedenburg (eds), *Palestine, Israel, and the Politics of Popular Culture* (Durham, NC and London: Duke University Press, 2005) 150–72.
17 Shohat, *Israeli Cinema*, 215ff.

with its Arab population, to a military regime until 1966.[18] A scene from the movie shows the solemn ceremony of the signing of the act of capitulation by the mayor of the city, in the presence of the Israeli military authorities. While the respect of the equality of the citizens is mentioned amongst the conditions of surrender, read out by the Israeli commander, this equality is emptied of its content by the other conditions, which submit the Nazarene population to the good will of the decisions of the military authority:

> **The Commander:** Your Honor Mr. Mayor, you are asked to sign the official act of surrender: 'Nazareth surrenders unconditionally to the army of Israel. The fighters of the Arab countries will be delivered to the army of Israel. The weapons and ammunition will be transferred to the army of Israel. The military commander may sentence any offender to death at his discretion. The mayor will be in charge of the civil affairs. However, only the army will distinguish between civil and military matters. Israel recognizes the civil rights of Nazarenes without distinction of race, language or religion'. Sign here please.

The director's depiction strikingly contrasts with that vehiculated by movies like *Exodus*: the equality proclaimed is a mere facade and the Palestinian minority, when it is not expelled, is in fact the object of discrimination.[19] This reality is reflected in many other productions.[20] Retrospectively, contemporary cinema thus gives reason to Taha's point of view, contrasting with the message conveyed by *Exodus*: the reality of power relations and interests takes precedence over formal law. An idealistic view of the law has given way to a critical approach, which recognizes the difficulties of effective implementation in the light of the relationship of domination.

The filmic revelation of the Palestinian exodus: 'Tell me Schmulik, don't you see what we're doing? We're sending people into exile'

Totally absent from American and Israeli fictions before the 1970s, the question of the 1947–49 Palestinian exodus was later depicted by various

---

18 See: Geremy Forman, 'Military Rule, Political Manipulation, and Jewish Settlement: Israeli Mechanisms for Controlling Nazareth in the 1950s' (2006) *Journal of Israeli History* 335ff.

19 See Haaretz, ' "We Look at Them Like Donkeys": What Israel's First Ruling Party Thought About Palestinian Citizens', 13 January 2018.

20 See *Chronicle of a Disappearance* (Elia Suleiman, Palestine/Israel, 1996); *Yom Yom* (Amos Gitaï, Israel/France,1998); *Jaffa* (Keren Yedaya, Israel, 2009); *Ajami* (Scandar Copti and Yaron Shani, Israel, 2009); *Miral* (Julian Schnabel, USA, 2010); *Man Without A Cell Phone* (Sameh Zoabi, Israel/Belgium/France, 2010); *The Promise* (Peter Kosminsky, UK, Channel Four, 2011, four episodes); *Inheritance* (Hiam Abbass, Israel/France, 2012); *Dancing Arabs* (Eran Riklis, Israel/Germany/France, 2014); *Junction 48* (Udi Aloni, Israel/Germany/USA, 2016); *Wajib* (Annemarie Jacir, Palestine, 2017).

movies.²¹ A pivotal production in this regard was the Israeli film *Khirbet Hiza'a*, made for television in 1978 by Ram Loevy. The film depicts, in a very crude way, the Israeli army's conquest of a Palestinian village during the 1948 war and the expulsion of its entire population beyond the borders of the State of Israel.²² Micha, one of the soldiers, wonders about the 'right' and the morality of an expulsion, which results in the creation of an entire people of refugees. Several dialogues of the film illustrate this questioning:

> **Micha:** We have no right to take them away from here.
> **Moishe:** Listen, Micha, what is this dump called? Immigrants will come here, work on this land and it will be great.
> **Schmulik:** Come on, Micha, don't play righteous. What we are doing is a necessary defense move.
> **Gabi:** Come on, stop all the crap, you are fighting for your existence. We can't keep a hostile population behind our lines.
> **Micha:** Your existence?
> **Gabi:** They should thank us for not killing them. I'd like to see how he'd react, if Arabs captured his village, he's an idiot.
> **Micha:** Tell me Schmulik, don't you see what we're doing? We're sending people into exile.

These conversations mark the confrontation between, on the one hand, the law and the ethical principles, invoked by Micha, and, on the other hand, the necessities, military or political, which must take precedence over the rules normally applicable in the name of higher goals. The film shows that this last conception prevails, since Micha is unable to prevent the expulsion of the population of the Palestinian village. We thus find here a more critical conception of international law rather than an idealistic one.

The Right of return on screen: 'They refuse us the Right of return, I take it'

The theme of the right of Palestinian refugees to return to their homes is also becoming more and more commonly depicted on the screen. While Israel's official position still consists in refuting any responsibility for the

---

21 See *Hannah K.* (Costa-Gavras, Israel/France, 1983); *Kedma* (Amos Gitai, Israel/Italy/France, 2002); *Bab el chams* (Yousry Nasrallah, Egypt/France, 2004); *Forgiveness* (Udi Aloni, Israel/USA, 2006); *Junction 48* (Udi Aloni, Israel/Germany/USA, 2016).
22 See Nurith Gertz and Gal Hermoni, 'The Muddy Path between *Lebanon* and *Khirbet Khizeh*: Trauma, Ethics and Redemption in Israeli Film and Literature' in Boaz Hagin, Sandra Meiri, Raz Yosef and Anat Zanger (eds), *Just Images: Ethics and the Cinematic* (Newcastle upon Tyne: Cambridge Scholars Publishing, 2011) 35ff.

creation of the Palestinian refugee problem in 1948 and denying them any 'Right of return',[23] the cinema, be it Palestinian, Israeli or foreign, comes to give substance to this claim by presenting its human dimension. Several documentaries, notably Palestinian and Israeli, evoke Palestinian villages destroyed or expropriated, to which Palestinian residents aspire to return or which they at least wish to visit.[24] This same topic is depicted in several fictional productions,[25] with as forerunner *Hannah K.* by Costa-Gavras, released in 1983.

In *Salt of this Sea*, Soraya, a Palestinian settled in New York, decides to go to Palestine for the first time, her family, originally from Jaffa, having been exiled since 1948.[26] Upon her arrival to Ramallah, she explains the reasons of her visit to two Palestinian businessmen:

> **Businessman 1:** Why does a pretty girl like yourself come back to Palestine?
> **Soraya:** They refuse us the Right of return, I take it.
> **Businessman 1:** The Right of return … You must be joking … Who would want to 'return' here?
> **Soraya:** Many people.
> **Businessman 2:** We will have to live with two States. Ours and theirs. Jaffa is long lost.
> **Soraya:** Are we supposed to thank them for leaving us 95% of the 20% of the 5% of our own ass?

This dialogue illustrates the tension between a more idealistic approach to the application of international law, in this case the Right of return, which should be fully implemented, and a more pragmatic approach agreeing to relinquish certain rights to ensure the establishment of a Palestinian State. After visiting her grandparents' house in Jaffa, Soraya is finally arrested by

---

23 Israel Ministry of Foreign Affairs, 'Israel, the Conflict and Peace: Answers to Frequently Asked Questions', http://mfa.gov.il/MFA/ForeignPolicy/Issues/Pages/FAQ_Peace_process_with_Palestinians_Dec_2009.aspx#Refugees1, accessed 1 December 2019.

24 *House* (Amos Gitai, Israel, 1980); *A House in Jerusalem* (Amos Gitai, Israel, 1998); *Ma'loul Celebrates its Destruction* (Michel Khleifi, Palestine, 1985); *Once I Entered a Garden* (Avi Mograbi, Israel/France/Switzerland, 2012).

25 *Salt of this Sea* (Annemarie Jacir, Palestine/Belgium/France/Spain/Switzerland, 2008); *When I Saw You* (Annemarie Jacir, Palestine/Jordan/Greece/United Arab Emirates, 2012); *Bab el chams* (Yousry Nasrallah, Egypt/France, 2004); *Zaytoun* (Eran Riklis, Israel/UK/France, 2012).

26 Jaffa was attributed to the Arab State in the UN Partition Plan in 1947. The city was conquered by the Zionist forces in May 1948, and a very large majority of the Palestinian population was driven into exile. See: Benny Morris, *The Birth of the Palestinian Refugee Problem Revisited* (Cambridge: Cambridge University Press, 2004) 212ff.

the Israeli police and deported to the United States: in the face of Israeli immigration rules, the Right of return is inoperative.

Movies that deal with the theme of the creation of the State of Israel and its consequences for the rights of the Palestinian population thus adopt, apart from the 'heroic-nationalist' wave, a critical approach to international law, privileging the consideration of factors related to the imbalance of power relations on the ground, explaining that the law cannot be fully taken into consideration and applied. The occupation of the Palestinian territories after 1967 is the second side of the Israeli–Palestinian conflict. Let us now examine how it has been shown by cinema, and how the question of its legal regime has been presented.

The depiction of the conflict after the Six-Day War of 1967: from the fight against Palestinian terrorism to the struggle against the Israeli occupation

After the conquest of Eastern Jerusalem, the West Bank and Gaza in 1967 as a result of the Six-Day War, Israel extends its control over the whole Palestinian territory covered by the British Mandate. Jerusalem is annexed and the West Bank and Gaza placed under military administration. A settlement policy is implemented by successive Israeli governments. At the same time, hijackings and attacks against Israeli interests are carried out by Palestinian organizations arising from the PLO. These events were presented on screen in an antagonistic manner, moving from films focusing on Palestinian terrorism to films criticizing the realities of the Israeli occupation.

The 'Palestinian terrorists' movies: 'Tell your Israeli friends that there will be no deal'

For a long time, the dominant vision of the conflict in Hollywood and Israeli cinema portrayed the struggle of the American or Israeli hero against Palestinian terrorists, as illustrated by numerous productions released in the 1970s and 1980s.[27]

---

27 *Rosebud* (Otto Preminger, USA, 1975); *The 'Human' Factor* (Edward Dmytryk, UK, 1975); *21 Hours at Munich* (William A. Graham, USA, 1976); *Raid on Entebbe* (Irvin Kershner, USA, 1976); *Victory at Entebbe* (Marvin J. Chomsky, USA, 1976); *Black Sunday* (John Frankenheimer, USA, 1977); *Opération Septembre noir* (Jack Morrison, Israel/Switzerland, 1977); *Operation Thunderbolt* (Menahem Golan, Israel, 1977); *The Ambassador* (Jack Lee Thompson, USA/Israel, 1984); *The Little Drummer Girl* (George Roy Hill, USA, 1984); *Delta Force* (Menahem Golan, Israel/USA, 1986).

This kind of Manichean production actually has the effect of removing the relevance of the issue of Palestinian rights. In the context of an imminent terrorist threat, there is no room for discussion, and the force of arms constitutes the right answer. *Rosebud* (1975), directed by Otto Preminger, is very illustrative of this view, blaming Palestinian terrorism for the lack of opportunity for peace negotiations.[28] The film narrates the story of five young women taken hostage by a commando of the Palestine Liberation Army, who then takes them to the region of Nice. This kidnapping is sponsored by Edward Sloat (Richard Attenborough), a leader of 'Black September', a Palestinian organization based in Lebanon. Larry Martin (Peter O'Toole), a former CIA agent, is hired by the families of the young women to negotiate their release with the leader of the kidnappers. After Larry Martin arrives in Black September's headquarters in Lebanon, he has the following discussion with Edward Sloat:

> **Larry Martin:** Release the girls and you will have what the Palestinians urgently wish to have: negotiations with Israel.
> **Edward Sloat:** Perhaps. But not I. I want the elimination of Israel.
> **Larry Martin:** Haven't you heard? Jews don't walk into gas chambers anymore. They fight. And they fight hard. The hope for the Palestinians is a deal.
> **Edward Sloat:** Oh, my plans go much further than helping the Palestinians. This is the beginning of Jihad. The Holy war. And I've been chosen to regain Arabia for all the faithful. I cannot compromise with this will [...] Tell your Israeli friends there will be no deal. They will have no peace until we have what we must have: all of Arabia, including Palestine, united under the flag of Islam. A muslim Holy land, where we can live in peace.

Following the refusal of any compromise, the hostage situation will have to be solved by force: an Israeli commando releases the young women in France, and a military operation conducted in Lebanon allows the capture of the leader of Black September. While the latter is being interrogated by the Israeli services, an agent states: 'But perhaps, without you and the scum like you who preach violence, both sides will be able to sit together, talk, and find a real solution for peace.' This possibility is however immediately refuted by the film itself, which ends in a sequence showing another Palestinian terrorist engaged in hijacking a plane. It is thus understood that the Israelis are perfectly willing to negotiate but are always confronted with the endless

---

28 See Jack G. Shaheen, *Reel Bad Arabs: How Hollywood Vilifies a People* (New York and Northampton: Olive Branch Press, 2001) 402–3.

cycle of Palestinian violence.²⁹ This presentation is in line with the 'heroic-nationalist' current, depicting Israel as ready to submit to the mechanisms provided by international law, while the Palestinians use illegal means. Such a vision, still based on a certain idealistic conception, again conceals another aspect of the legal reality of the Israeli–Palestinian conflict: that of the occupation and the rights recognized to the Palestinian people.

With the recognition of the PLO by Israel and the beginning of a negotiation process under the Oslo Accords (1993), the cinematic figure of the evil 'Palestinian terrorist' tends to fade.³⁰ As from the end of the 1970s, Palestinian, Israeli and foreign films will focus on the realities of the Israeli occupation.

The Palestinian militant cinema: 'Can we do anything? As long as there is occupation, no'

While in the 1960s and 1970s, Palestinian cinema is closely related to Palestinian organizations and is conceived mainly from a revolutionary perspective,³¹ as from the 1980s, a more personal Palestinian cinema is produced, notably led by Michel Khleifi (*Wedding in Galilee*,³² *Canticle of the Stones*³³).³⁴ The films will focus on describing the daily life of the Palestinians living under occupation, later joined by some foreign productions, in a militant perspective.

---

29 This conception will be called into question by the film *Munich* (USA, 2005), directed by Steven Spielberg, which challenges the legitimacy of the means used to fight Palestinian terrorism. See Yosefa Loshitzky, 'The Post-Holocaust Jew in the Age of the "War on Terror": Steven Spielberg's *Munich*' (2011) 40:2 *Journal of Palestine Studies* 77–87.
30 See, however: *The Siege* (Edward Zwyck, USA, 1996); *The Body* (Jonas Mccord, USA, 2001); *Mogadiscio* (Roland Suso Richter, Germany, 2009); *Carlos* (Olivier Assayas, France/Germany, Canal Plus/Arte, 2010, three episodes); *Fauda* (Lior Raz and Avi Issacharoff, Israel, Yes/Netflix, 2015–2020, three seasons); *Beirut* (Brad Anderson, USA, 2018); *7 Days in Entebbe* (José Padilha, UK/USA, 2018); *The Little Drummer Girl* (Park Chan-wook, UK, BBC/AMC Studios, 2018, six episodes).
31 See Nadia Yaqub, *Palestinian Cinema in the Days of Revolution* (Austin: University of Texas Press, 2018); Gertz and Khleifi, *Palestinian Cinema*, 20ff.; Alexander, 'Is There a Palestinian Cinema?', 154.
32 Michel Khleifi, Palestine/France/Belgium, 1987.
33 Michel Khleifi, Palestine/Israel/UK/France/Belgium, 1990.
34 See Gertz and Khleifi, *Palestinian Cinema*, 30ff. and 74ff.; Alexander, 'Is There a Palestinian Cinema?', 154ff.; Michel Khleifi, 'From Reality to Fiction: From Poverty to Expression' in Hamid Dabashi (ed.), *Dreams of a Nation: On Palestinian Cinema* (London and New York: Verso, 2006) 45–57.

Israeli oppression is presented in its most concrete manifestations through the portrayal of ordinary Palestinian characters,[35] who are subject to orders of expulsion,[36] house destruction and requisitions,[37] restricted access to health care,[38] curfew measures,[39] imprisonment,[40] repression of any form of resistance,[41] the policy of colonization.[42] As from the early 2000s and in view of the evolution of the situation, the films will place the figures of the checkpoint and the Wall at the centre of their stories,[43] showing the effects of these physical barriers on people's daily lives.[44]

It should be noted that these productions give little space for any form of legal discourse in the apprehension of occupation situations, even though the issues dealt with are governed by the rules of international law (the Hague Regulations of 1907, the Fourth Geneva Convention, UN Covenants on human rights, etc.). The rights of Palestinians only appear in the background, through the Israeli violations of which they are the object. Such portrayal of the occupation also underlines the submission of the Palestinian population to the orders imposed by the Israeli military authority, which are practically impossible to question, even when they are contrary to international law.[45]

---

35 See Lina Khatib, *Filming the Modern Middle East: Politics in the Cinemas of Hollywood and the Arab World* (London and New York: I.B. Tauris, 2006) 114–15 and 126–34.
36 *Hannah K.*; *Salt of this Sea*.
37 *Rana's Wedding* (Hany Abu-Assad, Palestine/Netherlands/United Arab Emirates, 2002); *Private* (Saverio Costanzo, Italy, 2005).
38 *Inch'Allah* (Anaïs Barbeau-Lavalette, Canada/France, 2012).
39 *Wedding in Galilee*; *Tale of the Three Jewels*; *Girafada* (Rani Masalha, Palestine/France/Italy/Germany, 2013).
40 *Tale of the Three Jewels*; *Miral*; *Omar* (Hany Abu-Assad, Palestine, 2013); *Girafada*.
41 *Wedding in Galilee*; *Canticle of the Stones*; *Tale of the Three Jewels*; *Miral*; *The Promise*; *Omar*; *Girafada*; *Palestine Stereo* (Rashid Masharawi, Palestine/France, 2013).
42 *Ticket to Jerusalem* (Rashid Masharawi, Palestine/France/Netherlands/Australia, 2002); *The Promise*; *Palestine Stereo*; *Girafada*.
43 See, amongst others, *Divine Intervention* (Elia Suleiman, Palestine/France/Germany/Morocco, 2002); *Rana's Wedding*; *Ticket to Jerusalem*; *Salt of this Sea*; *Time that Remains*; *Girafada*.
44 See Gertz and Khleifi, *Palestinian Cinema*, 152ff.; Dorit Naaman, 'Elusive Frontiers: Borders in Israeli and Palestinian Cinemas' (2006) 20 *Third Text* 511–21; Tanya Shilina-Conte, 'Imaginal Border Crossings and Silence as Negative Mimesis in Elia Suleiman's *Divine Intervention* (2002)' in Jakub Kazecki, Karen Ritzenhoff and Cynthia Miller (eds), *Border Visions: Identity and Diaspora in Film* (Lanham: Scarecrow Press, 2013) 3–21; Sean Carter and Klaus Dodds, *International Politics and Film: Space, Vision, Power* (New York: Columbia University Press, 2014) 28–33.
45 Carter and Dodds, *International Politics and Film*, 29.

This weakness in the face of the Israeli legal order is perfectly illustrated by the film *Omar*, directed by Hany Abu-Assad. In this film, the eponymous character is arrested by the Israeli police for alleged involvement in armed action against a military post. After being tortured during an interrogation throughout which he remained silent, his confession was secretly recorded by a Shin Bet agent, who pretended to be a Palestinian prisoner, a member of Al-Aqsa Brigades. This same agent, this time under his true identity, informs him that this recording will have value as a confession, 'according to our judges'. Omar then discusses this issue with his lawyer:

> **Lawyer:** At the court martial, where you will be judged, this stands for an admission of guilt.
> **Omar:** What are the consequences?
> **Lawyer:** You'll get 90 years, at least.
> **Omar:** Can we do anything?
> **Lawyer:** As long as there is occupation, no.

This kind of feeling of isolation, of inescapable confrontation with the occupation system, makes it possible to understand the absence of any reference to international law.[46] A (very) critical approach to international law thus prevails: the powerful impose the rules and the law proves unfit to change the course of things on the ground.

The Israeli critical cinema: 'It's not really legal, you know. – Maybe for the U.N., but fuck them'

In the 1970s, a 'critical' cinematographic trend emerges in Israel, stemming from the 'New sensitivity' movement.[47] Taking a different direction from the 'heroic-nationalism' analysed above, many films, until today, question the founding myths of the creation of Israel and the occupation policy conducted since 1967.[48]

---

46 See Richard Falk, '*Omar*: Uncovering Occupied Palestine', 4 February 2014, http://richardfalk.wordpress.com/2014/02/04/omar-uncovering-occupied-palestine/, accessed 1 December 2019.
47 See: *Beyond the Walls* (Uri Barabash, Israel, 1984); *On a Narrow Bridge* (Nissim Dayan, Israel, 1985); *Avanti Popolo* (Rafi Bukai, Israel, 1986). For an analysis of these films, see Shohat, *Israeli Cinema*, 215ff.; Ilan Pappé, 'Post-Zionism and its Popular Cultures', in Rebecca L. Stein and Ted Swedenburg (eds), *Palestine, Israel, and the Politics of Popular Culture* (Durham, NC and London: Duke University Press, 2005) 86–9.
48 See: *Time of Favor* (Joseph Cedar, Israel, 2000); *Rock the Casbah* (Yariv Horowitz, Israel/France, 2012); *Close to Home* (Vidi Bilu and Dalia Hager, Israel, 2005); *A Bottle in the Gaza Sea* (Thierry Binisti, France/Israel/Canada, 2010); *Policeman*

Albeit for different reasons, just like in Palestinian films, international law is not very present in the debates illustrated by these productions criticizing various aspects of the Israeli occupation. On the few occasions it is mentioned, it is to underline its setting aside in the minds of Israeli soldiers. In *Forgiveness*,[49] we witness a discussion between two soldiers with opposite visions of the question of the use of Palestinian civilians as a 'human shield'. One of them states: 'A real live bullet-proof vest, officer. Its not really legal, you know.' The other one replies: 'Maybe for the U.N., but fuck them. As far as they're concerned, we should be all dead.' Only for the first soldier to ironize: 'The court says it's legal if the Arab volunteers to die for you, eh Yoni?' The scene refers to the actual practice of the use of human shields by the Israeli army, confirmed, amongst others, by United Nations reports,[50] and intends to show that, ultimately, international law is of little weight in preventing it.

In most productions, the norms referred to are the mission orders and the rules of engagement laid down by the military authorities. When these rules are questioned, ethical principles come into play rather than international legal provisions. *Room 514* is symptomatic of this angle of analysis. Anna is a young investigator of the Israeli military police. She stubbornly pursues an investigation following a complaint by a Palestinian family, who claims to have been the victim of brutality committed by an Israeli patrol during a vehicle search. She conducts various interrogations to obtain the confession of Captain Davidi, the patrol commander. Through their exchanges, we note that what concerns Anna is not the protection of the rights of Palestinians, also invisible on the screen, but rather the proper application of the rules of conduct of the army and the preservation of its reputation:

Anna: Tell me, how has your violence served us?
Davidi: Us?
Anna: The army (...)
Davidi: It's the army you are accusing. I don't know if we're part of the same army.
Anna: In my army, nobody crosses the lines. Your attitude is unacceptable.

(Nadav Lapid, Israel/France, 2011); *Room 514* (Sharon Bar-Ziv, Israel, 2012); *Foxtrot* (Samuel Maoz, Israel/France/Germany/Switzerland, 2017).
49 Udi Aloni, Israel/USA, 2006. On this film, see: Yael Ben-Zvi-Morad, 'Borders in Motion: The Evolution of the Portrayal of the Israeli–Palestinian Conflict in Contemporary Israeli Cinema' in Miri Talmon and Yaron Peleg (eds), *Israeli Cinema: Identities in Motion* (Austin: University of Texas Press, 2011) 280–4.
50 See 'Report of the United Nations Fact-Finding Mission on the Gaza Conflict' (known as 'Goldstone Report'), 25 September 2009, A/HRC/12/48, 214–27.

It should be noted that Anna considers that she must absolutely carry out her mission of investigation because of her conception of the duties of the armed forces. And the moral implications of the acts of the various protagonists constitute the heart of the movie: Davidi commits suicide, Anna is challenged by her superiors for her extreme attitude. Palestinian rights remain out of scope. The same analysis applies to most of the Israeli films examined. Occupational policy is under severe criticism, but the discussion mainly focuses on the trauma inflicted on the participating soldiers and the ethical debates about the Israeli society.[51]

It would be misleading, however, to conclude that all Israeli films are necessarily critical of the occupation. Although they belong to a minority, quite a few productions favour a securitarian view of the occupation of the Palestinian territories,[52] as reflected in the recent TV series *Fauda*,[53] which recounts the missions carried out by an Israeli undercover commando unit in the West Bank in order to foil attacks planned by Hamas or even the Islamic State, without ever mentioning the existence of the occupation and even less the applicability of international rules governing this type of operation.

In sum, whether within the 'critical' or the 'securitarian' stream, Israeli films that address the issue of occupation usually do so by largely ignoring the question of the application of international law. The Israeli cinema thus offers little evidence of the analysis favoured by some organizations, such as B'Tselem[54] or Yesh Din[55] that base their criticism of the occupation mainly on respect for humanitarian law and human rights. The cinematic approach primarily evolves around societal ethics and personal morality, rather than the recognition of the rights of the Other. In this, they contribute to validating the critical perspective that emerges from Palestinian films: from

---

51 See Dorit Naaman, 'A Rave against the Occupation? Speaking the Self and Excluding the Other in Contemporary Israeli Political Cinema' in Miri Talmon and Yaron Peleg (eds), *Israeli Cinema: Identities in Motion* (Austin: University of Texas Press, 2011) 257ff.; Schweitzer, *Le cinéma israélien*, 45–6.
52 See *Double Edge* (Amos Kollek, Israel/USA, 1992); *Bethleem* (Yuval Alder, Israel/Germany/Belgium, 2013). See also the Hollywood film *World War Z* (Marc Forster, USA, 2013), which presents the Wall built by Israel around Jerusalem as a 'security' border (see Jesse Benjamin, 'Zombie Hasbara: "World War Z" and Hollywood's Zionist Embrace', Mondoweiss.net, 25 June 2013).
53 *Fauda* (Lior Raz and Avi Issacharoff, Israel, Yes/Netflix, 2015–2020, three seasons). On the controversies sparked by the series, see: Sayed Kashua, ' "Fauda" Creators Think Arabs Are Stupid', *Haaretz*, 12 January 2018; Hagar Shezaf, 'How "Fauda" Has Romanticized the Most Repugnant Aspects of Israel's Occupation', *Haaretz*, 11 March 2018.
54 The Israeli Information Center for Human Rights in the Occupied Territories, www.btselem.org/, accessed 1 December 2019.
55 Yesh Din, Volunteers for human rights, www.yesh-din.org/, accessed 1 December 2019.

the point of view of the occupying State and of its society, the rules of international law find little place in the debate on the Israeli–Palestinian conflict and there are other standards – political or moral – that will guide positions and behaviours.

In some films, Palestinian, Israeli and foreign, the question of the use of international law as a means of struggle against the occupation is explicitly raised. Once again, they reflect a rather disenchanted view on the possibility of effective application of the law in the light of the existing balance of power.

Law as a weapon against the occupation? 'At first, I would like to assure you that the Israeli occupation must comply with UN resolutions ...'

Mobilization of international law to challenge the decisions taken by the occupying Power is at the centre of the Israeli production *Lemon Tree*, directed by Eran Riklis.[56] The Israeli Defense Minister moves into a house situated on the 'green line', contiguous to a lemon plantation which belongs to Salma Zidane, a Palestinian widow. Pursuant to military orders, the lemon trees must be uprooted for 'security reasons'. With Zia Daud as her lawyer, Salma takes legal action aiming at having the orchard destruction order revoked and thus saving the lemon trees. This results in a legal battle all the way to the Supreme Court of Israel. The debate mainly evolves around the interpretation of Article 53 of the Fourth Geneva Convention, which prohibits the occupying Power from destroying property 'except in cases where such destruction is rendered absolutely necessary by military operations'. Ultimately, the Supreme Court makes the following decision:

> In our opinion, the right to housing that guarantees everyone's safety and physical integrity prevails over the right of ownership over land and its cultures, provided that the breach of the said right is minimal in the achievement of the desired goal. In order to fully meet the safety requirements, it is enough to cut, not to uproot, half of the trees of the plantation up to a height of 30 cm. This will clear the view of the orchard adjacent to the Minister's House.

The film presents three different visions of the role of international law in the context of occupation. The Supreme Court gives it a legitimizing function, by moderating the decision of the military command based on a proportionality test, while validating the security considerations that

---

56 Israel/Germany/France, 2008. See Ben-Zvi-Morad, 'Borders in Motion', 284–90; Anat Y. Zanger, *Place, Memory and Myth in Contemporary Israeli Cinema* (London: Vallentine Mitchell, 2012) 138–41.

constitute their foundation.⁵⁷ The occupation thus appears to be regulated by law and therefore more legitimate. The film here is very illustrative of the jurisprudence generally followed by the Supreme Court of Israel,⁵⁸ in particular of the decisions concerning the construction of the wall.⁵⁹ As for Salma, she sees the decision of the Supreme Court on a personal and concrete level: the modification of the order of destruction is of little consequence for the exploitation of her orchard and the recourse to the law ultimately appears as inoperative. Finally, the lawyer uses the law for militant and symbolic purposes and seeks to interpret the Court's judgment in a manner that is favourable to the Palestinian cause in general, beyond the particular case of Salma. The legal gain, even if minimal, is conceived as a 'first step towards the path of victory'. *Lemon Tree* concludes with a pessimistic view of the use of Israeli courts to try to enforce international law: the last scene reveals Salma's orchard with the cut trees, now isolated from the minister's property by the Separation Wall.⁶⁰

The means of struggle against the occupation are also discussed in the film *Palestine Stereo* (2013)⁶¹ where international law is derided and reduced to a purely incantatory discourse. The main character, Stereo, and his brother Samy develop a professional sound business to raise the money needed to leave Palestine and emigrate to Canada. As they work on the sound installation for the conference of a Palestinian minister, Stereo utters the text that the minister is yet to pronounce in his speech about the application of international law:

> At first, I would like to assure you that the Israeli occupation must comply with UN resolutions, especially 242 and 338, stating that Israel must withdraw from the land it occupied since 1967. Also, the resolution 194 concerning the Palestinian refugee's right to return to their home …

He then explains: 'I memorized this minister's speeches. Next time, he doesn't have to show up. I can do his speech for him.' This address, just like another one a little later about the illegality of the settlements, is disturbed

---

57 See also the documentary film *The Law in These Parts* (Ra'anan Alexandrowicz, Israel, 2011).
58 See David Kretzmer, *The Occupation of Justice: The Supreme Court of Israel and the Occupied Territories* (Albany: State University of New York Press, 2002).
59 See François Dubuisson, 'La construction du mur en Territoire palestinien occupé devant la Cour suprême d'Israël: analyse d'un processus judiciaire de légitimation' in *Mélanges offerts au professeur Jean Salmon* (Brussels: Bruylant, 2007) 889–927.
60 The films *Hannah K.*, *Miral*, *Omar*, *Junction 48* and TV series *The Promise* also show that the confrontation of the Palestinians with the Israeli judicial system is hardly favourable to the recognition of their rights.
61 Rashid Masharawi, Palestine/France, 2013.

by technical problems, which forces the minister to stop before attempting to resume: 'As I was saying ...'. International law is thus shown as entirely hollow words, purely rhetorical, repeated mechanically but without any connection to reality. The action on the ground, rather than words, must make it possible to fight the Israeli domination. This is illustrated by the conclusion of the movie: in the final scene, the two brothers are in charge of the sound system for a demonstration during which a participant is killed. This incident makes them reconsider their decision to emigrate to Canada as they choose to continue the struggle right where they are.

When international law is mentioned, its place in the fight against the occupation is thus presented with a certain scepticism as to its utility and effectiveness. The only bodies that one can seize are the Israeli courts, which implies that the rights invoked by the Palestinians will necessarily be interpreted through the securitarian prism of the Israeli military authorities. The powerful is thus in a position to impose his reading of international law upon the dominated, which reflects a critical conception, prevalent on the screen. International institutions are cruelly absent, and nothing seems to be expected of them in favour of a better application of international law.

The question of the application of international law also arises in the context of the peace process initiated by the Oslo Accords. Can the Israeli–Palestinian conflict be resolved through negotiation, and can the law serve as a point of reference, in line with an idealistic view? This theme is addressed by a series of cinematographic productions that deserve to be analysed.

The peace process at the cinema: between illusions and disillusions

For a long time, any direct negotiations between Israel and the PLO were made impossible by the lack of mutual recognition. Since 1993 and the conclusion of the Oslo Accords, a negotiation process with regard to the Israeli–Palestinian conflict meant to result in the conclusion of a final peace agreement and the establishment of a Palestinian State.[62] The issues to be resolved, as defined by the Oslo Accords, concern mainly the borders, the status of Jerusalem and the Palestinian refugee problem. The perspective of establishing peace between Israelis and Palestinians, and the ways for achieving it, is featured in several films and television series. Some productions bring forward the illusion of a diplomatic solution, thanks to the decided intervention of the United States, which manages to impose a

62 See Antonio Cassese, 'The Israel-PLO Agreement and Self-Determination' (1993) *EJIL* 564ff.

Pax Americana for the benefit of humanity. Most other fictions, however, present a disenchanted view of the peace process and the possibilities for the implementation of international law.

The Pax Americana: 'Palestinians will love it!'

In American fiction, it is very common to portray the United States as playing a vital role in preserving world peace. The context of the Middle East is not an exception, as illustrated by *The West Wing* series.[63] The first two episodes of season 6 (2004) are devoted to resolving the Israeli–Palestinian conflict, staging negotiations held at Camp David under the auspices of US President Josiah Bartlet and bringing together Palestinian President Farad and Israeli Prime Minister Efraim Zahavy.[64] While the series offers an idealized view of the role of the United States and of the possibility of resolving the conflict through a negotiation mechanism, it should be noted that the place given to international law is limited and that the main tool will consist of a power relations game. After a few days, discussions stumble over the question of the partition of Jerusalem. The American president presents a solution accepted by President Farad to the Israeli prime minister, but he faces a categorical refusal. The announced departure of the prime minister on the following day leaves President Bartlet only a few hours to come up with a compromise proposal. Kate Harper (Mary McCormack), one of the presidential counsellors, imagines the following formula:

> **Kate Harper:** After the Six-Day War, the Israelis offered to give the UN diplomatic status and immunities in the Holy sites in Jerusalem. If they were willing to do it in 1967, why not now? They give the Muslim holy sites the status of diplomatic missions. The Israelis keep all the sovereignty they want, they still can't enter without permission from the Palestinians.
>
> **President Bartlet:** So the Palestinians would have a sovereign like state that is inviolable. Like a foreign embassy.
>
> **Kate Harper:** Palestinians will love it! Because it gives them the same custodial status over the Haram that the Saudis have over sites like Mecca or Medina.

---

63 Aaron Sorkin, USA, NBC, seven seasons. See also *The Ambassador* (Jack Lee Thompson, USA/Israel, 1984).
64 For an analysis of these episodes, see Anna Bernard, 'Consuming Palestine: The Israeli–Palestinian Conflict in Metropolitan Popular Culture' (2012) *Journal for Cultural Research* 208–12; Philip Cass, 'The Never-Ending Story: Palestine, Israel and *The West Wing*' (2007) *Journal of Arab and Muslim Media Research* 31–46.

This proposal highlights the fact that rules of international law are a simple tool to cobble together a (totally absurd) solution designed to align with the Israeli position, rather than an element of reference defining the legal status of East Jerusalem. For example, there is no mention of the relevant UN resolutions, including Security Council Resolutions 242, 476 and 480, which provide for the withdrawal from 'occupied territories' by Israel in 1967 and characterize East Jerusalem as 'Palestinian occupied territory'.[65] Be that as it may, in the series, the solution is obviously attractive enough for the Palestinians to accept a peace deal announced at the end of the episode. Rather balanced in its approach to the conflict and the respective positions of the parties, *The West Wing* illustrates a rather paradoxical vision of the place of international law in the establishment of peace. On the one hand, it marks the belief in a possibility of reaching a solution through negotiation and mediation, the most usual tools for the peaceful settlement of disputes under international law (Article 33 of the UN Charter). But, on the other hand, when the solution is crafted, international law is discarded (the episode suggests that the 'Right of return' cannot be implemented either) to give way to the power balance, the United States ultimately aligning itself with Israel's positions.[66]

Not all the productions show the same faith as *The West Wing* in the possibility of negotiations likely to lead to a definitive solution, even imposed by the United States. The peace process is thus most often approached in a pessimistic way, highlighting the constraints linked to the geopolitical realities, which undermine the chances of success and evacuate considerations of international law.

The disenchantment of Oslo: 'They will sign something in Oslo, and we are going to have a country'

In general, Palestinian productions convey a harsh critical view of the peace process and the functioning of the Palestinian institutions created by the Oslo Accords,[67] a view shared by several contemporary Israeli films.[68] The same

---

65 See Bernard, 'Consuming Palestine', 210–11.
66 For a critical, ironic approach to the pro-Israeli bias of US policy, see the TV series *Veep* (Armando Ianucci, HBO) season 2, episode 2 (2013).
67 See, amongst others, *Chronicle of a Disappearance*; *Salt of this Sea*; *Palestine Stereo*; *Laila's Birthday*. See also Laure Fourest, 'Valse au pays de l'absence: le paradigme d'Oslo au prisme du cinéma palestinien contemporain' (2012) 106 *Cahiers de l'Orient* 57–74.
68 *Atlit* (Shirel Amitaï, Israel/France, 2014); *Rabin, The Last Day* (Amos Gitaï, Israel/France, 2015); *Self Made* (Shira Geffen, Israel, 2014).

pessimistic view is also found in international productions.[69] One example is the American film *Miral* (2010), which recounts the story of Hind Husseini (Hiam Abbass), the director of a boarding school in Jerusalem, and one of his protégées, Miral (Freida Pinto). Miral takes part in the first Intifada and spends time with PLO militants. She hopefully looks forward to the forthcoming conclusion of the Oslo Accords. She explains their content to Hind Husseini who is very ill at that moment:

> **Miral:** I think we're nearing a final agreement. They will sign something in Oslo, probably in a few months. There is already an agreement between both sides. And we are going to have a country. We are free. Israel agrees to give back 22% of the land. There are still certain things left on the table: borders, refugees, settlements, specifics about Jerusalem, water. The only sure thing is that West Bank and Gaza will be on the Palestinian State. And the PLO can come back. And we will govern ourselves.
> **Hind Husseini:** I didn't think I would see this in my lifetime.

The film ends, however, with the following words, highlighting the failure of a negotiated solution: 'The Oslo agreement set a plan for two independent states. It was signed in 1993. It has not been honoured yet.'

This kind of pessimistic portrayal of any chance of negotiated peace leads some productions to approach this issue from a burlesque angle, through comedy or even a practical joke.

The peace process as a practical joke: 'Do you, the Palestinians, agree to give the pyramids back to the Israelis?'

The absence of any illusions with regard to the perspectives of peace between Palestinians and Israelis is also translated into a comic form. This use of humour makes it possible to convey, in an indirect way, the idea that the conflict is intrinsically irresoluble, and that the principles normally applicable are incapable of resolving the contradictions between the parties.[70]

In *Brüno*,[71] the character by the same name (Sacha Baron Cohen) tries to 'fix the Middle East' to recover his blemished fame, by bringing both sides to conclude a peace agreement. To do this, he gathers Yossi Alpher,

---

69 A very cynical view of the Middle East peace process is presented in two TV series: *The Honourable Woman* (Hugo Brick, BBC, UK, 2014); *House of Cards* (Beau Willimon, Netflix, USA, season 3, 2015).
70 See also: *The 90 Minute War* (Eyal Halfon, Israel/Germany/Portugal, 2016), in which the result of a football match is supposed to determine the solution of the conflict.
71 Larry Charles, USA/UK, 2009.

Avraham Sela, Ghassan Khatib and Adnan Al-Husseini. After finding a point of convergence on the distinction to be maintained between *Hamas* and *humus*, the discussions stumble on the status of the pyramids:

> **Brüno:** Do you, the Palestinians, agree to give the pyramids back to the Israelis?
> **Adnan Al-Husseini:** This is in Egypt, not in Palestine.
> **Brüno:** I don't care where you put them. Give them back.

Despite all his 'best' intentions, Brüno's mediation remains unsuccessful. Beyond its silly humour, the sequence ultimately highlights the difficulty of achieving a solution based on a 'land for peace' solution, a task that appears as difficult as moving the pyramids.

The hopelessness of any perspective of an Israeli–Palestinian dialogue is once again presented in family contexts, in an amusing fashion, revealing that any discussion on this subject inevitably leads to disputes and dissension, whether between Jewish and Palestinian fiancés (*Only Human*[72]) or even within a Jewish family (*Simon Konianski*,[73] *Transparent*[74]).

Through the prism of humour, these comedies illustrate that the Israeli–Palestinian conflict refers to almost irreducible contradictions, not only between Palestinians and Israelis but also within each of the societies concerned.[75] International law does not seem to be able to provide a common language to overcome and resolve the dispute. This (very) critical viewpoint reflects the general tone of the productions evoking the negotiation process, which suggest that its constraints make the outcome highly improbable and marginalize the reference to international law.

Israeli–Palestinian conflict in cinema/cinema in the Israeli–Palestinian conflict

As illustrated by all the productions referenced in this chapter, the Israeli–Palestinian conflict is of a very singular nature, which has been accompanied and observed by cinema from its very beginning. In our analysis of its

---

72 Dominic Harari and Teresa De Pelegri, Spain/Argentina/Portugal/UK, 2004.
73 Micha Wald, Belgium/France/Canada, 2009.
74 Jill Soloway, Amazon Video, USA, four seasons, 2014–18. See, in particular, episode 5 of the third season and the entire season 4. See: *Haaretz*, 'How a Young Activist Shaped Attitudes on Israel and Palestine for "Transparent"', 11 October 2017.
75 In *Don't Mess with the Zohan* (Dennis Dugan, USA, 2008), humour makes it possible to imagine an Israeli–Palestinian reconciliation, but only in the limited context of a New York neighbourhood. For a detailed analysis of this film, see Bernard, 'Consuming Palestine', 203–7.

on-screen representation, we focused on the question of the role attributed to international law and the conceptions that were conveyed, oscillating between criticism and idealism. It is noteworthy that, in the end, questions of international law are rarely explicated in the cinematic representation of the various aspects of the conflict. At first glance, this may be surprising since the 'question of Palestine' is probably one of the conflicts for which the discourse of international law is used the most, by all the actors involved: international and regional organizations, States, NGOs, media, etc. In the films, primacy is given to producing a factual account, to constructing a 'narrative', rather than to an analysis taking into account the relevant legal aspects. This perspective, of course, first of all depends on the specificities of the cinematographic language, which favours the human experience over a more technical approach. This does not mean, however, that it is not possible to perceive, in most of these films, a discourse on the place and role of international law.

As we have seen, films that develop an idealistic view of international law are mainly those that are part of the 'national-heroic' trend, with a view to founding the creation and legitimacy of the State of Israel in the texts adopted within the United Nations, which were supposed to have resolved all aspects of the conflict with the Arab States. The formal reference to international law in this regard has been intended to hide other dimensions of the Palestinian question related to the rights of the Palestinian people, and their violation in practice. After the occupation of the Palestinian territories in 1967, and the adoption of United Nations resolutions calling for the withdrawal from those territories, condemning the settlement policy and recognizing the right of the Palestinian people to self-determination, the invocation of international law was no longer possible to support Israeli nationalist discourse. The wave of Palestinian terrorist films appeared in the 1970s, carrying a strictly security vision, with the effect of excluding any relevance of international law that would be invoked in favour of the Palestinian cause.

The emergence of Israeli and Palestinian films critical of the occupation in the late 1970s did not, however, lead to a return of an idealistic discourse on the capacities of international law to resolve the conflict. There are various reasons for this. As has been highlighted, and with a few exceptions,[76] Israeli cinema has been mainly concerned with the consequences of the continued occupation of Palestinian territories on its own society, the psychological impact on its soldiers and their families, the morality of the

---

76 In particular, the films of Eran Riklis and Udi Aloni, which feature Palestinian main characters.

Zionist project, social cohesion and respect for liberal values. In the internal political debate on the Israeli–Palestinian conflict and how to resolve it, legal discourse has a very limited place, with UN resolutions most often perceived as the product of an anti-Israeli bias. Cinema is probably a reflection of this marginalization, preferring to focus on political and moral issues. Palestinian films make more explicit or implicit reference to the relevant rules of international law, but generally present them as inoperative in light of the daily realities and ineffective because of the power balance in the international society. This vision is most likely consistent with the feelings of many people amongst the Palestinian population living under occupation. The numerous resolutions of the UN Security Council or the General Assembly, the repeated disapprovals by States, the Arab League or the European Union, the opinion of the International Court of Justice on the legality of the Wall[77] have not brought any tangible change on the ground, which has created a disillusioned perception of international law and the possibilities of its implementation. This largely explains the very critical view of international law that can be observed in Palestinian films, and in some foreign movies. The lost hope in the solution promised by the international community is best illustrated by a scene from Elia Suleiman's film *It Must Be Heaven* (2019),[78] in which the main character, a Palestinian director, consults a fortune-teller who, after drawing the cards, tells him: 'I see Palestine. But not during your lifetime.'

The Israeli–Palestinian conflict is probably the most represented contemporary dispute in film fiction. This intimate link, and the existence of both Israeli and Palestinian productions, means that the cinema itself has become an integral part of the conflict, even if it is a secondary one. In this respect, cinema has become a subject of political confrontations as well as a symbolic tool. It is frequently conceived as a means of struggle (especially the Palestinian cinema)[79] or a channel of debates. It is therefore hardly surprising that productions dealing with the Israeli–Palestinian conflict, such as *Munich, Paradise Now*,[80] *The Promise*, or *Fauda*[81] often provoke passionate polemics. Sometimes, disputes culminate in a diplomatic incident, revealing the power that is attributed to cinema. Two examples

---

77 ICJ, Legal Consequences of the Construction of a Wall in the Occupied Palestinian Territory, Advisory Opinion of 9 July 2004.
78 France/Qatar Germany/Canada/Turkey/Palestine, 2019.
79 See Massad, 'The Weapon of Culture', 32–44.
80 Hany Abu-Assad, Palestine/Israel/France/Germany/Netherlands, 2005.
81 *Haaretz*, 'BDS Movement Urges Netflix to Drop Fauda for "Supporting Israeli Occupation and Apartheid"', 29 March 2018, www.haaretz.com, accessed 1 December 2019.

can be mentioned in this regard. The first one concerns the formal protest by Israel against the authorization by the presidency of the UN General Assembly to host a screening of the film *Miral* (2010). The Israeli delegation to the UN claimed that the film had 'contentious political content' and that the decision revealed 'poor judgment and a lack of even-handedness'.[82] In a second case, upon the injunction of the Minister of Culture, Miri Regev, the Israeli Embassy in France boycotted the opening of the Israeli film festival in Paris, which projected the film *Foxtrot* (2017), in which Israeli soldiers are portrayed killing the Palestinian passengers of a car and covering up the traces of their act. The minister declared that the movie 'harms the good name of the IDF' and 'destroys the greatest celebration of the 20th century – the State of Israel'.[83]

Facing the disillusionment of Oslo and the ineffectiveness of international law, cinema itself can appear as a palliative to concretize Palestinian claims through the magic of pictures. In *Divine Intervention*, E.S. (Elia Suleiman) inflates a red balloon bearing the image of Yasser Arafat, which he sends to distract the Israeli soldiers and thus cross a checkpoint while deceiving their vigilance. The balloon continues its flight to land at the top of the Dome of the Rock in Jerusalem, symbolically representing Palestinian sovereignty. And in *Time that Remains*, the Wall built by Israel, which the opinion of the International Court of Justice in 2004 did not allow to remove on the ground, is crossed by Elia Suleiman with a pole vault. The filmmaker's very particular style, made of distant humour and surrealism, ultimately only reveals the desperate nature of the real situation. It is only through film that Palestinians can achieve the victory that international law is unable to offer them.

---

82 'Israel Condemns Screening of Film about Palestinian Journalist at UN HQ', *Guardian* (14 March 2011).
83 *Haaretz*, 'Movie Theater of the Absurd: Regev's Boycott of "Foxtrot" Snubs Israeli Culture', 13 February 2018.

6

Is cinema the handmaid of international criminal justice?

Anne Lagerwall

In the opening scene of the first episode of British TV series *Black Earth Rising*,[1] the Prosecutor of the International Criminal Court has just finished giving a conference and accepts a few questions from the audience. A black young adult asks her, rather daringly:

> **Jay:** What motivates you to vomit up all this neocolonialist bullshit?
> **Moderator:** You don't have to answer this question …
> **Prosecutor Ashby:** I am motivated to see justice done, wherever the crime took place.
> **Jay:** Oh … it just so happens, all these crimes, they take place in Africa?
> **Prosecutor Ashby:** We only prosecute those cases a country is unable or unwilling to prosecute for itself.
> **Jay:** What about the West Bank?
> **Prosecutor Ashby:** I believe that's an active situation.
> **Jay:** … situation? … But when it comes to action, they are at least 40 individuals being prosecuted by the International Criminal Court right now. And each and everyone of them are Africans, black Africans.
> **Prosecutor Ashby:** And I am sure that they all have a case to answer, properly represented in a court of law.
> **Jay:** But you are telling us you successfully prosecuted one of these cases. And that doesn't make you feel embarrassed?
> **Prosecutor Ashby:** Embarrassed? Not at all.
> **Jay:** Really? Why not? After all, isn't what you do just the latest example of self-righteous Western paternalism of exactly the same sort that for hundreds of years has systematically decimated that continent of its wealth, its government, its religions and most of all its peoples. And now, having done it, you have the temerity to expect them to turn to you for justice, for justice that only you can provide, for a crime that surely would never have happened had your world not gone there in

---

1 *Black Earth Rising* (Hugo Blick, 2018, BBC Two-Netflix, UK), season 1, episode 1.

the first place. So you are right, I wouldn't feel embarrassed. Cause if I was you, I would feel fucking ashamed. African problems deserve African solutions, they don't deserve you.

Prosecutor Ashby: This is not the time.

Young man: Then when is the time?

Prosecutor Ashby: Not now. I am sorry, I have to leave, I am running late ...

[silence]

Prosecutor Ashby: Just a minute. Can I just say one thing? I stand by my record because it is a record of justice. All right? Whatever the cause, whatever the history, we delivered justice to the people who needed it most when otherwise they might not have had it at all. And I'm proud to have done that and I'm proud to keep doing that.

This scene stages two representations of international criminal justice which can be found more generally in cinema. On one hand, it appears as a necessary means to fight impunity 'wherever the crime takes place' and to 'deliver justice to the people who need it most'. On the other, it is shown as an institution commanded by Western States' interests and their neocolonialist reflexes. It is hard to tell which representation *Black Earth Rising* finally endorses. In the long run, the Prosecutor certainly does not appear as a naive or idealistic agent of international criminal justice, unaware of what the International Criminal Court is causing through her decisions and policies. Rather she is pictured as a clever and dedicated women, trying her best in a complicated world where highly tense situations generate crimes the prosecution of which requires more than simple solutions. As John Powers affirms, 'we see how hard it is to define justice in a world where onetime heroes start doing bad things and fate transforms villains into victims'.[2] In that, the critique of neocolonialism is not upheld by the TV series taken in its entirety, leaving the viewer with a rather positive image of international criminal justice, without denying its ambiguities. More generally, cinema can be very supportive of what international criminal justice is and how it works, either by conveying romanticized images about its aims and achievements or by explaining – not to say justifying – its weaknesses. Fundamental scepticism is sometimes voiced and valued in films. But it does not quite override the heroic role that cinema generally entrusts international criminal justice with, for reasons that will be suggested below.

---

2 J. Powers, 'Black Earth Rising is a Fascinating, if Clunky, Take on the Rwandan Genocide', *National Public Radio*, 30 January 2019, www.npr.org, accessed 7 December 2020.

The material that has fed this analysis consists of films and series in which international criminal justice is expressly mentioned, whatever the importance of this evocation. All have been subject to equal attention, whatever their quality, which it would be difficult to assess without making a value judgement, and whatever the validity of the legal interpretations that they propose. In other words, no film or series has been excluded or neglected because it supposedly is a 'bad' film or because it would present an 'incorrect' image of international criminal justice. On the contrary, legal interpretations suggested in cinema – and perhaps especially when they deviate from expert analyses – seem relevant in that they are likely to reveal the possible desires and fears nourished about it. This work has tried to cover a significant number of films, but is limited by their availability and their production or translation in a language mastered by the author.

Romanticized images of international criminal justice

The romanticized images of international criminal justice conveyed in movies or TV series correspond fairly to those circulated by its promoters, staging it as an important tool in a 'global fight to end impunity' and a quest of justice for the victims.[3] Films also allocate to international criminal justice powers and means as well as a jurisdiction incomparable to those enjoyed in reality, granting it a form of omnipotence which participates in its idealization. Whether feared by perpetrators or desired by victims, international criminal justice is staged as a meaningful project which proves to be both adequate and functional.

Fighting impunity: 'This is about making sure every political leader knows when they make a decision they will be held to account by international law'

International criminal justice can be depicted as an important tool to fight impunity for those who have committed the gravest crimes, whatever

---

3 See the messages entitled 'The fight against impunity continues' and 'Victim's voices are heard' on the website of the International Criminal Court, www.icc-cpi.int/about, accessed 7 December 2020; see also, for similar messages with regard to the fight against impunity, the website of the International Criminal Tribunal for Rwanda on '20 years challenging impunity', https://unictr.irmct.org and the website of the International Criminal Tribunal for Former Yugoslavia stating that 'in its precedent-setting decisions on genocide, war crimes and crimes against humanity, the Tribunal has shown that an individual's senior position can no longer protect them from prosecution', www.icty.org/en/about, accessed 7 December 2020.

their functions. This image certainly emerges from *The Interpreter*,[4] in relation to abuses committed in the fictitious African state of Matobo by the government in power. The Head of State, Edmond Zuwanie, loosely reminiscent of the late Robert Mugabe, is expected to be brought to justice throughout the film while it remains unclear whether the United States will let this happen given its opposition to the International Criminal Court.[5] The decision finally adopted by the United Nations Security Council to refer President Zuwanie to the Court is therefore the high point of the film, a scene particularly dramatized by a shot over New York City at sunset showing the UN buildings, featuring grandiloquent music and a voiceover stating: 'Let the record show that the Security Council has unanimously commanded that President Edmond Zuwanie of Matobo be tried in the International Criminal Court in The Hague for crimes against humanity.' A similar sense of victory comes out in *Hunt for Justice,* a TV movie portraying Louise Arbour as the chief prosecutor at the International Criminal Tribunal for Former Yugoslavia (ICTY), especially when she finally succeeds in having President Slobodan Milosevic indicted for crimes against humanity and war crimes, leading to his arrest and transfer to The Hague in order to stand trial.[6]

An international criminal justice entrusted with a fight against impunity for the most powerful is also at work in *The Ghost Writer*.[7] Based on a book by Robert Harris partly inspired by the calls for Tony Blair to face trial for war crimes, the film depicts how the International Criminal Court is calling into question the alleged permission granted by former British Prime Minister Adam Lang to arrest four UK nationals on Pakistani territory and hand them over to CIA agents for brutal interrogation.[8] The prospect of a politician of his rank appearing before the ICC seems serious enough to worry the former tenant of number 10 on Downing Street and affect his travel plans.[9] When legal proceedings become more than likely, Adam Lang (Pierce Brosnan) and his wife Ruth (Olivia Williams) meet with his American lawyer to discuss the risks he faces and the options he has left:

---

4 *The Interpreter* (Sydney Pollack, UK/US/France/Germany, 2005).
5 A. Louwette, 'L'interprète de Sydney Pollack: l'ONU, la Cour pénale internationale et les Etats-Unis', 7 November 2013, www.cdi.ulb.ac.be, accessed 4 November 2019.
6 *Hunt for Justice* (Charles Binamé, Germany/Canada, 2005).
7 *The Ghost Writer* (Roman Polanski, UK/France/Germany, 2010).
8 B. Plett, 'How Realistic is New Polanski Film *The Ghost*', *BBC*, 19 March 2010, http://news.bbc.co.uk/2/hi/uk_news/politics/8576156.stm, accessed 7 December 2020.
9 A. Lagerwall, 'The Ghostwriter de Roman Polanski: Un thriller politique ou un film d'anticipation?', 17 September 2014, www.cdi.ulb.ac.be, accessed 7 December 2020; J. Fernandez, 'Puissance réelle et puissance fictive de la Cour pénale internationale: The Ghost Writer de Roman Polanski', *Mélanges Serge Sur* (Paris: Pedone, 2014) 335–46.

Sidney: If it's any comfort, you are in no jeopardy as long as you stay here amongst friends.
Adam: Are you saying I can't leave the United States?
Sidney: As your attorney, I strongly advise you not to travel to any of the countries that recognize the jurisdiction of the International Criminal Court.
Ruth: Just about all the countries of the world recognize the ICC.
Sidney: America doesn't.
Ruth: Who else?
Legal assistant: Iraq, China, North Korea, Indonesia, Israel and parts of Africa.

Realizing how complicated things are for him, Adam Lang becomes even more worried when the former minister for foreign affairs publicly announces that he would testify before the Court if invited to do so. When journalists ask the latter whether he will cooperate in the investigation, he states that 'this is about justice, this is about making sure every political leader knows when they make a decision they will be held to account by international law'. In reducing States which are not party to the ICC in number and importance and evoking States' cooperation as being beyond doubt, the film sketches the image of a powerful Court able to bring the most powerful to trial, including European leaders. This idealized picture deserves attention as it starkly contrasts with reality. Far from limited to 'Iraq, China, North Korea, Indonesia, Israel and parts of Africa', States that have neither signed nor ratified the Rome Statute amount to dozens, including India, Pakistan, Saudi Arabia and Turkey.[10] As for the cooperation of States Parties, it has proven far from infallible as illustrated by the reluctance shown by several States Parties to the Rome Statute to arrest and surrender Omar Al Bashir, although requested by the Court to do so.[11] But more fundamentally, in the film, the Court appears truly determined to investigate the acts of a Westerner, something it has not yet shown itself capable of in reality,[12] even

---

10 In December 2020, 123 States are parties to the ICC Rome Statute and 137 are signatories, UNTS database, https://treaties.un.org, accessed 7 December 2020.
11 See the decisions rendered by the ICC about the lack of cooperation by Sudan, Chad, Kenya, Djibouti, Malawi and the Democratic Republic of Congo, https://asp.icc-cpi.int, accessed 4 November 2019. See also M. Falkowska and A. Verdebout, 'L'opposition de l'Union africaine aux poursuites contre Omar Al Bashir' (2012) 1 *Revue belge de droit international* 201–36. After Omar Al Bashir was ousted in a military coup, Sudan's transitional authorities agreed in February 2020 to hand over the former President to the ICC.
12 Concerning the alleged crimes committed by United Kingdom nationals in the context of the Iraq conflict and occupation from 2003 to 2008, the Office of the Prosecutor has not yet issued its admissibility assessment which might lead the Court to open an

if the recent decision to authorize the opening of an investigation in relation to the situation in Afghanistan opens concrete perspectives in that respect.[13]

Political leaders are not the only ones targeted by international criminal justice on screen. In *Largo Winch II* subtitled *The Burma Conspiracy*,[14] the International Criminal Court investigates a powerful billionaire – whose character was imagined by Belgian comic book writer Jean Van Hamme – and its possible involvement in crimes committed against Karen people. Showing the relentless investigation of the prosecutor, brought to the screen by Sharon Stone, the film underlines that international criminal justice does not spare the influential world of finance. She embarks aboard a speedboat and intercepts Largo Winch's yacht in the South China Sea to seize important documents with the assistance of local authorities. She meets with judges in Geneva and convinces them to lift banking secrecy concerning the suspect. She flies to Thailand to lead the interrogation of Largo Winch, played by Tomer Sisley, in the presence of a testifying victim. This interrogation gives the prosecutor the opportunity to explain what motivates her:

> **Largo Winch:** But who do you really work for, Miss Francken?
> **Prosecutor:** For people like that young woman. So the people like you and groups like you do not exploit them and slaughter them for pocket change.

The prosecutor is actually being played and Largo Winch will finally prove his innocence. But it remains that the International Criminal Court certainly appears very determined to prosecute any criminal, no matter how influential he might be. By depicting judicial proceedings against heads of State, former heads of government and magnates, whatever their nationality and wherever they are, these films all fuel the idea that international criminal justice resolutely intends to lead a universal fight against impunity for the powerful.

---

inquiry, Office of the Prosecutor, Report on Preliminary Examination Activities 2018, para 213, www.icc-cpi.int/itemsDocuments/181205-rep-otp-PE-ENG.pdf, accessed 7 December 2020. The same is true for the alleged crimes committed in the occupied Palestinian territory, including East Jerusalem, for which the Court is still studying the observations related to the scope of the Court's territorial jurisdiction, order setting the procedure and the schedule for the submission of observations, ICC-01/18-14, 28 January 2020.

13 Judgement on the appeal against the decision on the authorization of an investigation into the situation in Afghanistan, ICC-02/17-138, 5 March 2020.
14 *Largo Winch II – The Burma Conspiracy* (Jérôme Salle, France/Belgium/Germany, 2010).

Seeking justice for the victims: 'I have the fate of this family on my conscience'

International criminal justice is also frequently portrayed as a quest for justice led for the benefit of victims, an image that is predominant in the international courts and tribunals' self-representation.[15] The salient place of victims is often illustrated by the way in which prosecutors and inspectors care about their fate. For *Storm*,[16] the poster was even composed of the respective portraits of an ICTY prosecutor, played by Kerry Fox, and one of the victims, played by Anamaria Marinca, with whom the prosecutor builds an intense relationship. At all times, the prosecutor appears adamant to uncover the whole truth about the actions committed by General Goran Duric, in the interests of the victims and, in particular, of this woman who agrees to testify about what she endured in his presence.[17] The plan however comes up against considerations linked to Serbia's forthcoming accession to the European Union. Her superior, the chief prosecutor, agrees to a deal: the prosecution is not to mention the sexual crimes for which Duric could be held responsible, so as not to damage the reputation of Duric's acolyte, a political figure likely to ensure a smooth transition for the country and, in return, Duric accepts to testify against other war criminals. The deal sparks an argument between the prosecutor Hannah Maynard who had assured the witness that she would be able to tell her story in court and her boss Keith Haywood:

> **Keith:** Hi. It's done. It's done. Duric will testify against his former comrades. Anderson agrees, the politicians are happy so everyone is happy.
> **Hannah:** And the witness?

---

15 See the exhibition in the ICC, 'Justice Matters', a description is available at www.icc-cpi.int/get-involved/Pages/-Display-exhibit.aspx, accessed 7 December 2020. See also the presentation of the ICTY stating that 'by bringing perpetrators to trial, the ICTY aims to deter future crimes and render justice to thousands of victims and their families, thus contributing to a lasting peace in the former Yugoslavia', www.icty.org/en/about, accessed 7 December 2020.
16 *Storm* (Hans-Christian Schmid, Germany/The Netherlands/Denmark, 2010).
17 M.-L. Hébert Dolbec, 'Storm-La révélation de Hans-Christian Schmid, 2010: sons et images sur les victimes et les limites de la justice internationale pénale', 16 December 2015, http://cdi.ulb.ac.be/storm-la-revelation-hans-christian-schmid-2010-sons-et-images-sur-les-victimes-et-les-limites-de-la-justice-internationale-penale-une-analyse-de-marie-laurence-hebert-dolbec/, accessed 7 December 2020; E. Espinoux and M. Flores-Lonjou, 'Le long cheminement de la rédemption en Bosnie Herzégovine', Lauren Lydic and Bertrand Westphal (eds), *Le silence et la parole au lendemain des guerre yougoslaves* (Limoges: Pulim, 2015) 131–45.

Keith: What?

Hannah: This agreement damages the witness. She becomes a pawn in a political trick.

Keith: That was the deal.

[...]

Hannah: You don't understand. I have the fate of this family on my conscience.

Hannah will finally break the deal during the hearings and allow for the witness to tell her story, in a defiant move towards her hierarchy which is staged in the film as a heroic decision to ensure justice for the victims.

Such a strong commitment is also shown in the depiction of Louise Arbour in the TV movie *Hunt for Justice*. Not only does she care for an interpreter working in her investigation team, whose wife has been missing since the war, but she also dearly keeps a family picture gifted to her, during a visit to the mass graves, by a group of mothers who ask for the remains of their sons. This same commitment is also embodied by the French inspector Calvez (Benoît Magimel) from *Resolution 819*.[18] The title of the movie refers to the decision adopted by the UN Security Council which required 'that all parties and other concerned treat Srebrenica and its surroundings as a safe area free from any armed attack or any other hostile act'.[19] Investigating for the ICTY what happened in Srebrenica, the inspector – whose character is directly inspired by Commissioner Jean-René Ruez[20] – speaks regularly with the victims and seems profoundly moved by their testimonies. He also keeps in his coat pocket a photograph of a missing girl, which appears to symbolize the *raison d'être* of his work. When he finally leaves Yugoslavia full of bitterness, the inspector explains how he feels in a letter that he sends to a colleague, the content of which is delivered by a voiceover with the music composed by Ennio Morricone for the film playing:

> The tribunal dresses the words – violation of the law of war, crime against humanity – but it is hatred we are talking about, the terrible banality of hatred. Even though many defendants, many criminals have been convicted, I share with the Yugoslav victims, whatever their camp, a feeling of incompleteness.[21]

---

18 *Resolution 819* (Giacomo Battiato, France/Poland/Italy, 2008).
19 UN Doc, SC Resolution 819 (1993), para 1.
20 'The Inquiries of the ICTY: Interview with Jean-René Ruez' (2007) 65 *Cultures et Conflits* 19–35; M. Bortin, 'The Policeman Who Dug Out the Horrors of Srebrenica', *New York Times* (11 July 2008), www.nytimes.com, accessed 7 December 2020.
21 [Author's translation].

If prosecutors regularly express disappointment with the work of international courts and tribunals, they usually embody the will to seek justice for the victims and the belief that this is what international criminal justice is about.

Fighting all crimes universally: 'A world without borders needs justice without borders'

International criminal justice sometimes works much more effectively and broadly in films than in reality, enjoying the full cooperation of States or even its own police forces in order to arrest those responsible for crimes which do not fit the classical definition of crimes under international law. A particularly powerful international criminal justice is notably pictured in the series *Crossing Lines*,[22] featuring a team of police officers from diverse European states, united to fight crime under the authority of the International Criminal Court. As the trailer claims, 'A world without borders needs justice without borders'. The team tracks criminals wherever they are, without ever wondering whether the States on whose territory they intervene have ratified the Rome Statute or not.[23] Police officers deploy easily across borders, benefiting from the help of national police forces or substituting for them during delicate operations according to a logic very different from the complementarity recognized in the Statute of the Court.[24] Their means are remarkable, including futuristic technologies allowing for reconstructing a crime scene in the form of a hologram. The police officers undoubtedly appear as heroes engaged in the fight against crime, reminiscent of Superman, Batman, Flash and Wonder Woman in *Justice League*, originally a series of comic strips to which *Crossing Lines* explicitly refers.[25]

This image of a particularly effective International Criminal Court is often coupled with its jurisdiction being considerably extended in films. In *Crossing Lines* particularly, the Court is not only concerned with crimes of aggression, war crimes, crimes against humanity or genocide, the only crimes within the jurisdiction of the Court under article 5 of its Statute. It is also prosecuting serial killers, art dealers, abductors, bank robbers, drug dealers

---

22 *Crossing Lines* (Edward Allen Bernero, France/Germany/US/Belgium, 2013).
23 A. Lagerwall, 'La répression des crimes internationaux à l'écran: l'apologie d'une justice sans frontières' in E. Espinoux, V. Lefebve and M. Flores-Lonjou (eds), *Frontière(s) au cinéma* (Paris: Mare-Martin, 2019) 403–26.
24 Article 1, Rome Statute of the International Criminal Court, 17 July 1998, *UNTS*, vol. 2187, 3; J. Stigen, *The Relationship between the International Criminal Court and National Jurisdictions* (Leiden and Boston: Martinus Nijhoff, 2008).
25 *Crossing Lines*, pilot, part 1 (Edward Allen Bernero, TF1, France/Germany/US/Belgium, 2013).

and various murderers.²⁶ The series thus offers legal interpretations that no scholar in the field would endorse.²⁷ This is certainly the case, for example, when two police officers, during an interview with Court inspector Michael Dorn, played by Donald Sutherland, claim that the murders committed by a serial killer should be investigated:

> **Agent Vittoria:** I read something you wrote once in a report on Kosovo. The mothers and wives of missing Serbs are begging for their loved ones to be found. But they never will be. This Court is the only ...
> **Inspector Dorn:** ... is the only place for them to turn. We weep for those no one else weeps for.
> **Agent Vittoria:** Exactly. Four women have been butchered by the same man in four different countries. That man will never be caught because the authorities in Rome don't talk to Dublin who don't talk to Paris who don't talk to London. I mean, it's not their fault. But that's the way it worked until Major Daniels brought us together. And maybe one day we won't need it. But right now, this Court is the only place for these women to turn. No one else weeps for them, no one.
> **Major Daniels:** It is a crime of aggression that is ongoing, systematic and cross-border. This is exactly what the ICC does.²⁸

In *The Ghost Writer* already mentioned, the Court also enjoys a rather extensive jurisdiction. Former Prime Minister Adam Lang is wanted by the ICC for rendering four British nationals to CIA agents in order to be interrogated. Contrary to what the Court's prosecutor asserts in the film, these facts hardly qualify as crimes against humanity or war crimes. According to article 7 of the Rome Statute, acts are considered crimes against humanity only 'when committed as part of a widespread or systematic attack directed against any civilian population', a context totally absent from the scenario.²⁹ To constitute war crimes, exactions should be committed during

---

26 The ICC is after serial killers (pilot, part 1 and 2, 2013), art dealers using radioactive polonium as a weapon ('The Terminator', season 1, episode 3, 2013), abductors ('Special Ops', season 1, episodes 5 and 6, 2013; 'The Rescue', season 2, episode 1, 2014; 'The Homecoming', season 2, episode 2, 2014), bank robbers ('The Animals', season 1, episode 7, 2013), drug dealers ('Desperation and Desperados', season 1, episode 8, 2013) and various types of murderers ('The Kill Zone', season 2, episode 3, 2014 ; 'Home Is Where the Heart Is', season 2, episode 5, 2014).
27 K.J. Heller, 'The Problem with Crossing Lines' (24 June 2013) and 'Crossing Lines Is Going to be a Disaster' (12 May 2013), *Opinio Juris*, http://opiniojuris.org/2013/06/24/the-problem-with-crossing-lines/, accessed 7 December 2020.
28 *Crossing Lines*, pilot, part 2, 2013.
29 K. Ambos, 'Article 7' in O. Triffterer and K. Ambos (eds), *The Rome Statue of the International Criminal Court: A Commentary* (München and Baden-Baden: C.H.

an armed conflict which seems equally absent from the situation depicted.[30] Maybe the film implicitly refers to the 'war on terror', in the name of which the United States launched several military operations following the attacks of 11 September 2001.[31] But this concept is not similar to that of an 'armed conflict' and is not in itself sufficient to qualify Adam Lang's alleged acts as war crimes. In any case, the facts mentioned in the film are far from meeting the gravity threshold required for the Court to enjoy jurisdiction over them.[32]

This idealized depiction of an omnipotent international criminal justice contrasts with the representations of its limits found in many other films. While various productions show the tense relations between international criminal justice and politics as a straightjacket to the ability to reach its aims, they equally fuel the legitimacy of international criminal justice by providing justifications to its shortcomings and inabilities, as will be illustrated below.

Apologetic representations of international criminal justice

The fragility of international criminal justice in the face of politics is frequently shown and denounced on screen, particularly in films recounting the search for criminals, whether Nazi officials in South America in the aftermath of the Second World War or Serb commanders in the context of the Yugoslav wars in the 1990s.

> Beck, Hart, Nomos, 3rd edn, 2016) 167–72; Y. Jurovics, 'Article 7 – Crimes contre l'humanité' in J. Fernandez and X. Pacreau (eds), *Statut de Rome de la Cour pénale internationale* (Paris: Pedone, 2012), 465–73; A. Cassese, 'Crimes against Humanity' in A. Cassese, P. Gaeta and J. Jones (eds), *The Rome Statute of the International Criminal Court* (Oxford: Oxford University Press, 2002) 356–60.
> 30 M. Cottier, 'Article 8' in O. Triffterer and K. Ambos (eds), *The Rome Statue of the International Criminal Court: A Commentary* (München and Baden-Baden: C.H. Beck, Hart, Nomos, 3rd edn, 2016) 314–16; M. Eudes, 'Article 8 – Crimes de guerre' in J. Fernandez and X. Pacreau (eds), *Statut de Rome de la Cour pénale internationale* (Paris: Pedone, 2012) 493–503; M. Bothe, 'War Crimes' in A. Cassese, P. Gaeta and J. Jones (eds), *The Rome Statute of the International Criminal Court* (Oxford: Oxford University Press, 2002) 388–9.
> 31 Olivier Corten and Barbara Delcourt (eds), 'Les Guerres antiterroristes' (2004) 105 *Contradictions*; M. Sassoli, 'La "guerre contre le terrorisme", le droit international humanitaire et le statut de prisonnier de guerre' (2002) 39 *Canadian Yearbook of International Law* 211–52.
> 32 Article 1, 17 and Preamble, Rome Statute of the International Criminal Court, 17 July 1998, *UNTS*, vol. 2187, 3; see also *The Handmaid's Tale*, season 3, episode 12, 'Liars', where Mrs Waterford is accused of war crimes for one single conduct (Bruce Miller, Hulu-Bravo, 2017).

In *La traque*,[33] which tells the struggle by the Klarsfeld to have Klaus Barbie face justice, the complicit indifference of several States – of their prosecutors and their administrations – is underlined throughout the film, exposing the Latin American States, the United States, the Vatican, Germany and above all France, primarily concerned by the crimes committed by 'the butcher of Lyon'.[34] If justice is initially dysfunctional in the movie, it is finally able to triumph as soon as political arrangements between States are reached. The constant dependence on politics never leads, however, to delegitimize international criminal justice or its promoters on screen. Rather, the film shows that political obstacles can be overcome with sufficient persistence.

A similar story is told in the *Labyrinth of Lies* and *The People versus Fritz Bauer* where Germany appears unwilling to secure the arrest and the trial of Adolf Eichmann and Josef Mengele as well as many other Nazis who have comfortably reintegrated the amnesic German society of the 1960s.[35] These films mostly denounce the unwillingness of German intelligence, police and prosecutors who believe that the country should not dwell on the past. In both cases, justice finally prevails, at least partly thanks to a few tenacious and idealistic prosecutors including Fritz Bauer who succeeds in having Eichmann arrested by the Mossad and other SS officers working in Auschwitz tried before German courts. In *The Labyrinth of Lies*, the struggle for justice is embodied in the young and determined prosecutor Radmann who strives to convince his colleagues, and particularly his superior prosecutor Friedberg, of the necessity to prosecute former Nazi criminals:

> **Prosecutor Radmann:** These men must pay for their crimes. It's a question of justice.
> **Prosecutor Friedberg:** Of course, justice is your exclusive domain. Parading around some small fish, while millions of others are allowed to carry on. How is this justice?
> **Prosecutor Radmann:** Your small fish are criminals.
> **Prosecutor Friedberg:** Are you aware of the consequences? Do you want every young German to ask if their father was a murderer?
> **Prosecutor Radmann:** Yes, that's exactly what I want. I want these lies and this silence to end.

---

33 *La Traque* (Laurent Jaoui, France, 2008).
34 These complicities have also been exposed in the documentary *Hôtel Terminus* (Marcel Ophüls, France/Germany/US, 1988); see also T. Bower, *Klaus Barbie, the Butcher of Lyons* (Pantheon, 1984).
35 *Labyrinth of Lies* (Guilio Ricciarelli, Germany, 2014); *The People versus Fritz Bauer* (Lars Kraume, Germany, 2015). See also on the subject of Nazis from Hungary integrated in United States, *Music Box* (Costa-Gavras, US, 1989).

Tensions between international criminal justice and politics also lie at the heart of several films dealing with the prosecution of war criminals involved in the Yugoslav wars. In *Storm, Resolution 819* or *Hunt for Justice* which have already been mentioned as well as in *The Hunting Party* inspired by a true story of three reporters trying to find Ratko Mladic themselves, the unwillingness of States and international organizations or the arrangements which justice is capable of when it renounces, for political reasons, to fight against impunity as fully as it should are heavily criticized.[36] This emerges clearly for example in *Hunt for Justice*, when ICTY prosecutor Louise Arbour meet with the British, French and American generals in charge of post-war Yugoslavia during a cocktail party in Sarajevo:

> **British General:** I understand you have just returned from Vukovar.
> **Louise Arbour:** And I understand suspects for crimes committed in Vukovar and elsewhere are at large in all your zones. I was hoping you gentlemen might help me understand that.
> **British General:** The situation is quite complicated as I am sure you realize.
> **Prosecutor Arbour:** I can't try them until you arrest them. Seems simple enough to me.
> **American General:** Are we policemen now? I thought we were soldiers.
> **Prosecutor Arbour:** Any reason you can't be both?
> **American General:** (…) This is not our war.
> **Prosecutor Arbour:** I am not talking about war, I am talking about war crimes, the Geneva Conventions, the very laws that separate soldiers from common killers. Don't you all have a vested interest in helping me uphold that?

Justice seems very fragile at the mercy of politics but generally the former is less criticized than the latter to which cinema attributes greater responsibility for any shortcomings. If the reluctance of States as well as international organizations comes under heavy fire in these films, the ambition embodied by the prosecutors and their colleagues to fight impunity remains intact, an ambition that is finally realized in many of these films, leaving the viewer with the impression that the good will of a few people can and does override political obstacles. In that, the legitimacy of international criminal justice is not profoundly called into question. More fundamental criticism rather comes in other shapes, as will now be illustrated.

---

36 *The Hunting Party* (Richard Shepard, US/Bosnia/Croatia, 2007); S. Anderson, 'What I Did on My Summer Vacation: Inside the Hunt for Ratko Mladic', *Esquire*, October 2000.

Fundamental criticism of international criminal justice

Many of the critiques which have been addressed by scholars to international criminal justice are voiced and valued in films and TV series.[37] The idea that justice is a spectacle working as a diversion from our collective responsibilities in the commission of international crimes or as a legitimizing device for States to tell their own version of history is regularly expressed in movies. Cinema also denounces international criminal justice as an enterprise governed by Western interest, echoing a critique that has been expressed by scholars as well as the African Union.[38]

Justice as a spectacle: 'It's just a diversion'

Doubts as to the exact ambitions of international criminal justice have been expressed in films dealing with the prosecution of crimes committed in African countries. In *Sometimes in April*, a former Rwandan soldier played by Idris Elba makes a trip to Arusha to confront his brother accused before the International Criminal Tribunal for Rwanda because of his involvement in Radio Télévision Libre des Milles Collines, a radio station which played a significant role in the perpetration of the genocide against the Tutsis.[39] During his stay in Arusha, he is shocked by the fair treatment and medical care offered to the instigators of the genocide and wonders about the meaning of the international criminal justice in a conversation with his wife:

---

37 C. Schwöbel-Patel, 'Spectacle in International Criminal Law: The Fundraising Image of Victimhood' (2016) *London Review of International Law* 1–28; P. Hazan, *Juger la guerre, juger l'Histoire* (Paris: PUF, 2016); J. Allard, O. Corten, M. Fałkowska, V. Lefebve and P. Naftali, *La vérité en procès. Les juges et la vérité politique* (Issy-Les-Moulineaux: LGDJ, 2014); T. Krever, 'International Criminal Law: An Ideology Critique' (2013) *Leiden Journal of International Law* 701–23; C Schwöbel, *Critical Approaches to International Criminal Law: An Introduction* (London: Routledge, 2014).

38 A. Anghie and B.S. Chimni, 'Third World Approaches to International Law and Individual Responsibility in Internal Conflicts' (2003) 2 *Chinese Journal of International Law* 77, esp. 88–92; African Union, Decision on the International Criminal Court, 30th Ordinary Session of the Assembly, 28–29 January 2018, Addis Ababa, Ethiopia; African Union, Decision on the International Criminal Court, 28th Ordinary Session of the Assembly, 30–31 January 2017, Addis Ababa, Ethiopia; 'African Union Condemns "Unfair" ICC', *BBC*, 11 October 2013, www.bbc.com/news/world-africa-24489059, accessed 7 December 2020.

39 *Sometimes in April* (Raoul Peck, US/France, 2005); see the 'media case', ICTR, *Prosecutor v. Ferdinand Nahimana, Jean-Bosco Barayagwiza and Hassan Ngeze*, case n°ICTR-99-52, decision 3 December 2003.

Martine: I guess the killers are the stars of the show.
Augustin: Is this what this is? A show? A big show?
Martine: We need the tribunals. I know they have their shortcomings but it is a way to get through it, a way to move on.
Augustin: It is a way for everybody to wash their hands. So nobody has to feel bad, so we can pretend that we have justice. Where is our dignity?

The image of justice as a device to elude our own responsibility by trying only the most obvious perpetrators of international crimes is blatant in *L'oeil du cyclone*.[40] The film tells the story of a former rebel leader named Blackshouam, once a child soldier, being tried before a domestic court for the war crimes he committed while part of the rebellion. His lawyer Emma Tou, through the discussions she has with the accused, comes to understand that the rebels benefited greatly from the help of influential political figures who happen to be part of her family. As Maïmouna N'Diaye, the actress playing the lawyer, comments in an interview:

> Emma realizes that the same wealth that allowed her to become a lawyer made him a warlord. We all have a mobile phone, but it is to the detriment of the lives of some people who dig the basement to extract the raw material used to make this phone. Out of a thirst for justice, fairness and a sense of guilt, she agreed to defend Blackshouam.[41]

These representations can also be found in films relating to the Holocaust. *The Reader* tells the story of an illiterate woman played by Kate Winslet who worked as a guard in a concentration camp during the Second World War and is tried in the 1960s before a German court for letting dozens of prisoners die in a fire while she could have help them escape.[42] Law students attend her trial and discuss the court sessions with their professor in class:

Student: I started up believing in this trial, I thought it was great. Now I think … it's just a diversion.
Professor: Yes, a diversion from what?
Student: You choose six women, you put them on trial, you say 'They were the evil ones, they were the guilty ones'. Because one of the victims happened to write a book! That's why they're on trial and nobody else. Do you know how many camps there were in Europe? People

---

40 *L'œil du cyclone* (Sékou Traoré, France, 2015).
41 Author's translation, 'L'oeil du cyclone: les ex-enfants soldats, des bourreaux comme les autres?', 22 November 2017, available at www.francetvinfo.fr/monde/afrique/societe-africaine/l-oeil-du-cyclone-les-ex-enfants-soldats-des-bourreaux-comme-les-autres_3060011.html, accessed 7 December 2020.
42 *The Reader* (Stephen Daldry, US/Germany, 2008).

go on about how much did everyone know? 'Who knew?' 'What did they know?' Everyone knew. Our parents. Our teachers. That isn't the question. The question is 'How could you let it happen?' And better. 'Why didn't you kill yourself when you found out?' Thousands! That's how many there were. Everyone knew.

Another form of critique consists in evoking the political instrumentalization of such trials to enhance the legitimacy of the State conducting them. Such a critique has been particularly voiced in films made about the arrest and trial of Adolf Eichmann in Jerusalem. In *Hannah Arendt*, the German philosopher intends to prevent such risk, as she did in her book *Eichmann in Jerusalem*.[43] In the film, after hearing the opening discourse of prosecutor Gideon Hausner, which the film reproduces using original film archives, Hannah comments on his performance and, more generally, on the trial:

Hannah Arendt: And Hausner struts around like he's competing with Eichmann for a part in the theatre!
Friend: His dramatic opening speech was predictable.
Hannah Arendt: Did Ben Gurion demand it? He's the one pulling the strings, right? Israel must ensure that this does not become a show trial.

The image of an international criminal justice moulding what and who is to be judged is also sketched in *Operation Finale*, telling the story of Eichmann's abduction in Buenos Aires by the Mossad.[44] As he is held in captivity before his transfer to Jerusalem, Eichmann, played by Ben Kingsley, criticizes his possible trial in Jerusalem:

Eichmann: You want me to stand trial in place of an entire regime.
Mossad agent: I am offering you a fair trial.
Eichmann: These are German crimes, they should be tried in German courts.
Mossad agent: That's not an option.
Eichmann: Ask your superiors to negotiate. If they refuse, I do too. I have no desire to be a scapegoat.
Mossad agent: I'd argue that the architect of the final solution has plenty to answer for.
[…]

---

43 *Hannah Arendt* (Margarethe von Trotta, France/Germany, 2013); H Arendt, *Eichmann in Jerusalem: A Report on the Banality of Evil* (New York: Viking Press, 1963); V. Lefebve, 'Penser la justice pénale internationale avec Hannah Arendt (Margarethe Von Trotta, 2013)', 4 April 2013, http://cdi.ulb.ac.be/penser-la-justice-penale-internationale-avec-hannah-arendt-margarethe-von-trotta-2013-une-analyse-de-vincent-lefebve, accessed 7 December 2020.
44 *Operation Finale* (Chris Weitz, US, 2018).

> **Mossad agent:** Come to Israel. Make your case to the world.
> **Eichmann:** I would rather die than have my history told the way someone else would like it to be. You have no interest in what I have to say unless it confirms what you think you already know.

It cannot be said that the character of Eichmann triggers sympathy from the viewer but his views are certainly expressed in a fashion that retains the attention and are not discarded because of the horrendous crimes he is responsible for. In that, he can be listened to much more than in the film *Eichmann*, which depicts him exclusively as a barbarous murderer.[45]

Justice as an Western enterprise: 'If it is a international crime to take territory by force, who convicted the British, the French, the Dutch and the American leaders?'

The idea of an international criminal justice governed by Western interests can be found in particular in films recounting the work of the International Military Tribunal for the Far East established at the end of the Second World War to hold the Japanese leaders responsible for the crimes committed during the conflict.[46] In *Emperor*, the Supreme Allied Commander General MacArthur, played by Tommy Lee Jones, would prefer to avoid bringing Emperor Hirohito before the Tribunal in order to maintain the fragile stability of Japan just recovering from Allied bombardments, a position which comes out as rather reasonable in the film.[47] The investigation to decide whether or not to prosecute him is entrusted to General Fellers, played by Matthew Fox, who decides to meet with Prince Konoe, a former Japanese prime minister and close adviser to the emperor. During the conversation, he asks him about the involvement of the emperor in the outbreak of hostilities:

> **Prince Konoe:** It is not a black and white issue, General.
> **General Fellers:** Millions of people died in his name. Your skies were filled with kamikazes. Atrocities were committed everyday as he expanded his Empire. Invading, conquering, decimating.

---

45 *Eichmann* (Robert Young, UK/Hungary, 2007); *The House on Garibaldi Street* (Peter Collison, UK, 1979); *The Man Who Captured Eichmann* (William Graham, US, 1996).
46 International Military Tribunal for the Far East, Special proclamation by the Supreme Commander for the Allied Powers at Tokyo, 19 January 1946, www.un.org/en/genocideprevention/documents/atrocity-crimes/Doc.3_1946%20Tokyo%20Charter.pdf, accessed 7 December 2020.
47 *Emperor* (Peter Webber, US/Japan, 2012); in contrast, see *Blood Oath* (Stephen Wallace, Australia, 1990).

Prince Konoe: You incinerated two of our cities, turning our children into shadows on the walls. We are both guilty. Yes, we seized territories in China. Did not Great Britain and even Portugal precede us? Yes, we took Singapore and Malay. But we took it from the British. We did not take the Philippines from the Philipinos, but from the Americans who themselves took them from the Spanish. If it is a international crime to take territory by force, who convicted the British, the French, the Dutch and the American leaders? Nobody. And what is different with Japan? Nothing. You see, General, we were simply following your fine example.

The film does not support this critique when taken in its entirety but it certainly does not downplay it, allowing for the viewers to reflect on the double standards which seems to govern international criminal justice. This is all the more true that the film validates the decision to spare the emperor, just as Prince Konoe wishes. In that, it feeds a narration very different from that of several historians who have shown how much this decision was taken through a construction of imperial innocence strongly called into question by the archives.[48] Besides, the position and influence exercised by the emperor could have led to his inclusion amongst the defendants, as Justice William Webb sitting on the bench stated in his separate opinion.[49] None of these reflections find echo in the film.

On the contrary, the mini-series *Tokyo Trial* fundamentally questions the choice to spare the emperor and takes, more generally, a critical stance on the work accomplished by the International Military Tribunal for the Far East.[50] Films and series rarely stage international judges. They rather focus on prosecutors, lawyers, victims and sometimes perpetrators, as we have seen. The series stands out as a remarkable exception in that respect.[51] What is unusual also in its depiction of judicial activity is that it uncovers the political affinities of the judges, their concerns for their respective States' position, the internal dissension and the struggle for power on the bench. In particular, it shows that Western judges are more influential on the whole than others, and especially more than Justice Pal whose views are regularly dismissed because of their contravention to Western interests

---

48 J. Dower, *Embracing Defeat: Japan in the Wake of World War II* (New York: Norton, 2000); H. Bix, *Hirohito and the Making of Modern Japan* (New York: HarperCollins, 2000); P. Wetzer, *Hirohito and War: Imperial Tradition and Military Decision Making in Pre-War Japan* (Honolulu: Univerity of Hawai'i Press, 1998).
49 Opinion of honourable Justice William Webb in Bernard Victor Aloysius Röling and Christiaan F. Rüter, *International Military Tribunal for the Far East* (Amsterdam: University Press Amsterdam, 1977).
50 *Tokyo Trial* (Pieter Verhoeff and Rob King, Canada/Japan/Netherlands, 2017).
51 I. Tallgren, 'Watching Tokyo Trial' (2017) *London Review of International Law*.

and to the Western judges' views to which the Russian and Indonesian judges rally in their own interests. This emerges, for example, from a discussion about a motion introduced by the defence of former prime minister Tojo to dismiss the charge for the crime of aggression, arguing that the crime did not exist as such at the time of the facts. Justice Pal is convinced by the argument, technically but also politically because it rallies his understanding of international criminal law as a set of rules conceived of in a way that would not call into question the responsibility of Western States for their colonial enterprise. Other judges however are very attached to the idea of seeing Japanese leaders condemned for invading foreign territories:

> **Lord Patrick:** Charging the accused for crimes of aggression is allowed in our Charter.
> **Justice Pal:** The Charter is wrong.
> **Justice Cramer:** It was a precondition to our appointment on this Tribunal.
> **Justice McDougall:** We cannot and we should not debate whether the Charter is right or wrong.
> **Justice Zaryanov, translated by his assistant:** The general supports what Justice McDougall says and you all should support that.
> **Justice Pal:** Yes, but not by making up laws at will.
> **Justice Bernard:** I agree, but why are we here, Justice Pal? We are here because we should be able to discuss what is the right step for humanity to take and based on the outcome of that discussion, we make the best decisions for the law.
> **Justice Pal:** Respected gentlemen, I certainly believe law has the power to guide mankind. So its principles must be upheld. That is why we must acquit all the defendants on the charge of crimes of aggression for this is a law which does not truly exist yet.
> **Lord Patrick:** If you cannot follow the Charter, you should return to Calcutta.
> **Justice Pal:** I did not come from a country that struggles to gain its independence in order to have my arguments discarded or to be told to go home.

Another image of justice preserving the interests of Western States emerges from *A War*, a film in which the commander of a Danish military unit deployed in Afghanistan is tried for having ordered the bombing which resulted in the death of eleven civilians.[52] The film shows the circumstances in which Commander Claus Michael Pedersen orders to bomb 'section 6',

---

52 *A War* (Tobias Lindholm, Denmark, 2015).

his unit being suddenly caught under heavy fire during a regular patrolling operation and one of his soldiers being critically wounded. There is great uncertainty as whether the attack originates from 'section 6'. He nevertheless calls for the bombing by a helicopter, which triggers simultaneously a rescue operation for the wounded soldier whose life will be saved. During the trial, everything points at his culpability, until one of his soldiers surprisingly testifies before the court that he had identified 'section 6' as a military target. The court finally acquits him. What is quite remarkable in this film is that, even though the viewer is convinced the commander is guilty, the acquittal does not come out as unreasonable or unjust given the extremely tense and chaotic circumstances in which he took the decision under scrutiny. More fundamentally, his attitude – ready to take responsibility for his act and bearing guilt for the loss of lives even after the acquittal – tends to convince the viewer that no further punishment is needed. Somehow, the film calls into question the very idea of an individual criminal responsibility for international crimes which seem largely linked to the tense and complex situation in which States like Denmark send their army to begin with.

If fundamental scepticism about international criminal justice is thus sometimes expressed in movies, it does not quite override the heroic role that cinema generally entrusts international criminal justice with. This unavoidably triggers interrogations as to the reasons why cinema works so often as the handmaid of international criminal justice.

Why does cinema work so often as the handmaid of international criminal justice?

First, this might be explained by the influence exerted on filmmakers by the laudatory discourse efficiently conveyed about international criminal justice in films and documentaries by organizations or people who support this judicial project.[53] The ICTY Outreach Programme has issued a series of documentaries aiming at 'making the ICTY's work more visible and comprehensible' which are particularly telling of self-representations of international criminal justice being pursued in the interests of the victims.[54] The documentaries produced

---

53 Wouter Werner, 'Justice on Screen: A Study of Four Documentary Films on the International Criminal court' (2016) 29 *Leiden Journal of International Law* 1043–60.
54 See the documentaries made by the ICTY in the context of its outreach program and, in particular, 'Through Their Eyes: Witnesses to Justice' and 'Sexual Violence and the Triumph of Justice', www.icty.org/en/outreach/documentaries, accessed 7 December 2020.

by Skylight Pictures[55] and Bullfrog Films[56] constitute vibrant pleas in favour of the International Criminal Court. Directors sometimes openly express admiration for international criminal justice and, in particular, for the work done by prosecutors. When a journalist asks Hans-Christian Schmidt if he thinks it is too early to close the doors of the ICTY and if he tries to change the situation with his film *Storm*, he replies:

> I don't think my film can change anything, but I wish it could be possible. I did not know that prosecutors were under pressure from this closure, I learned this by talking to them. It is now up to journalists to intervene to make things change.

Several of his film previews were sponsored by people like Bernard Kouchner or Daniel Cohn-Bendit and sometimes took place in the presence of his adviser in writing the screenplay, Florence Hartmann, the former spokeswoman of ICTY prosecutor Carla del Ponte. During one of these previews, Hartmann answered a question about *Storm*: 'I must say that the film speaks more than any book, any story. And I am impressed every time I see him'.[57] Such proximity between directors and people whose commitment to international criminal justice is well known reveals how much cinema can be imbued with the discourse of the promoters of such justice, and in turn permeate it. Television film *Resolution 819*'s script is directly inspired by Jacques Massé's book *Nos chers criminels de guerre*, which is described as a 'chronicle of a struggle to defend the law against barbarism'.[58] When Jean-René Ruez, who inspired the main character in the film, was asked whether he thought that this type of cinema could change mentalities, he replied that:

> at first, the idea of making a film of these events didn't seem interesting to me. On arrival, I think exactly the opposite. A film will reach a much wider audience than a documentary and will have the merit of reminding people that the horror happened next door to them.[59]

---

55 *The Reckoning: The Battle for the International Criminal Court* (Pamela Yates, Skylight Pictures, US, 2009); *Law or War: The Creation of the International Criminal Court* (Skylight Pictures, US, 2010); *Seeking Peace and Seeking Justice: The ICC and Uganda* (Skylight Pictures, US, 2010); *International Law Testing Limits: The ICC and Darfur* (Skylight Pictures, US, 2010).
56 *In Search of International Justice* (Judy Jackson, Judy films, Canada, 2006).
57 La Révélation – Storm: Reportage Avant-première, www.allocine.fr/video/player_gen_cmedia=18978920&cfilm=136376.html, accessed 7 December 2020.
58 Author's translation, Jacques Massé, *Nos chers criminels de guerre. Paris, Zagreb, Belgrade en clase affaires* (Paris: Flamarion, 2006).
59 Author's translation, Interview with Ruez, Telerama, 17 October 2008, www.telerama.fr/television/penetrer-dans-un-charnier-ca-bouleverse-la-conception-de-l-etre-humain,34833.php, accessed 7 December 2020.

The evocatively named Canadian television film *Hunt for Justice* was produced by Galafilm, which presents this production in the following terms:

> Louise Arbour's story is nothing less than a crusade waged by one woman to uphold an international standard of human dignity. What is her most effective weapon? The law. Arbour's successful indictment of war criminals at The Hague is of tremendous historical significance. While *Hunt for Justice* is fictionalized, due to the dictates of dramatic exposition, it's infused with Arbour's real-life passion, warmth and charm. She is driven by the desire to save future generations from suffering the indignities that scarred the Balkan and Kosovo regions.[60]

As these examples illustrate, filmmakers are receptive to the discourse disseminated about international criminal justice by its promoters and sometimes seem perfectly aware of it.

Second, and in line with the first point, cinema can be understood as a reflection of the idealistic formalism that often characterizes lawyers and academics writing on the subject. *The Interpreter* embodies a faith in international institutions and particularly in the United Nations which is certainly that of Sydney Pollack. The latter made considerable efforts to obtain permission to film on UN premises and was finally authorized to do so by Kofi Annan, assuring the latter 'that there would be nothing embarrassing for the United Nations in this film, that history would be a plea in favour of diplomacy against violence, a plea in favour of words against weapons'.[61] This faith is generally shared by internationalists who prove to be ardent defenders of international institutions and international criminal tribunals, which they frequently portray as devices which, although they can be bettered, remain legitimate and adequate for fighting impunity. Fewer are those who formulate a critique which fundamentally challenges international criminal justice and reveals its biases, prejudices, the dynamics at work in its functioning or the ideologies to which its objectives and methods refer.

Third, fundamental questions are rather articulated in films and documentaries which leave space for the accused and the accused's lawyers to express their views. *War Don Don* recounts the trial of one of the leaders of the Revolutionary United Front before the Special Court for Sierra Leone.[62] Not only does it question international criminal justice and its

---

60 Presentation of *Hunt for Justice: The Louise Arbour Story*, http://galafilm.com/en/pages/productions/2/7/68, accessed 7 December 2020.
61 Warren Hoge, 'A Coup de Hollywood at the United Nations; Persistent Sydney Pollack Succeeds Where Hitchcock Failed, in Getting Nod to Shoot on Location', *New York Times* (2 August 2004).
62 *War Don Don* (Rebecca Richman Cohen, US, 2010).

way of forging a certain reality, but it also leads the viewer to reflect on the meaning of the nearly sixty-year prison sentence handed down to the young leader of the rebel forces, Issa Sesay, who had worked to disarm them in collaboration with the United Nations. The director's experience as a trainee defending some of the accused before the special court probably explains why she produced a less idealistic discourse about the work being done there. The accused are generally portrayed in movies in their monstrous dimension, implicitly encouraging any attempt to hold them accountable before the courts and tribunals. From Mladic who slits a pig to signify the fate of the Bosnian Muslims in a particularly chilling scene of *Resolution 819* to a character evoking Karadzic crossing a village with a smile on his face after the perpetration of heinous crimes in *The Hunting Party*, the Yugoslavian war criminals and their henchmen are often shown as abominable murderers. Similarly, Nazi leaders are usually portrayed as cruel torturers. In *La Traque*, Klaus Barbie shares his expertise on the most effective techniques of torture to Bolivian military preparing a coup. Films offering a more equivocal picture of the accused are usually the ones bearing the most fundamental critique towards international criminal justice. In *The Reader*, Hanna Schmitz presents herself, during her trial in Germany in the 1960s, as a modest woman, having found during the war a job as a guard in a detention camp which she tried to carry out the best she could. Although she is certainly responsible for the deaths of several dozen prisoners placed under her responsibility, she manages to elicit from the viewer something other than only contempt, the film being criticized for being complacent towards her.[63] The mini-series *Nuremberg* is also remarkable in that respect.[64] Hermann Göring clearly appears as the least repentant of the Nazis accused before the International Military Tribunal instituted by the Allied forces at the end of the Second World War. Yet, the mini-series draws a complex portrait of him that is certainly not reduced to that of a monster.[65] The performance of the actor who plays him, Brian Cox, is not unrelated to the density of Göring, a performance that some critics felt largely outweighed that of Alec Baldwin in the role of prosecutor Robert Jackson. Brian Cox explained how he tried to play the Nazi dignitary:

> My job is to examine the detail of lives. That detail takes into account motivation, excuse, mindlessness, emotions such as envy, malice and resentment. But when these motives are examined, they actually become quite fine and nobody is exempt. In consequence, evil does dwell within us all.[66]

63 Ron Rosenbaum, 'Don't Give an Oscar to the Reader', *Slate*, 9 February 2009.
64 *Nuremberg* (Yves Simoneau, Canada/US, 2000).
65 Julie Alamon, 'Humanized, but not Whitewashed, at Nuremberg', *New York Times* (14 July 2000).
66 Brian Cox, 'The Face of Evil', *Guardian* (21 May 2001).

L'œil du cyclone and *A War*, mentioned earlier, should finally be mentioned in this respect as both portray the accused in ways which induce the viewers to sympathize, if not identify, with him. Although the crimes committed by the former rebel leader in *L'œil du cyclone* are odious and his character rather unpleasant, the viewer comes to understand that he was forcefully enrolled as a child soldier. The film indicates that joining and leading the rebellion became the only way for him to survive and blurs the line that distinguishes the criminal from the victim. This is even more so with the Danish commander of *A War* who, despite ordering an attack which resulted in eleven civilian deaths, principally appears as a loving father, a caring husband and a commander taking care of his soldiers. Identification with the accused of international crimes remains exceptional though.[67] This could partly explain why radical criticism towards international criminal justice remains comparatively limited.

Finally, the predominance of romanticized images about international criminal justice might be explained in light of where the directors and the financial backing for these films come from. An overwhelming majority of these movies have been directed by North American and European filmmakers and produced by Western States. This is not the case with *Sometimes in April*, which was directed by Haitian filmmaker and former Haitian minister of culture Raoul Peck, also known, amongst others, for *I Am Not Your Negro* and *Lumumba*. This is not the case either of *L'œil du cyclone* made by Burkinabe director Sékou Traoré. Unsurprisingly, these two films are amongst the most critical about international criminal justice. This reminds us that what films say about international criminal justice is to a large extent what Western filmmakers think about it and that diversity amongst film directors and producers remains the safest means of ensuring that diverse stories be told about it.

---

67 Compare with description of Eichmann by Arendt, *Eichmann in Jerusalem* or Duch by Marcel Lemonde, *Un juge face aux Khmers Rouges* (Paris: Le Seuil, 2013).

7

The fog of law in the fog of war: international humanitarian law in war movies

Martyna Fałkowska-Clarys* and Vaios Koutroulis

A drone is flying over the territory of Yemen. The image transitions to show the inside of the compound in Las Vegas which serves as a base for the US pilots who are operating the drones. Directing the strikes under the codename *Langley*, the CIA instructs the team of pilots, led by Lieutenant Colonel Johns, to fire at a group of people gathered by a market:

> **CIA:** The target is the Al-Qaeda cell gathered by the market.
> **Lt Col. Johns:** We see the crowd. [incredulously] You want us to kill a crowd?
> **CIA:** Al-Qaeda unsurprisingly tend to congregate with Al-Qaeda or associated forces. Consequently, we've determined that it is militarily more effective to eliminate a group than an individual.
> **Airman Vera Suarez:** Does that include the underage boy, Sir?
> **CIA:** Our analysts see only military aged males. In our assessment, this Al-Qaeda cell represents an imminent threat. Permission to prosecute [*sic*]. Please cease recording.

The strike is launched, killing everyone present on the ground. One member of the team, Vera Suarez, voices her objection to the justification given by the CIA about the strike: ' "Imminent threat"? They couldn't live any further from us', only to have another member of the team reply: 'It depends on your definition of imminent'. According to him, a boy who may turn into a terrorist when he grows up constitutes a sufficiently 'imminent' threat to justify such a strike.[1]

---

* The opinions expressed in this chapter do not in any way reflect the views of the Belgian Judicial Training Institute.

1 See Pardiss Kebriaei, 'Justifying the Right to Kill: Problems of Law, Transparency, and Accountability' in David Cortright, Rachel Fairhurst and Kristen Wall (eds), *Drones and the Future of Armed Conflict: Ethical, Legal, and Strategic Implications* (Chicago and London: University of Chicago Press, 2015) 89–93.

This scene comes from the 2014 film *Good Kill*,² which focuses on US military operations conducted exclusively by drones in the context of the war against the Taliban and Al-Qaeda. From a legal point of view, the central question of whether the people at the market constituted military targets and could thus be lawfully killed falls within the scope of the law of armed conflict, otherwise known as international humanitarian law (IHL),³ and more specifically under the principle of distinction. Part of the rules regulating the conduct of hostilities,⁴ this principle sets out the fundamental distinction between, on the one hand, persons and objects which constitute military objectives and, on the other hand, persons and objects which have a civilian character.⁵ While military objectives can be attacked by the adverse party, civilians and civilian installations are immune from attacks, except in cases of participation (for persons) or use (for objects) in hostilities. Moreover, when a party to the conflict targets a military objective, it must not provoke damage to civilians or civilian objects, which is excessive to the concrete and direct military advantage anticipated from the attack (principle

---

2 Andrew Niccol, USA, 2014. For a commentary of this movie with regard to various aspects of international law, technology and ethics, see Vaios Koutroulis, '*Good Kill*: la guerre à l'époque des assassinats ciblés', Amélie Férey, 'Transparence et effets de Parallax dans *Good Kill*' and Chris De Cock, 'L'utilisation de drones: un faux débat?' (ULB, Centre de droit international, dossier ' "Culture-pop" et droit international', 27 April 2016) http://cdi.ulb.ac.be/3312-2/, accessed 1 December 2019.

3 Marco Sassòli, Antoine A. Bouvier and Anne Quintin, *How Does Law Protect in War?*, vol. 1 (Geneva: ICRC, 3rd edn, 2011) 93; Christopher Greenwood, 'Historical Development and Legal Basis' in Dieter Fleck (ed.), *The Handbook of International Humanitarian Law* (Oxford: Oxford University Press, 2009) 11.

4 Called by some scholars 'the Hague Law', François Bugnion, 'Droit de Genève et droit de La Haye' (2001) 83 *RICR* 905; Yoram Dinstein, *The Conduct of Hostilities under the Law of International Armed Conflict* (Cambridge: Cambridge University Press, 2010) 14–15.

5 Protocol additional to the Geneva Conventions of 12 August 1949, and relating to the protection of victims of international armed conflicts (Protocol I), adopted on 8 June 1977 (hereafter: AP I) 1125 UNTS 25 (article 48). This rule is part of customary international law and applies both to international and non-international armed conflicts; see Jean-Marie Henckaerts and Louise Doswald-Beck, *Customary International Humanitarian Law*, vol. I: Rules (Cambridge: Cambridge University Press, 2005) 3 (rule 1). Sassòli et al., *How Does Law Protect in War?* 250ff.; William H. Boothby, *The Law of Targeting* (Oxford: Oxford University Press, 2012) 60–2, 77ff.; Nils Melzer, 'The Principle of Distinction Between Civilians and Combatants' in Andrew Clapham and Paola Gaeta (eds), *The Oxford Handbook of International Law in Armed Conflict* (Oxford: Oxford University Press, 2014) 296–331; Jean d'Aspremont and Jérôme de Hemptinne, *Droit international humanitaire* (Paris: Pedone, 2012) 177–216; Robin Geiß and Michael Siegrist, 'Has the Armed Conflict in Afghanistan Affected the Rules on the Conduct of Hostilities?' (2011) 93 *IRRC* 12.

of proportionality).⁶ These rules constitute one of the cornerstones of IHL, which 'rests upon the simple moral premise that one should never harm someone who has no means of harming you'.⁷ Soldiers have to apply them based on a more or less subjective appreciation even under extremely difficult combat conditions.

Wars in Afghanistan and Iraq that followed the attacks on the World Trade Center and the Pentagon on 11 September 2001 (the 9/11 attacks) brought about a range of criticisms towards IHL, which has repeatedly been branded as outdated and inadequate to regulate modern warfare: 'This new kind of war cannot be forced into the mold of existing international law; rather [...] the law must adapt and advance to accommodate the metamorphosis in the nature of conflict'.⁸ A particularly salient element of these 'new wars' seems to be the blurring, if not disappearance, of the distinction between those who participate in combat and those who do not, since in many cases, civilians become direct actors of the armed combat. In situations where combat takes place amongst a civilian population, identifying the enemy becomes much more difficult than in classical combat where two armies in uniform confront each other. In wars such as the ones in Iraq and Afghanistan, the question 'who is the enemy?' becomes essential. This is partly due to the disembodied and demonized portrayal of the enemy from the very outset of the conflict, through the characterization as terrorist and evil.⁹ The Taliban and Al-Qaeda, for example, are repeatedly described

---

6   Article 51§5(b), AP I 26; Henckaerts and Doswald-Beck, *Customary International Humanitarian Law*, 46 (rule 14).

7   Hugo Slim, 'Civilians, Distinction, and the Compassionate View of War' in Haidi Willmot, Ralph Mamiya, Scott Sheeran and Marc Weller (eds), *Protection of Civilians* (Oxford: Oxford University Press, 2016) 23.

8   William K. Lietzau, 'Combating Terrorism: Law Enforcement or War?' in *Terrorism and International Law: Challenges and Responses* (San Remo: International Institute of Humanitarian Law, 2003) 80, www.dphu.org/uploads/attachements/books/books_3763_0.pdf, accessed 1 December 2019. For the same argument, see also George Bush, 'Humane Treatment of al Qaeda and Taliban Detainees', Memorandum for the Vice President *et al.*, 7 February 2002, in Karen J. Greenberg and Joshua L. Dratel (eds), *The Torture Papers: The Road to Abu Graib* (Cambridge: Cambridge University Press, 2005) 134.

9   See, for example, the following speeches by George W. Bush, 'Address to a Joint Session of Congress and the American People' (Office of the Press Secretary, 20 September 2001) https://georgewbush-whitehouse.archives.gov/news/releases/2001/09/20010920-8.html, accessed 1 December 2019; 'President Delivers State of the Union Address' (Office of the Press Secretary, 29 January 2002) https://georgewbush-whitehouse.archives.gov/news/releases/2002/01/20020129-11.html, accessed 1 December 2019: 'Our cause is just, and it continues. Our discoveries in Afghanistan confirmed our worst fears, and showed us the true scope of the task ahead. We have seen the depth of our enemies' hatred in videos, where they laugh about the loss of innocent life. And the

as outlaws, extremists and enemies of humanity.¹⁰ These descriptions are invoked to justify depriving such 'outlaws' of certain rights under humanitarian law.¹¹ Following this logic, the principle of distinction, and IHL more generally, is rendered useless – and seen as such – since it fails to offer reliable benchmarks for its application¹² and even to clearly draw a 'morally relevant line between those who fight and those who do not'.¹³

This chapter will seek to determine whether and to what extent this view of IHL as an outdated body of rules, irrelevant to present-day conflicts, finds an on-screen reflection in the representation of rules relating to the conduct of hostilities in war movies and TV series, and more specifically in movies depicting scenes of combat in the field.¹⁴ The material analysed

depth of their hatred is equaled [sic] by the madness of the destruction they design'; 'President Bush Discusses Global War on Terror in Las Vegas, Nevada' (Office of the Press Secretary, 31 January 2008) https://georgewbush-whitehouse.archives.gov/news/releases/2008/01/20080131-2.html, accessed 1 December 2019: 'We're involved in an ideological struggle [...] between those of us who love freedom and human rights and human dignity, and those who want to impose their dark vision on how people should live their lives'.

10 For relevant speeches, see John B. Bellinger III, 'Legal Adviser Remarks at the Symposium in Honor of Edward R. Cummings on Lawyers and Wars' (George Washington University Law School, 30 September 2005) https://2001-2009.state.gov/s/l/rls/73075.htm, accessed 1 December 2019; Georges W. Bush, 'Presidential Address to the Nation' (Office of the Press Secretary, 7 October 2001) https://georgewbush-whitehouse.archives.gov/news/releases/2001/10/20011007-8.html, accessed 1 December 2019.

11 Tim Blackmore, 'Eyeless in America: Hollywood and Indiewood's Iraq War on Film' (2012) 32 *Bulletin of Science, Technology & Society* 308: 'Who, after all, were and are the enemies in these two wars? According to the Bush White House, they were "terrorists," "evildoers," "insurgents," but never soldiers, never human beings with their own coherent belief systems. Denied that status, they could be and were excluded from treatment accorded combatants and prisoners under the Geneva Conventions.'

12 Tim Blackmore speaks of the 'jam into which military and civilian command put soldiers where they must interpret the standing rules of engagement, the guidelines for how to deal with the enemy (Is a car driving toward a check-point hostile? Should the car's occupants be shot at, killed, even if they're civilians? What if there are children in the car?)', 'Eyeless in America', 308.

13 Larry May, 'Killing Naked Soldiers: Distinguishing between Combatants and Noncombatants' (2005) 19 *Ethics & International Affairs* 39.

14 Thus, several categories are excluded from the scope of this contribution: movies focusing on the political or diplomatic aspects of war (such as *In the Loop* (Armando Iannucci, UK, 2009), *Lions for Lambs* (Robert Redford, USA, 2007) or *Quai d'Orsay* (Bertrand Tavernier, France, 2013)), movies dealing with the social dimension of conflicts, such as the disappearance and return of soldiers from war and the influence this has on their families, etc. (*Brothers* (Jim Sheridan, USA, 2009) or *In the Valley of Elah* (Paul Higgis, USA, 2007)), and movies focusing on the treatment of persons

is composed of TV series and narrative movies,[15] including those based on or inspired by actual events.[16] War documentaries are therefore excluded, even though the distinction can sometimes be delicate.[17] Of course, war documentaries are not devoid of interest.[18] However, we decided not to include them in the present analysis as they are possibly less suited for evaluating ideological overtones conveyed through movies seen as part of 'pop culture'.[19] Our filmography does however include 'docudramas' as they implement certain documentary film techniques in narrative movies thereby reinforcing the viewers' impression of reality.[20] Far from being innovative,[21] this mixture of genres has been used extensively in widely distributed films on the Iraq and Afghanistan wars, such as *Redacted*[22] or *The Hurt Locker*.[23] In view of the large number of existing war movies, we certainly cannot pretend to have exhausted the relevant material. However, the movies that we have viewed allowed us to formulate cross-cutting

---

who have fallen in the hands of the enemy such as prisoners of war (*The Bridge on the River Kwai* (David Lean, UK/USA, 1957) or *The Great Escape* (John Sturges, USA, 1963)).

15 Jean-Sébastien Chauvin, 'Fiction' in Antoine de Baecque and Philippe Chevallier (eds), *Dictionnaire de la pensée du cinéma* (Paris: PUF, 2012) 298–9.

16 See e.g. *The Road to Guantanamo* (Mat Whitecross and Michael Winterbottom, UK, 2006). More generally, see Steven N. Lipkin, Derek Paget and Jane Roscoe, 'Docudrama and Mock-Documentary: Defining Terms, Proposing Canons', in Gary Don Rhodes and John Parris Springer (eds), *Docufictions: Essays on the Intersection of Documentary and Fictional Making* (Jefferson and London: McFarland & Co, 2006) 14.

17 See, amongst many, *The Ground Truth* (Patricia Foulkrod, USA, 2006), *Standard Operating Procedure* (Errol Morris, USA, 2008), *Taxi to the Dark Side* (Alex Gibney, USA, 2007), *Armadillo* (Janus Metz, Denmark, 2010), *Restrepo* (Tim Hetherington and Sebastian Junger, USA, 2010), *Off to War: From Rural Arkansas to Iraq* (Brent Renaud and Craig Renaud, USA, 2005), *Soldiers of Conscience* (Catherine Ryan and Gary Weimberg, USA, 2007), *Winter Soldier* (Winterfilm Collective, USA, 1972). On the notion of 'documentary', see Cindy Wong, 'Documentary' in Roberta Pearson and Philip Simpson (eds), *Critical Dictionary of Film and Television Theory* (London and New York: Routledge 2001) 196–7; Maria Muhle, 'Documentaire' in Antoine de Baecque and Philippe Chevallier (eds), *Dictionnaire de la pensée du cinéma* (Paris: PUF, 2012) 239.

18 Wong, 'Documentary', 197.
19 See the methodological introduction to this book.
20 Lipkin et al., 'Docudrama and Mock-Documentary', 18, 23.
21 For examples of docudramas dating from the inter-war period and the Second World War, see Lipkin et al., 'Docudrama and Mock-Documentary', 18–19.
22 Brian De Palma, USA, 2007.
23 Kathryn Bigelow, USA, 2009.

observations concerning the on-screen representation and place reserved to the IHL rules regulating the conduct of hostilities and, by extension, to IHL more generally. Indeed, the rules relating to the distinction that must be made at all times during a conflict between persons and objects that can and cannot be attacked are so central to IHL, so emblematic of the role humanitarian law is called upon to play in hostilities, that the way they are depicted (or not) in movies and TV series can be seen as reflecting, more broadly, the way 'pop culture' views IHL.

Generally speaking, alluding to or more directly portraying IHL or situations it governs can either bring the rules themselves into focus – making them the object submitted to the viewers' scrutiny – or be of a more functional nature. In this second approach, IHL is no longer the object of observation but rather a tool – sometimes in the form of a rhetoric discourse – that helps (de)legitimizing an armed conflict as such or a specific State-led operation.

As for the first approach, there are several ways of organizing and presenting the material we have viewed depending on the element that will be chosen as the point of reference. For the purposes of this contribution, it is useful to start from the main division between films and TV series that mention IHL explicitly and those that do not. As will be shown, this division does not imply that all movies that do not mention IHL reject its relevance or utility, nor, conversely, that all movies that do refer to IHL rules present them under a positive light. Upon analysis, a number of subtleties appear, which is why it is necessary to look more closely into both the *way* the rules are represented (when they are mentioned) and the general message of the makers of a movie or series, in order to identify their stance on IHL. This task is of course somewhat easier when it comes to the analysis of the way IHL rules are depicted in movies and series that mention them explicitly.

Explicit reference to IHL: between irrelevance and criticism of military operations

Direct and concrete references to IHL rules in movies are rather exceptional, especially if we consider the number of productions depicting combat situations. However, when these rules are mentioned, they are used in different ways: while sometimes they are portrayed as irrelevant and ill-adapted to modern warfare, in other cases they are invoked in order to criticize specific actions.

IHL as a set of rules irrelevant and ill-adapted to modern warfare

The Lone Survivor[24] by Peter Berg, a film based on true events, is set in Afghanistan in 2005. It follows a four-member unit of the US Navy SEALs, sent to capture a Taliban leader. Before the mission, the rules of engagement (RoE) are explained to the soldiers. In one of the scenes, the following rule is projected and discussed during a briefing: 'US forces will comply with the Law of Armed Conflict. Only combatants and other military objectives may be attacked.' During their mission, the four soldiers encounter three goatherds – an elderly man, an adolescent boy and a child – who carry a radio transmitter. Given the circumstances and the potential threat to the mission, the SEALs engage in a heated discussion over what to do with the three Afghans. One of them presents the three possible scenarios:

> The way I see it, we've got three options. One: we let them go, hike up. We'll probably be found [i.e. by the Taliban] in less than an hour. Two: we tie them up, hike up, roll the dice. They'll probably be eaten by fucking wolves or freeze to death. Three: we terminate the compromise.

When one of the soldiers suggests that the Afghans be killed, another replies that if their bodies were found the incident would be made public and become problematic to the SEALs' reputation. Faced with this argument, a third soldier asserts: 'It's nobody's fucking business what we do up here. We do what we do, what we have to do.' The soldier who objects to killing the Afghans adds that this is contrary to the RoE. His comrade replies: 'I understand … and I don't care'. He reminds everyone of the US soldiers already killed by the Taliban leader. All he cares about is the life of his fellow soldiers. He wants to avoid that they end up beheaded by the Taliban. Pointing at the young Afghan boy, he says: 'Look at them. That's not a kid. That's a soldier. That's death. Look at death. Look at that soldier.' For him, the second the goatherds run down to their village, they will inform the Taliban of the unit's position, bringing certain death to the SEALs. Nevertheless, the other soldier insists: they are unarmed prisoners, they cannot be killed. The mission's chief takes the final decision: since the operation has been compromised, it should be aborted. The prisoners will be released in accordance with the RoE. The following scene shows the adolescent Afghan hurrying down the mountain, hopping from rock to rock with the dexterity of a child who grew up in those mountains. The viewer then witnesses almost an hour of Taliban attacks against the SEALs, who, despite heroic resistance, will fall one by one. Choosing to act within the bounds of humanitarian law – and thus materializing their '*belief* in the

---

24 Peter Berg, USA, 2013.

value of the restrictions placed upon them by the ROE and the law'[25] – has proven to be fatal.

This movie scene is one of the rare ones in which IHL rules are respected by the main actors on the battlefield. The consequences and final outcome of such choice is of course indicative of the message the movie conveys: had the US soldiers not respected IHL, they would all be alive, having probably succeeded in their mission as well. The constraints imposed by IHL are not only unrealistic and impracticable for certain operations – they are outright detrimental to the success of the mission, and – even more directly – to the soldiers' survival.[26]

A similar representation of IHL is found in the twenty-first episode of the seventh season of the TV series *JAG (Judge Advocate General)*.[27] In this episode, aired in 2002, a high-level member of Al-Qaeda is captured by US forces in Afghanistan. The detainee is brought before a military tribunal aboard a ship of the US Air Force in order to be judged for his participation in the 9/11 attacks. His defence counsel tries to establish that the accused did nothing more than participate in what should be considered legal acts of war. In this context, the defence calls an Oxford University professor of humanitarian law as expert witness. Interrogated by the counsel, the academic claims that Al-Qaeda 'is a militia group of international membership akin to the French Foreign Legion'. He then goes on to assert that the buildings attacked on 11 September 2001 were in fact military objectives: 'The World Trade Center could be characterised as key to US financial infrastructure and thus key to its war effort. Obviously, there is no question that the Pentagon was a military target.' However, when questioned by the prosecution, the professor is forced to admit that only the infrastructure *directly* linked to the war effort may be legally targeted during an armed conflict. Nevertheless, he insists that, in this case, the World Trade Center fulfilled this condition. The professor's arguments sound profoundly artificial and are hardly convincing. This is particularly evident during the expert's cross-examination by the prosecution. Here, the abstract and artificial reasoning is confronted with the prosecutor's counter-arguments

---

25   Michael W. Lewis, 'Battlefield Perspectives on the Laws of War' in Geoffrey S. Corn, James A. Schoettler, Jr., Dru Brenner-Beck, Victor M. Hansen, Dick Jackson, Eric Talbot Jensen and Michael W. Lewis (eds), *The War on Terror and the Laws of War: A Military Perspective* (Oxford: Oxford University Press, 2015) 265.

26   The same point is made in *Band of Brothers* (HBO, USA, 2001), episode 4, where a British soldier driving a tank refuses to fire a mortar shell and destroy a house blocking his view, because his orders prohibit any unnecessary destruction of property. This results in the British tank getting destroyed by an enemy tank hiding behind the house.

27   Donald P. Bellisario, NBC, USA, 1995–2005.

solidly grounded in realism and military common sense. In this case, it seems manifestly absurd to consider the attacks against the World Trade Center as attacks against a military objective. The prosecution denounces an academic image of humanitarian law presented as a set of abstract rules detached from reality and incarnated by the Oxford University professor, with his suit, glasses, noticeable British accent, moralistic tone and legal pedantry.

The reader should not however be left with the impression that every time IHL is explicitly mentioned in films it is to contest its relevance. Indeed, some films and TV series refer to IHL rules in order to denounce their violations and criticize actions undertaken by belligerents.

IHL as the legal basis for criticism of military operations

Two examples of clearly articulated criticism of violations of IHL are found in Andrew Niccol's *Good Kill* (2004), already mentioned in this chapter. The first one comes from the scene referred to above, which is interesting because without positively taking a position against the drone strike, it does present the incident in a bad light. This can be deduced from a number of elements such as the debate on the notion of 'imminent' threat, the reference to the act of 'killing a crowd' when there is no affirmative proof of any wrongdoing of its members, the qualification of an underage boy as a 'military aged male', as well as the request by the CIA to stop the recording of the incident pointing to the uneasiness provoked by the attack. The counter-argument of military effectiveness (and necessity) in targeting groups rather than individuals is not sufficient to neutralize this uneasiness, and justly so since the legality of the strike is problematic under IHL. Indeed, targeting a person simply because he is a 'military aged male' completely flouts the rule according to which, in case of doubt, a person is considered as a civilian and thus protected from attack.[28]

In a second example, the drone pilots are instructed by the CIA to fire at a building where 'Al-Qaeda's number one bomb-maker' is to be found. Once the strike is successfully completed and the building is destroyed, the CIA requests a second strike:

> CIA: Our compliments Colonel. That was a high card you and your people just pulled out of the deck. Al-Qaeda's number one bomb-maker will never again harm one of us ... [a few seconds pass by] ... Please do a follow-up.

---

28 For the presumption of civilian character in general, see Article 50 para 1, AP I 26; recommendation VIII of the ICRC recommendations concerning the interpretation of international humanitarian law relating to the notion of direct participation in hostilities in Nils Melzer, *Interpretative Guidance on the Notion of Direct Participation in Hostilities under International Humanitarian Law* (Geneva: ICRC, 2009) 17.

The members of the team operating the drones exchange worried looks before Lieutenant Colonel Johns replies:

Lt Col. Johns: Did I hear you correctly, Langley?
CIA: There are other combatants in the vicinity.
Lt Col. Johns: Double-tap …
CIA: We prefer the term 'follow-up'.

Vera Suarez, once again voices her protest: 'Sir, they are rescuers. We can't …' Another member of the team, Mission Intelligence Coordinator (MIC) Joseph Zimmer, reacts immediately: 'The fuck we can, they're Taliban. Who do you think their first responders are going to be? Quakers? Those rescuers have RPGs.'[29] The image focuses on what is happening on the ground. Through the smoke and dust, we see people digging, presumably in order to find any person who may have survived the attack. Vera Suarez insists: 'I see people with shovels.' Zimmer immediately throws back at her: 'Then just hit the ones with the RPGs.'

Lieutenant Colonel Johns asks the CIA to confirm the order only to hear the following reply:

CIA: In our opinion, it's proportionate.
Lt Col. Johns: Forgive me Sir but what the hell does that mean?
CIA: It means that in our assessment the combatants we are targeting pose a grave enough threat to the United States to justify potential civilian casualties. Not to mention that this pre-emptive self-defense is approved and ordered by the administration. Please engage.

Muttering 'Orders …', Lieutenant Colonel Johns caves and the team half-heartedly conducts the strike which of course results in more casualties. At the end of the scene, Suarez asks Lieutenant Colonel Johns 'Was that a war crime, Sir?'. The only answer she gets is 'Shut the fuck up, Suarez!'.

This scene is openly critical of the practice of 'double-tapping', which indeed has been considered by international lawyers as problematic under IHL.[30] Not only does it clearly highlight the possibility of this practice resulting in a war crime, but it also hints at the absurdity of referring to the act in question as a 'follow up', as if a change in the name would make the conduct less of a violation of humanitarian rules. Nevertheless, the film is not completely blind to the arguments in favour of double-tap

---

29 'RPG' stands for 'rocket-propelled grenade' and is a shoulder-fired anti-tank weapon.
30 ICRC, *Commentary on the First Geneva Convention* (Cambridge: Cambridge University Press, 2nd edn, 2016) para 1404; Human Rights Council, Report of the Independent International Commission of Inquiry on the Syrian Arab Republic, UN Doc. A/HRC/34/64, 2 February 2017, 33, para 49; Gary D. Solis, *The Law of Armed Conflict* (Cambridge: Cambridge University Press, 2nd edn, 2016) 359–60.

strikes. The CIA's justification relating to proportionality is not presented as being extremely convincing, as demonstrated by Lieutenant Colonel Johns' reaction, focusing on the fact that this is an order they are expected and required to execute. Much more interesting is the dialogue between the two members of the team, Suarez and Zimmer, who represent, respectively, the narrow and the broad interpretation of the rules of war protecting civilians and persons *hors de combat* during active hostilities. Where Suarez insists the persons on the ground should not be targeted because they are rescuers and there is nothing indicating that they are combatants, Zimmer replies that they should be presumed to be members of the Taliban carrying RPGs. Since there is no way to conclusively verify the status of these persons, it all boils down to the presumption that will prevail as a starting point: are the persons in question to be considered as civilians unless proven otherwise – as humanitarian law dictates – or as enemy combatants that can be the object of an attack? The final provocative statement by Zimmer – 'Then just hit the ones with the RPGs' – clearly refers to the impossibility of realistically achieving a conclusive assessment of the status of the persons targeted. It also highlights the necessity to prevent one's enemies from getting away by adopting overly cautious and humane behaviour. Although this reasoning is not definitively disavowed in the film, the production clearly adopts a critical stance with respect to double-tap strikes.

Drone strikes via live videostream are also depicted in a critical manner in the 2016 movie *Snowden* by Oliver Stone. In one of the scenes, sitting around a fire at a birthday party, Snowden – who works as a contractor for the National Security Agency (NSA) – and his colleagues are relaxing with a few drinks. In the background, one of them, a drone pilot, describes a drone operation, which resulted in the death of a child whose entire family is killed, a few days later, by another strike while attending the boy's funeral: 'Poof, and they are gone in a cloud of dust. I mean all of them, the whole fucking family.' After a short reflection, the same colleague adds: 'but the crazy thing is, you come home after work, kiss your wife, the kids, back to work the next day. Pretty soon, you know, it all just becomes a routine'. A short conversation, which follows these revelations, illustrates the underlying critical tone of the production regarding the lack of respect for international rules governing the conduct of hostilities.

> **Trevor James (one of Snowden's NSA colleagues):** [...] you make it sound criminal, man. It's war, it's a job.
> **Drone pilot:** Oh, I don't know, man. And jobs can't be criminal?
> **Trevor James:** Not if you're working for the government.
> **Edward Snowden:** Have you ever heard of the Nuremberg trials, Trev? They weren't that long ago.
> **Trevor James:** Yeah, and we hang the Nazi bigshots, right?

Edward Snowden: Well, the bigshots were the first trial. But the next trial, were just the judges, lawyers, policemen, guards, ordinary people following orders. That's where we got the Nuremberg principles, which then the UN made into international law just in case ordinary jobs become criminal.

To illustrate this critical position, we could also cite the US TV series *Generation Kill*[31] and the British TV mini-series *The Promise*,[32] where abusive interpretations of IHL rules suggested respectively by US Marines deployed in Iraq in 2003 and the Irgun militia[33] in 1947 Palestine, are presented in a critical light. In neither case are such interpretations depicted as being 'correct'[34] and, more generally, neither of the TV series may be considered complacent towards the actions of the Irgun (in *The Promise*) or of the US troops (in *Generation Kill*).

In all the cases analysed above, the explicit reference to IHL rules makes it easier to identify the representation and role played by these rules in the relevant films and TV series. However, as will be shown in the analysis below, even where no such explicit reference exists, the absence of IHL may be equally important for the message a production tries to convey.

The absence of explicit reference to IHL: letting the violations speak for themselves

Relatively few war films or series put forth, even implicitly, legal interpretations of the IHL rules applicable during combat. Most often law is not mentioned, even in cases where one would expect it to be. For example, films criticizing the excesses of the Vietnam war, such as *Platoon*[35] or *Full Metal Jacket*,[36] feature many attacks against civilians without any specific principle of humanitarian law being debated, or, *a fortiori*, interpreted. In such cases, the general critical overtone of the movie seems to convey a criticism of the violation of IHL in the way they depict combat actions. However, in other cases, the absence of any meaningful reference to IHL is

---

31 Susanna White and Simon Cellan Jones, HBO, USA, 2008.
32 Peter Kosminsky, Channel 4, UK, 2011.
33 Zionist armed organization operating from 1931 to 1948 in Palestine during the Mandate; see www.larousse.fr/encyclopedie/divers/Irgoun/125151, accessed 1 December 2019.
34 Concerning *Generation Kill*, see Thibaut de Saint-Maurice, *Philosophie en séries* (season 2, Ellipses, 2010) 131–44, esp. 142.
35 Oliver Stone, USA, 1986.
36 Stanley Kubrick, USA, 1987.

rather the symptom of it being discarded as ill-adapted to modern warfare, unable to offer any meaningful guidance as to how hostilities ought to be conducted.

The absence of explicit reference to IHL as proof of its irrelevance to modern warfare

Overall, war films which focus on combat action in the field, aiming to make the viewer identify with the soldiers in a military campaign, usually promote an approach favourable to the necessity to adapt IHL principles, such as the principle of distinction or of proportionality, to the realities on the ground.

The view that the realities on the ground do not allow for the luxury of scrupulously respecting humanitarian law is conveyed by the Danish film *Krigen (A War)*.[37] The production recounts an attack conducted by Danish soldiers operating in Afghanistan against the Taliban, potentially constitutive of a war crime. The main character, Commander Claus Pedersen, and his soldiers find themselves under relentless fire by the Taliban forces, with one of the soldiers badly wounded. Pedersen requests the supporting forces to carry out an airstrike against the compound from which the Taliban are believed to charge. As soon as the strike is conducted, the Taliban fire stops. The Danish unit is extracted and the wounded soldier transported to safety. However, a few weeks later, Pedersen – and the viewers with him – discovers that the compound was not a military objective and that the attack resulted in the death of eleven civilians, thus potentially making it a war crime. During Pedersen's trial in Denmark, two main arguments are put forth in his defence: first, the need to save the lives of the Danish troops and to bring everyone, included the wounded soldier, back home safe and sound; and second, the 'fog of war' which makes it extremely difficult, if not impossible, to avoid civilian casualties. Although IHL and the principle of distinction are not discussed in the movie (the second part focuses on the criminal trial and procedure), it is clear that these are the rules underlying the conduct of the Danish forces during combat. The justifications pointing to military necessity are directly linked to IHL and used in order to excuse its violation.

The same element is found in Gillo Pontecorvo's *The Battle of Algiers*[38] on the Algerian War of Independence against France. The movie carefully illustrates the methods used by the Algerian National Liberation Front (FLN), consisting mainly of terrorist attacks launched by women transporting bombs in their carrying baskets. During a press conference

---

37 Tobias Lindholm, Denmark, 2015.
38 La Battaglia di Algeri, Gillo Pontecorvo, Italy/Algeria, 1966.

held following the capture of an FLN leader, a French journalist asks about these methods: 'Don't you think it is rather cowardly to use the bags and baskets of your women to transport your bombs; these bombs that result in so many innocent victims?' Without hesitation, the FLN leader replies:

> What about you? Don't you think it is cowardly to launch napalm bombs on defenceless villages, killing a thousand times more innocents? Of course, it would have been easier for us if we had airplanes. Give us your bombers, Sir, and we will give you our baskets.

The reference to the use of napalm by the French army is connected to the idea of reciprocity. Of course, in this context, there is no mention of the rules as such but the violations of humanitarian law are denounced. However, the reference to the atrocities committed by one of the parties to the conflict and to the underlying violations of humanitarian law mainly serves as a justification of the other party's disregard for the same rules. Along the same lines, the FLN leader's reply highlights the impossibility of respecting IHL in the context of asymmetric conflicts,[39] when the means of combat are not the same for both sides. This type of conflict makes it impossible for the weaker party to respect humanitarian law if it is to have any chance at winning the war.

The same excuse, relating to the impossibility of respecting the prohibition of torture when confronted with a terrorist group, is expressed by Colonel Mathieu, the paratrooper commanding the French forces involved in the conflict in Algeria. Thus, although the film is positively predisposed towards the Algerian war of national liberation and denounces the methods employed by the French army in their efforts to quench the uprising, it does convey the message that one may not aspire to achieve the objective of prevailing over the adversary and scrupulously apply the rules of IHL at the same time.[40]

---

39 On the challenges posed by asymmetric conflicts to compliance with humanitarian law see amongst many, Karine Bannelier, 'L'influence de la guerre asymétrique sur les règles du *jus in bello*', in Karine Bannelier, Olivier Corten, Théodore Christakis and Pierre Klein (eds), *L'intervention en Irak et le droit international* (Paris: Pedone, 2004) 145–70; Toni Pfanner, 'Asymmetrical Warfare from the Perspective of Humanitarian Law and Humanitarian Action' (2005) 87 *IRRC* 149; Geiß and Siegrist, 'Armed Conflict in Afghanistan', 17–43; Michael L. Gross, 'Asymmetric War, Symmetrical Intentions: Killing Civilians in Modern Armed Conflict' (2009) 10 *Global Crime* 320.
40 Along the same lines, at an earlier point in the film, during the first briefing of the first paratroopers, Colonel Mathieu warns his soldiers about the impossibility of identifying the enemy combatants: 'The enemy is cunning and dangerous. It is an enemy that moves in the surface and in depth, with well-tested revolutionary methods and original tactics [...] It is an anonymous enemy, unrecognisable, blended within hundreds of other people. He is everywhere, in cafés, in the casbah alleys or in the streets of the European part of the city, in stores, in workplaces.'

Several productions about contemporary conflicts illustrate the limits of humanitarian law in general. They depict the enemy in a similar manner: disembodied, difficult to single out and identify, possibly hiding behind anyone and everyone. Any person, however innocent he or she may appear at first, is potentially dangerous. The Oscar-winning movie *The Hurt Locker* (2009) or the UK-produced *The Mark of Cain* (2007[41]) are two clear examples of such depiction. The second film focuses on events involving UK troops present in Iraq in 2003.[42] Following the killing of one of their officers by a roadside bomb, the soldiers violently mistreat captured Iraqi civilians (supposedly terrorists). As the soldiers try to determine who were the people behind the ambush, they engage in an illustrative exchange: 'What did those militants look like to you?', a soldier asks. Another replies: 'Everybody else'. The first then exclaims: 'Exactly. From now on, as far as I am concerned, every civilian has got an RPG wrapped inside his prayer mat.' These last words eloquently express the complete reversal of the humanitarian rule according to which, in case of doubt, a person is presumed civilian.

Other movies also abound with scenes illustrating the difficulty of identifying the enemy, a difficulty resulting in death and unreasonable outbursts of violence. The emblematic *Apocalypse Now*,[43] while placed in Vietnam, can be seen as illustrating how every soldier confronted with certain conflicts cannot avoid being progressively immersed into 'the heart of darkness'.[44] The film *Go Tell the Spartans*[45] is yet another example in this respect. The enemy in this film is elusive: by day he is barely visible, impossible to distinguish amongst the frightened faces of farmworkers; by night, he appears only briefly, against the light of the explosions caused by his attacks; when he finally reveals himself, he takes various forms, sometimes that of a desirable young girl smilingly carrying a basket full of ammunition, sometimes that of an old one-eyed man, half-Indian, half-zombielike.[46] This

---

41 Marc Munden, UK, 2007.
42 For the political, legal and judicial context of the events having inspired this movie, see: Rachel Kerr, 'The UK in Basra and the Death of Baha Mousa' in David W. Lovell (ed.), *Investigating Operational Incidents in a Military Context: Law, Justice, Politics* (Leiden and Boston: Brill/Nijhoff, 2015) 71–85.
43 Francis Ford Coppola, USA, 1979.
44 Laurent Tessier, *Le Vietnam, un cinéma de l'apocalypse* (Paris: Cerf-Corlet, 2009) 110–23.
45 Ted Post, USA, 1978. About this movie, see Tessier, *Le Vietnam*, 99–103.
46 André Muraire, *Hollywood – Vietnam. La guerre du Vietnam dans le cinéma américain: mythes et réalités* (Paris: Michel Houdiard, 2010) 70: 'À peine visible le jour, où on le confond facilement avec ces visages apeurés de paysans tassés sous leur chapeau conique, mais illuminé la nuit par intermittence grâce à la lueur apocalyptique des fusées éclairantes et des explosions, l'ennemi apparaît pour la première fois dans

image of a disembodied, unidentified, quasi-symbolic enemy appears in later productions such as *Black Hawk Down*,[47] where the Somali militiamen (referred to as 'skinnies') are depicted as faceless, disembodied shadows amidst urban warfare in Somalia. The same image materializes in the last scene of *Platoon*, where the viewer gets only a furtive glimpse of the Vietcong soldiers, who appear as interchangeable shadows.[48] Along the same lines, in the Danish film *Krigen* (*A War*) (2015), aside from one initial incident, we do not see the Taliban when they attack the Danish soldiers.[49]

Such depiction of the enemy results in an inversed paradigm. Instead of the presumption of civilian status, everyone is presumed to be a potential enemy. In some movies, this shift leads to the complete abolishment of any limits to the conduct of attacks or the treatment of detainees. The movies depicting abuses (*The Mark of Cain* (2007), *Battle for Haditha* (2007),[50] *In the Valley of Elah* (2007)) 'erase the distinction between civilians and combatants, the carrying of arms being their lowest common denominator'.[51] These productions show how soldiers who have been attacked cease to think in terms of the distinction between civilians and combatants and, as they suffer more and more losses of fellow soldiers, perceive every situation through a 'prism of evil'. Thus, the disregard of minimal humanitarian rules is often presented as a *fact*, as the seemingly inevitable result of the modern warfare typical to the 'war on terror'. A broadly understood concept of necessity – to win, to survive, to beat the enemy – becomes the dominant factor on the ground. Sometimes, this broad concept of necessity seems to simply replace any potential reference to the applicable (international) law. In the first season of *Fauda*,[52] an Israeli TV series in which the commander of a Mista'arvim unit, Doron Kavillio, comes out of retirement and re-joins

---

ce film sous toutes les formes qui vont hanter les soldats américains par la suite. Visage de cette jeune fille tellement désirable qui transporte en souriant un panier plein de munitions, ou marque de vieux hibou borgne mi-Indien, mi-zombie [...] [a]utant de représentations qui nourriront les cauchemars des *grunts*'. See also *Full Metal Jacket* (Stanley Kubrick, USA, 1987).

47 Ridley Scott, USA, 2001.
48 Jean-Michel Valantin, *Hollywood, le Pentagone et le monde. Les trois acteurs d'une stratégie globale* (Paris: Éditions Autrement, 2010) 51, 149: 'les soldats viêt-congs ne sont qu'entraperçus, semblables à des ombres interchangeables'.
49 See also Bénédicte Chéron, 'Représenter les conflits asymétriques par le cinéma de fiction (éthique, légitimité, légalité)' in Stéphane Boiron, Nathalie Goedert and Ninon Maillard (eds), *Les lois de la guerre. Guerre, droit et cinéma* (Paris: Institut Universitaire Varenne, 2015) 121–36.
50 Nick Broomfield, UK, 2007.
51 Valantin, *Hollywood*, 125: 'gomm[e]nt la différence entre civils et combattants, le port d'armes étant leur plus petit commun dénominateur' (translated by the authors).
52 Lior Raw and Avi Issacharoff, *Yes Oh*, Israel, 2015.

the Israel Defense Forces (IDF) to track a Hamas terrorist known as the Panther, the idea of necessity is tangible throughout superseding any potential argument drawn from applicable international law.

When the reality of war takes over and the distinctions between combatants and civilians are blurred, IHL becomes impracticable and ill-adapted, and necessity seems to prevail over any applicable rules. Movies and TV series that point out the difficulties relating to the identification of the enemy on the battlefield, and more broadly, to the application of IHL in practice, seem to criticize this paradigm shift. It is however important to note that in some cases, the presentation of the violations under a negative light is associated with a critical message about the lack of respect for IHL rather than with the denunciation of its uselessness and unfitness to the realm of war.

The absence of IHL as an element of criticism against the way military operations are conducted

Several movies and TV series illustrate military operations conducted in a way that violates IHL, linking these illustrations to a general critical message about the lack of humanity in warfare and, thus, implicitly, about the lack of respect for applicable international law.

Apocalypse Now (1979) with its iconic scene of the napalm attack against a Vietcong village is a good example in this respect. Lieutenant Colonel Kilgore demands that the surroundings be 'cleaned up' with napalm. After the orders have been executed and the smoke from the bombs has covered up the place, Kilgore says rather casually:

> I love the smell of napalm in the morning. You know, one time we had a hill bombed for 12 hours. When it was all over, I walked up. We didn't find one of them, not one stinking dink body. The smell, you know that gasoline smell, the whole hill. It smelled like ... victory.

Even though the script contains no explicit reference to the use of napalm bombs being in violation of applicable IHL rules, the film is certainly critical of such bombings. *Platoon* (1986) and *Full Metal Jacket* (1987) can also be listed in this category. *Platoon*'s reference to crimes committed in Vietnam by US troops and the generally unfavourable depiction of US soldiers deprived the production of the Pentagon's support. An article published in 1987 by the *Washington Post* refers to a confidential memo of the Pentagon dating back to 1984, which explains why the US army did not approve of the script (written by Oliver Stone based on his own experience in the Vietnam war):

> We have reviewed the script, 'The Platoon', and have found the Army cannot support it as written. In its present form, the script presents an unfair and

inaccurate view of the Army. There are numerous problem areas in the script. They include: the murder and rape of innocent Vietnamese villagers by U.S. soldiers, the coldblooded murder of one U.S. soldier, rampant drug abuse, the stereotyping of black soldiers and the portrayal of the majority of soldiers as illiterate delinquents. The entire script is rife with unrealistic and highly unfavorable depictions of the American soldier.[53]

The movie *Battle for Haditha* (2007), which narrates the macabre events from November 2005 when over twenty Iraqi civilians – men, women and children – were killed by US Marines looking to avenge one of their colleagues who perished during an ambush,[54] is another example in this respect. While the film illustrates the difficulty inherent in identifying the enemy in a situation of armed conflict, this factor is not used by the film as an excuse for the war crimes committed later by the US soldiers which are portrayed in all their frightening magnitude underlying the critical tone of the production towards the violations.

This critical tone is also put forth in productions where international law is mentioned, almost *en passant*, only to be discarded and ridiculed. *Vice*[55] narrates Dick Cheney's political career up to his US vice presidency in the George W. Bush administration. In the context of the infamous 'torture memo' and the revelations regarding the acts of torture committed by American troops in Afghanistan during the operations which followed the 9/11 attacks, Cheney and Bush engage in a dialogue with their collaborators.

> **George Tenet:** What about the Geneva Convention?
> **Dick Cheney:** The Geneva Convention is open to interpretation.
> **George Tenet:** What exactly does that mean?
> **David Addington:** Stress positions, water boarding, confined spaces, dogs.
> **Donald Rumsfeld:** We're calling it enhanced interrogation.
> **George W. Bush:** We're sure none of this fits the definition of torture?

---

53 Jack Anderson and Dale Van Atta, 'Why the Pentagon didn't like "Platoon"', *The Washington Post* (30 August 1987), www.washingtonpost.com/archive/opinions/1987/08/30/why-the-pentagon-didnt-like-platoon/b638371d-0dbf-4810-9483-898fa8b68cfe/, accessed 1 December 2019.

54 For more on that massacre, see Charlie Savage and Elisabeth Bumiller, 'An Iraqi Massacre, a Light Sentence and a Question of Military Justice', *New York Times* (27 January 2012), www.nytimes.com/2012/01/28/us/an-iraqi-massacre-a-light-sentence-and-a-question-of-military-justice.html?_r=0, accessed 1 December 2019; Tom Ayres, 'Haditha: A Case Study in Response to War Crimes' in David W. Lovell (ed.), *Investigating Operational Incidents in a Military Context: Law, Justice, Politics* (Leiden and Boston: Brill/Nijhoff, 2015) 87–97.

55 Adam McKay, USA, 2018.

> **David Addington:** The U.S. doesn't torture.
>
> **Dick Cheney:** Therefore, if the U.S. does it, by definition, it can't be torture.

During the scene, the viewer is confronted with the discrepancy between the legal interpretation and the realities of the war as the camera alternates between the comfort of the Oval Office in Washington and the scenes of torture in Afghanistan. The next scene is a satirical depiction of other, equally problematic, legal interpretations and opinions endorsed by Cheney and his collaborators. As we see the protagonists dining in a high priced, gourmet restaurant, the waiter presents them with 'the menu':

> **Waiter:** Good evening, gentlemen. Tonight we are offering the enemy combatant: whereby a person is not a prisoner of war or a criminal. Which means of course that he has absolutely no protection under the law. We are also offering an Extraordinary Rendition where suspects are abducted without record, on foreign soil and taken to foreign prisons in countries that still torture.
>
> **Donald Rumsfeld:** Oh, that sounds delicious!

As we see, IHL is generally alluded to but only to show that it is simply ignored and mocked by the protagonists or subject to very problematic interpretations, at best. The clear satirical tone of the production conveys its critical stance towards such attitude. It highlights the fact that the rules and principles of humanitarian law were not given any serious consideration and might as well have not been mentioned at all.

In all of the productions we have just mentioned, even where there is no explicit mention of IHL rules, the means and methods of combat used during the military operations are decried. The inhumanity of combat is omnipresent and the need to inject some humanity into warfare – the very purpose for the existence of IHL rules – becomes apparent to the spectator. Paradoxically, the absence of IHL in these productions seem to awaken its presence in the mind of the audience.

Using explicit or implicit references to rules of humanitarian law conveys a message. Either the existing rules are presented as irrelevant and unfit to effectively regulate armed conflicts, or they serve as a basis for criticizing operations carried out by the protagonists of a given conflict. Often, a properly articulated legal argument is replaced with justifications of possible violations of the relevant rules. These justifications or excuses take the form of a broadly understood concept of necessity and the general idea of the unavoidability of horror in the fog of war where the enemy is difficult to identify and where the prism of evil takes over.

Keeping in mind the stance – be it critical or otherwise – that films and TV series adopt with respect to IHL rules and their potential violations, it is important to take a step back and try to determine the more general role played by the explicit or implicit references to IHL in these productions. Indeed, aside from illustrating problems pertaining to the (in)applicability or (un)fitness of the rules, the references to IHL can play a central role in articulating a general discourse of a film with respect to a specific conflict, mainly by legitimizing or delegitimizing its protagonists or its very *raison d'être*.

The use and abuse of IHL for legitimacy purposes

The productions mentioned so far put IHL – explicitly or implicitly – under the magnifying glass, presenting it in accordance with the message they wish to convey about its suitability and applicability to the realm of the combat. A functional – if not instrumental – use of references to IHL can be found in other movies. Humanitarian law is no longer the object of scrutiny but rather an argument, or a tool, helping the director to legitimise a given armed conflict or to justify a specific operation that is more broadly problematic under international law (and not just under IHL).

Certain movies choose to ignore and hide or simply omit the violations committed by a State's armed forces in an effort to present a positive image of those forces (*The Green Berets*,[56] *Bombardier*,[57] *Twelve O'Clock High*[58]). In those productions, the principles of IHL are not criticized as such. Rather, the viewer is under the impression that the on-screen soldiers naturally comply with the rules. Clint Eastwood's *American Sniper* presents a suitable example in this regard.[59] It narrates the story of Chris Kyle, considered to be the deadliest sniper in the US forces. During the entire film, which follows

---

56 John Wayne, Ray Kellog, Mervyn LeRoy, USA, 1968. The movie depicts an idealized image of the US troops without mentioning the violations committed by them (Tessier, *Le Vietnam*, 58), and in general focuses more on justifying the war than on the application of the principle of distinction as such.
57 Richard Wallace and Lambert Hillyer, USA, 1943.
58 Henry King, USA, 1949. See Frank J. Wetta and Martin A. Novell, 'Good Bombing, Bad Bombing: Hollywood, Air Warfare, and Morality in World War I and World War II' (2008) 22 *Organization of American Historians Magazine of History* 25–9.
59 Clint Eastwood, USA, 2014. See Vaios Koutroulis, 'American Sniper (Clint Eastwood, 2014): une apologie de la guerre en Irak?' (ULB, Centre de droit international, dossier '"Culture-pop" et droit international', 19 November 2018), http://cdi.ulb.ac.be/american-sniper-clint-eastwood-2014-apologie-de-guerre-irak-analyse-de-vaios-koutroulis/, accessed 1 December 2019.

the protagonist through four consecutive deployments in Iraq, there is not one single incident in which Kyle seems to use lethal force in a manner contrary to the law of armed conflict: all those killed are legitimate targets, whether they are Iraqi rebels or women and children who try to throw a grenade at a convoy of US soldiers, and thus lose their protection as civilians because they participate directly in hostilities.[60] On the contrary, all of the IHL violations portrayed in the film – some are very graphic – are committed by the rebels against which the US soldiers are fighting. Combined with the complete absence of any mention or hint of violations committed by the US troops in Iraq, the movie ends up conveying a positive message about the US intervention and military operations in Iraq.

Indeed, it is not uncommon for movies and TV series to show the violations of the principle of distinction, and of IHL in general, committed by the adversary in order to charge the enemy and, in some cases, to justify violations committed by own troops. This objective is either that of the film as such (*Breaker Morant* (1980);[61] *The Pacific* (2010),[62] first episode), or that of one of the parties to the conflict and whose discourse is presented in the film (*Battle for Haditha* (2007); *The Battle of Algiers* (1966)).

In this sense, the political dimension of Hollywood productions, assisted sometimes by the Pentagon's active implication, can be highlighted with respect to some movies. This 'military-cinematographic' complex, already referred to in this book,[63] is not a recent phenomenon. On the contrary, military logistics have often been placed at the disposal of Hollywood, specifically at the end of the Second World War. The phenomenon intensified in the 1960s[64] and, after the 9/11 attacks, the US government has supported film-making focusing on recent conflicts, as illustrated by movies like *Act of Valor* (2012),[65] *The Lone Survivor* (2013)[66] and *Black*

---

60 Article 51 para 3, AP I 26; Henckaerts and Doswald-Beck, *Customary International Humanitarian Law*, 19 (rule 6): 'Civilians are protected against hostilities unless and for such time as they take a direct part in hostilities.'
61 Bruce Beresford, Australia, 1980.
62 HBO, USA, 2010.
63 See the chapter by Olivier Corten on the representation of the UN Charter in action movies.
64 Valantin, *Hollywood*, 25–6. *The Green Berets* (1968) is amongst the movies cited as flagrant examples of propaganda; Valantin, *Hollywood*, 33–4.
65 Mike McCoy and Scott Waugh, USA, 2012. The film was commissioned by the Pentagon and some of the characters are played by real SEALs members; Jordan Zakarin, ' "Act Of Valor" And The Military's Long Hollywood Mission', *Huffington Post* (21 February 2012), www.huffingtonpost.com/2012/02/17/act-of-valor-military-hollywood_n_1284338.html, accessed 1 December 2019.
66 The SEALs were authorized to act as consultants to the movie; Rowan Scarborough, 'What is the Pentagon's Policy on Artistic Aid? It Depends ...', *Washington Times*

Hawk Down (2001).⁶⁷ This 'coordination of US foreign policy, dominated by the "war against terrorism", with Hollywood productions'⁶⁸ results in cinematographic productions that are generally pro-military (pro-soldier), that evade the problems linked to the reasons and causes of a given conflict, and that focus instead on presenting a collective hero: *the armed forces*.⁶⁹ Even in films where armed forces torture or kill civilians, the soldiers are depicted as the victims of an unbearable situation, of the 'fog of war' and the personal and collective suffering it brings about.⁷⁰

Taking things one step further, in some cases, IHL rules are used as a way of justifying actions that, if committed outside a war zone, would constitute violations of other rules of international law, thus legitimizing resort to force in general. An excellent example of a film where IHL serves as an element of legitimization of State action is *Eye in the Sky*.⁷¹ This British film about drone warfare narrates the efforts of UK military intelligence officer, Colonel Katherine Powell (Helen Mirren), to capture three high-level Al-Shabaab members, including a British couple, in Nairobi.⁷² The operation is supervised by Lieutenant General Frank Benson, Deputy Chief of UK's Chief of Staff, as well as two British government ministers and a ministerial under-secretary. The evolving situation on the ground makes capture impossible. A drone strike targeting the house, which serves as a gathering place for the three individuals, becomes the only available option. Suicide vests and explosives found inside the house indicate that more suicide attacks are being planned. As the authorities stall, the situation gets even more complicated: an innocent girl selling bread sets up camp next to the house soon to become the target of the strike. This is where the film climaxes with intense discussions between Colonel Powell – wishing to proceed

---

(3 December 2012), www.washingtontimes.com/news/2012/dec/3/just-what-is-the-pentagons-policy-on-artistic-aid/?page=all, accessed 1 December 2019.

67 Scarborough, 'What is the Pentagon's Policy?'.
68 Valantin, *Hollywood*, 137: 'coordination de la politique étrangère américaine, dominée par la "guerre contre le terrorisme", avec les productions hollywoodiennes'.
69 Blackmore, 'Eyeless in America', 297, 300, 302–5. Even when the reasons for getting involved in the conflict are criticized, the army is still represented in a positive light, the criticism being mainly directed against politicians (*Green Zone* (Paul Greengrass, France/Spain/UK/USA, 2010)).
70 Blackmore, 'Eyeless in America', 303.
71 Gavin Hood, UK, 2015.
72 On the questions relation to the applicability of IHL in this situation, see: Ntina Tzouvala, 'Eye in the Sky: Drones, the (Human) Ticking-Time Bomb Scenario and Law's Inhumanity', *Critical Legal Thinking* (19 April 2016), http://criticallegalthinking.com/2016/04/19/eye-sky-drones-human-ticking-time-bomb-scenario-laws-inhumanity/, accessed 1 December 2019.

with the strike in order to eliminate the three dangerous individuals – the Army Legal Services – insisting on the rules of engagement and the need to minimize the collateral damage of the operation – and the politicians – factoring in the political cost of civilian victims, especially the potential death of a little girl. Eventually, the strike is authorized and executed, leaving the girl to pass away at the end of the movie. The movie portrays a quagmire of moral and legal nature.[73] Leaving aside the technicalities of the legal evaluations suggested, on a more general level, the movie takes for granted the applicability of IHL to the operation. At no moment is there any explanation of why the relevant States are involved in an armed conflict with Al-Shabaab. The film appears therefore to subscribe to the US vision of a generalized 'war on terror', an armed conflict against every terrorist group, and to which IHL would apply without any geographical constraint. This broad view of the geographical applicability of IHL is problematic in at least two respects. First, it has been rejected by the majority of States and thus does not represent the dominant interpretation of humanitarian law.[74] Second, it has been coupled with the invocation of IHL rules to justify actions that normally constitute violations of other rules of international law (State sovereignty, the prohibition to use force in the territory of other States without their consent, human rights). IHL is used as a smokescreen, covering up the fact that other rules of international law are relevant to drone strikes and may be violated by them. The underlying message of the film is that IHL is the only relevant legal framework and, as long as a drone strike does not violate the relevant rules – and we have seen how complicated this legal evaluation may prove to be – the strike is lawful and therefore justified.

The way of depicting or using IHL – and the principle of distinction, in particular – and its violations in films and TV series plays a multifaceted role that ultimately finds a reflection in the perception the general public has not only of the suitability of this body of law to regulate armed conflicts but also of the legitimacy of certain conflicts in particular, and the dehumanizing phenomenon of war, in general.

---

73 See also: Marko Milanovic, 'Eye in the Sky', *EJILTalk!* (9 May 2016), www.ejiltalk.org/eye-in-the-sky/, accessed 1 December 2019; Deane-Peter Baker, 'Eye in the Sky and the Moral Dilemmas of Modern Warfare', *The Conversation* (31 March 2016), http://theconversation.com/eye-in-the-sky-and-the-moral-dilemmas-of-modern-warfare-56989, accessed 1 December 2019.

74 See ICRC, *International Humanitarian Law and the Challenges of Contemporary Armed Conflicts*, Document prepared for the 32nd International Conference of the Red Cross and Red Crescent (October 2015) 15.

Concluding remarks

Whether explicit or not, critical or looking to legitimize a given operation or conflict, references to IHL and the portrayal of its violations penetrate – even indirectly – the common understanding and reading of the current situations of war. Directors and producers tend, of course, to minimize the role their films might play in legitimizing State actions. For example, Kathryn Bigelow rejects the criticism voiced against *The Hurt Locker* (2009) and *Zero Dark Thirty* (2012), seen as apologetic and glorifying the US armed forces' actions, by asserting that 'depiction is not endorsement'.[75] Clint Eastwood made similar statements with respect to *American Sniper*.[76] It is a fact that war movies have turned to a more realistic representation of warfare since the end of the 1970s,[77] with movies on the war in Vietnam. Thus, many productions are inspired by actual events and recount incidents that really took place. They pretend to expose the true, raw nature of conflict, in all its horror and atrocity, without considering it necessary to offer a justification – or to criticize – such actions. However, even if we accept that the director's intention is not to justify violations committed in wartime, presenting such violations as unavoidable is not neutral; far from it. In his famous book *From Apology to Utopia*, Martti Koskenniemi highlights the dilemma between apology, i.e. reducing legal rules to the mere reflexion of actual conduct on the ground, and utopia, i.e. defining the ideal legal rules that are bound to remain inapplicable on the ground. Cinematographic productions depict the disregard for the principle of distinction as an objectively – read, independent of any value judgement – unavoidable result in situations of conflict. They thus distance themselves from utopia, and appear to tend more towards apology. In that sense, they do more than describe or depict; they indirectly justify the principle's weakening and/or demise.

---

75 Kathryn Bigelow, 'Kathryn Bigelow Addresses "Zero Dark Thirty" Torture Criticism', *Los Angeles Times* (15 January 2013), http://articles.latimes.com/2013/jan/15/entertainment/la-et-mn-0116-bigelow-zero-dark-thirty-20130116, accessed 1 December 2019; Ben Child, 'Kathryn Bigelow and Mark Boal Respond to Zero Dark Thirty Torture Row', *Guardian* (8 January 2013), www.theguardian.com/film/2013/jan/08/bigelow-zero-dark-thirty-torture?guni=Article:in%20body%20link, accessed 1 December 2019.
76 When asked about *American Sniper*'s glorifying war and snipers, Clint Eastwood replied that, to him, his film was anti-war because it shows the difficulties the soldiers deployed on the ground and their families go through; Stephen Galloway, 'Clint Eastwood Describes His Near-Death Experience, Says 'American Sniper' is Anti-War (Exclusive)', *The Hollywood Reporter* (16 March 2015), www.hollywoodreporter.com/news/clint-eastwood-describes-his-death-781618, accessed 1 December 2019.
77 Pierre-Emmanuel Barral, 'Le guerre du Vietnam au cinema' in Philippe d'Hugues and Hervé Coutau-Bégarie (eds), *Le cinéma et la guerre* (Paris: Economica, 2006) 157. See in this respect Tessier, *Le Vietnam*, 160–5.

Along the same lines, showing the atrocities committed by armed forces may result in their trivialization, influencing both the public and the soldiers themselves. Progressively, 'by its dynamic and visual qualities, and due to all the cinematographic past rooted in the soldiers' memory, war may [...] appear itself as a movie not only to the public [...] but also to the soldiers participating in it'.[78] Soldiers could thus start viewing the horrors of war in a detached way, which may lead to putting aside their notions of humanity and to succumb to the primary instinct of vengeance or, simply, survival. The vision of war conveyed in movies may lead to a feeling of 'being in a movie'. Accordingly, soldiers may find it difficult to accept that the horrors of war to which they are both parties and viewers are real. The end result could be a massive resort to firepower.[79] As for the public, movies shape, to a certain extent, the common perception of what is acceptable and prohibited in situations of armed conflict. Trivializing humanitarian law violations engenders the risk that, in the end, such actions be perceived as acceptable behaviour in time of war. Such an evolution may influence not only the interpretation of rules of humanitarian law but also the content of some rules. The famous 'Martens clause' comes to mind in this respect. The clause sets out that, in situations not regulated by humanitarian law conventions, combatants and civilians 'remain under the protection and empire of the principles of international law, as they result from the usages established between civilised nations, from the laws of humanity and *the requirements of public conscience*'.[80] Movies can certainly influence and shape the public conscience.[81] Their potential impact on IHL should thus be kept in mind.

---

78 Muraire, *Hollywood – Vietnam*, 64: 'par sa dynamique et ses qualités visuelles, et en raison de tout le passé cinématographique ancré dans la mémoire des soldats, la guerre peut [...] paraître elle-même comme un film non seulement au public [...] mais aux soldats qui y participant'.
79 Valantin, *Hollywood*, 126–7.
80 See Convention (II) with Respect to the Laws and Customs of War on Land, Annex: Regulations concerning the Laws and Customs of War on Land, preamble, The Hague, 29 July 1899 (emphasis added), https://ihl-databases.icrc.org/applic/ihl/dih.nsf/Article.xsp?action=openDocument&documentId=AF4868EA2C79E A8EC12563BD002B95CF, accessed 1 December 2019. The clause was inserted in many subsequent humanitarian law conventions, namely, and most importantly, the 1949 Geneva Conventions, the 1977 Additional Protocols, the 1980 Convention on Prohibitions and Restrictions on the Use of Certain Conventional Weapons which may be deemed to be excessively injurious to of to have indiscriminate effects, and the 2008 Convention on cluster munitions. On the Martens clause, see, amongst many, Antonio Cassese, 'The Martens Clause: Half a Loaf or Simply a Pie in the Sky?' (2000) 11 *EJIL* 187; Michael Salter, 'Reinterpreting Competing Interpretations of the Scope and Potential of the Martens Clause' (2012) 17 *JCSL* 403.
81 See Achilles Scordas, 'Hegemonic Custom?' in Michael Byers and Georg Nolte (eds), *United States Hegemony and the Foundations of International Law* (Cambridge: Cambridge University Press, 2003) 317–47.

8

Science fiction cinema and the nature of international law

Nicolas Kang-Riou

One of the main functions of legal academia is to examine the operation of legal institutions and existing norms. As many movies represent legal professionals and rules in action, in particular criminal trials, this is actually what most of the juridical law and cinema scholarships does.[1] What many legal scholars attempt when they study cinema and popular culture is to continue doing what they are the most adept at: analyse legal actors and legal rules, albeit focusing on representations rather than on the rules and actors themselves. The idea resting upon the 'film's ability to provide an apparently credible account of the operation and personnel of law'.[2]

Science fiction cinema is quite different in this respect. Science fiction is based on worlds, though still following (most of) the natural rules of our universe, which are dramatically altered compared to what we know. As Marco Benatar describes, 'science fiction is replete with scenarios set in the future extrapolating from contemporary knowledge and experience'.[3] He usefully adds 'not only in the realms of science and technology but also in respect of societal structures'.[4] Thus, it is difficult to say that science fiction cinema can produce a 'credible account' of known international law due to the radically transformed nature of the 'international' society.

Then is writing as legal scholars on international law in science fiction cinema an impossibility? Did the editors of this book fail to notice that science fiction movies do not deal with any of our current world international legal institutions or rules? Or are we in an alternate universe where publishers give free rein to authors to write without following the genre[5] which they

---

1 See P. Bergman and M. Asimow, *Reel Justice: The Courtroom Goes to the Movies* (Kansas City: Andrews McMeel Publishing, 2006).
2 Peter Robson, 'Law and Film Studies: Autonomy and Theory' in Michael Freeman (ed.), *Law and Popular Culture* (Oxford and New York: Oxford University Press, 2005) 23.
3 Benatar in this volume, p. 20.
4 Benatar in this volume, p. 20.
5 See on the distinction between fantasy and science fiction in the publishing industry: Orson Scott Card, *How to Write Science Fiction and Fantasy* (New York: F+W Media, 1990) 45.

have been assigned to? Now I am very glad that the editors, Olivier Corten, François Dubuisson and Martyna Fałkowska-Clarys, as well as Vincent Chapaux and Marco Benatar who wrote two very stimulating chapters from the perspective of legal theory (Chapter 2) and interspecies relations (Chapter 3), have not been afraid of this and decided that there was actually scope to write something meaningful, as legal scholars, about international law in science fiction cinema.

So, what is that something? Agreeing with Corten and Dubuisson (Chapter 1), it is not the role of the legal doctrine to discuss how the various film professionals have used their technical skills, though there is much to be admired[6] or critiqued, as that would demand an expertise not part of the legal domain. What can be done, according to the editors, is trying to come up with perspectives from legal philosophy (see Chapter 1), in particular in terms of ideology. Cinema, as a form of popular culture *par excellence*, is a great indicator of the ideology and how people make up the 'hodge-podge of notions about rights and duties'[7] that they 'carry round in their head'.[8] In science fiction cinema, several elements completely transform the common analysis of international law: there are very few texts to be analysed,[9] the underlying legal doctrines do not refer to known international law and the legal actors, in particular the figure of the lawyer, have substantially changed.[10]

Nevertheless, the sci-fi imaginary of cinematic universes like *Star Trek* or *Star Wars* enable several useful analysis from the perspective of international law. Indeed, science fiction is not only about imagining a radically different world but 'science fiction is amongst other things a mode of theorizing that seeks to disclose often-tacit assumptions about the manner and dynamics of the contemporary social world'.[11] Applied to international law, sci-fi cinema

---

6 For exceptions see, Jessica Silbey, 'Patterns of Courtroom Justice' (2001) 28 *Journal of Law and Society* 97; Michael Böhnke, 'Myth and Law in the Films of John Ford' (2001) 28 *Journal of Law and Society* 47.
7 Lawrence M. Friedman, 'Law, Lawyers, and Popular Culture' (1989) 98 *The Yale Law Journal* 1579, 1605.
8 Robson, 'Law and Film Studies', 23.
9 For an exception see the world of Star Trek: F. Defferrard, *Le Droit Selon Star Trek* (Paris: Mare & Martin, 2015); R.H. Chaires and B.S. Chilton, *Star Trek Visions of Law and Justice* (Dallas: Adios Press, 2003).
10 See, for instance, how the key legal actor is the ship captain in *Star Trek* rather than a professional lawyer, Paul Joseph and Sharon Carton, 'The Law of the Federation: Images of Law, Lawyers, and the Legal System in Star Trek, the Next Generation' (1992–93) 24 *University of Toledo Law Review* 43.
11 N.J. Kiersey and I.B. Neumann, Battlestar Galactica *and International Relations* (London and New York: Routledge, 2013) 10.

narratives are 'touching upon the fundamental or more technical aspects of international law'.[12] Whereas for Chapaux[13] movies interestingly embrace the same anthropocentred speciesism of international law, meaning that they generally place the development of humanity at the centre and its value above other species. In both instances, despite fundamental differences, one can still recognize legal concepts typically associated with what Chapaux calls 'Earth international law'. In doing so, we need to question whether science fiction cinema only offers a recognition of patterns and themes similar to 'Earth international law'. Sci-fi cinema does more than this. It enables not only a recognition but also a questioning of some of the fundamental characteristics and assumptions of international law.

If we want to apply international law doctrines, institutions or theories to science fiction universes, key features of international law need to be adapted, as sci-fi worlds radically transform our known societal landscape. Modern international law requires the existence of the tenets of equal sovereignty of States and of humanity as the final beneficiaries. In most of the movies used as illustrations by Benatar and Chapaux, States are no longer major social structures, nor human beings the sole members of the groups, nor the only end beneficiaries of the law. Despite this, for Benatar, the core elements of international law are sufficiently flexible to be recognizable in such situations. Indeed, for him, the inherent structural tensions of international law between idealism and realism, apology and utopia or unity and plurality can be apprehended in these new environments. Chapaux, for his part, illustrates how the liberal view of the human groups' inter-relations found in international law is usually extended to extra-terrestrial sentient species. Despite the lack of States, or humanity not being the sole dominant protected species, both authors recognize that (a form of) international law is still used in science fiction cinema. In other words, the speculative freedom afforded to sci-fi cinema allow us to visualize, in 'concrete' instances, how much the environment can change for structures associated with international law to still be recognizable, and applied as a meaningful explanation of the underlying ideology carried by this popular art form.

This leads us to the key question this chapter addresses: what does the encounter between science fiction cinema and international law reveal about the nature of international law as accepted by the international legal community?

Two aspects come to the fore. The first is the flexibility of the potential scope of application of international law even through the alteration of key

---

12 Benatar in this volume, pp. 20–39, esp. p. 22.
13 Chapaux in this volume, pp. 40–57.

assumptions. The second is that despite the plasticity of the international legal language, in some situations international law is no longer a useful frame of reference. This chapter concludes by understanding that both its flexibility and disappearance reveal a non-conventional result: the nature of international law is embedded not in States, not even in humanity, but in the equality of rights of groups displaying a sufficient number of anthropomorphic features, including the capacity to communicate with humans.

The flexibility of the nature of international law revealed by science fiction

Star Trek is a useful starting point in the analysis of how international law can underscore a rich science fiction cinematic world. Indeed, though science fiction has seldom been analysed by lawyers, quite a few have concentrated on *Star Trek*,[14] because of extensive materials, popular success as well as an underlying liberal ethos.[15] There seems to be very little opposition to imagine *Star Trek* from the point of view of international law. For instance, Wingfield sees it as a perfect tool for teaching international law.[16] In the *Star Trek* universe as depicted in the original television series, the films or the most recent series, the human domain is controlled by the United Federation of Planets (the Federation) which looks much more like a federal State than a loose confederation. Several elements indicate this: the existence of Starfleet, the unified military arm of the Federation, the enactment of a specific Federation criminal code and criminal courts, the possibility of imposing martial law, etc. Thus internally, there are no sovereign planets ('States'), despite the fact that they are self-governing. Externally, the Federation has rules to deal with non-federated planets governed by other alien races. Then we could say that both the internal and external rules of the Federation seem like an advanced vision of international law, the (internal) realization of the Kantian dream of

---

14 Chaires and Chilton, *Star Trek Visions*; Defferrard, *Le Droit Selon Star Trek*; Richard Peltz-Steele, 'On a Wagon Train to Afghanistan: Limitations on Star Trek's Prime Directive' (2003) 25 *University of Arkansas at Little Rock Law Review* 635; Michael P. Scharf and Lawrence D. Roberts, 'The Interstellar Relations of the Federation: International Law and Star Trek – The Next Generation' (1994) 25 *University of Toledo Law Review* 577.
15 Barry Buzan, 'America in Space: The International Relations of Star Trek and Battlestar Galactica' (2010) 39 *Millennium* 175, 176.
16 Thomas C. Wingfield, 'Lillich on Interstellar Law: U.S. Naval Regulations, Star Trek, and the Use of Force in Space' (2001) 46 *South Dakota Law Review* 95.

perpetual peace through law (Benatar), or a peaceful vision of (external) coexistence (Chapaux). Neither fulfil some of the most basic requirements of international law, Federation rules apply internally to non-State entities, and externally the rules benefit non-humans which goes against anthropocentric speciesism. There are rules of engagement, diplomacy etc. dealing with substantive issues usually linked with international law, but here it is about the Federation in relation to non-human empires (Klingon, Romulan, etc.). Both have been the basis for analysis of the law, the internal dimension from an international human rights law perspective, the external one from a more traditional view of international law centred on international or inter-spatial relations.[17]

The other cinematic references to international law chosen by Benatar and Chapaux include a series of works where key features of traditional international law are missing both in terms of the existence of States, and in terms of human beings being the sole ultimate beneficiary of the law. Regarding the States, they can be replaced for instance by: a Federation of planets (*Star Trek*), individual planets (*Star Wars*), alien civilizations or empires (*Babylon V*[18]).[19] If the international law concepts can be usefully applied, then this process underlines how States are not that crucial for our understanding of the mechanisms of international law. What really matters is the existence of autonomous social groups disposing of a certain amount of sovereignty. Now the minimum content of that sovereignty is as difficult to assess as what is currently debated in the context of the EU integration[20] or the transition from a confederation of States to a federal State. These social groups must nevertheless be able to exercise some of the powers normally attributed to States, in particular regarding self-determination of the people. But other key elements of the definition of the State, such as territory (space-wandering species can be easily imagined[21]) or even population[22] can be overlooked. In these contexts, substantive branches of international law are applicable. One such example could be the breach of the law of wars through the experimentation of bio-agents on a human

---

17 Scharf and Roberts, 'The Interstellar Relations of the Federation'.
18 Joe Michael Straczynski, USA, 1993–98, five seasons.
19 Roy Balleste, 'The Earth Alliance Constitution: International Human Rights Law and Babylon 5' (2008) 10 *Florida Coastal Law Review* 33.
20 R Schütze, *European Constitutional Law* (Cambridge: Cambridge University Press, 2015) 46–73.
21 This is actually what happens to humanity in *Battlestar Galactica*, as humanity is pursued by the Cylons. See Buzan, 'America in Space'.
22 See the special existence of Dax, a character and a species actually made of a host and a symbiote, see Chaires and Chilton, *Star Trek Visions*.

colony, which turned out to be deadly bio-weapons as in *Serenity*,[23] the movie outshoot of the sadly short-lived *Firefly*[24] TV show.

If States are not needed for the international legal analysis to be usefully applied to sci-fi cinematic worlds, neither are humans the necessary sole beneficiaries of the rights. From a teleological view of international law, humans are given a privileged status above other species (Chapaux). They are the ones that the States ultimately should be protecting. It is clearly embedded in international human rights law or international humanitarian law. However, when similar doctrines are used in science fiction cinema, they are often extended to non-human groups. The *Star Trek* Federation of Planets is premised upon the equality between alien and human races. The governing body depicted in *Star Wars* episodes I to III[25] is constructed on the same principle. In the pre-empire setting of *Star Wars: The Phantom Menace*, each member of the Senate of planets is independent and recognized equal without any connection to the species involved.

Interestingly, even when the situation is reversed, when there are discriminations in place, the ethos of most movies is to get the audience to pine for equality. This is particularly true in relations to intelligent robots where movie directors try to get us to empathize with them. In *I, Robot*,[26] AIs are both villains and heroes. Sonny the robot, who is no longer bound by Asimov's three laws of robotics,[27] ends up being the redeemer of humanity. In *Battlestar Galactica*,[28] the Cylons, sentient AIs originally created by humanity, have developed in a way to mimic humans. Though they have tried to destroy humanity twice, they also display deeply human characteristics of love, hope or passion. As they have the capacity to take human form, the interactions between humans and Cylons, when humans are not aware of their nature, cannot be distinguished from traditional human relations. In *Artificial Intelligence: A.I.*,[29] the story is centred around David, the first robot with feelings, who is trying to get full acknowledgement and love from his adoptive 'mother'. Again, here the plot suggests the close resemblance of the desires of AIs and humans. In these stories, robots do

---

23 Joss Whedon, USA, 2005.
24 Joss Whedon, Fox, USA, 2002, 14 episodes.
25 *Episode I: The Phantom Menace* (George Lucas, USA, 1999); *Episode II: Attack of the Clones* (George Lucas, USA, 2002); *Episode III: Revenge of the Sith* (George Lucas, USA, 2005).
26 Alex Proyas, USA, 2004.
27 For an ethical analysis, see R. Clarke, 'Asimov's Laws of Robotics: Implications for Information Technology-Part I' (1993) 26 *Computer* 53.
28 Ronald D. Moore and Glen A. Larson, USA, 2004–9. See Kiersey and Neumann, *Battlestar Galactica*.
29 Steven Spielberg, USA, 2001.

not have equal rights, but they push us to reflect towards a horizon where it would happen. It is also the case for imagined mutated human species. In the *X-Men* franchise,[30] the general population has a deep distrust towards powerful and dangerous human mutants. Still, they are globally depicted as neither good nor evil but as human with flaws and qualities; mutants are both heroes and villains. Again, the general metaphor is liberal, the necessity to accept differences in a modern society (Chapaux).

From an interspecies relation prism, most movies display a liberal worldview where rights such as auto determination or basic fundamental rights should be also extended to alien species. For instance, *Babylon V* or *Star Trek: Deep Space Nine*[31] are created on such premises. Both are TV series in which the main characters are based in a space station which is partly designed to support species interaction on an equalitarian basis. Taking the lives of any of them is prohibited; and their rights are protected.[32] The list of movies in which it is the case is growing with the popularity of the sci-fi genre. In the recent blockbuster franchise *Guardian of the Galaxy*,[33] the main team is composed of various species where none is given more rights or discriminated on that basis. *Star Wars Episodes VII to IX*[34] have continued in this vein, with the inclusion of human traits in robots. In the original *Star Wars* trilogy,[35] C-3P0 and R2-D2 were given a real prominence in the story line. They possess individual identity traits and quirks not normally associated with androids. R2-D2 is stubborn and inventive; C-3P0 is clumsy and extremely talkative. BB-9, one of the main characters of the recent *Star Wars: The Last Jedi*, is faithful and self-sacrificial. In essence, they are quasi-human.

30 *X-Men* (2000); *X-Men 2* (Bryan Singer, USA, 2003); *X-Men: The Last Stand* (Brett Ratner, USA, 2006); *X-Men Origins: Wolverine* (Gavin Hood, USA, 2009); *X-Men: First Class* (Matthew Vaughn, USA, 2011), *The Wolverine* (James Mangold, USA, 2013); *X-Men: Days of Future Past* (Bryan Singer, USA, 2014); *X-Men: Apocalypse* (Bryan Singer, USA, 2016); *Deadpool* (Tim Miller, USA, 2016); *Logan* (James Mangold, USA, 2017); *Deadpool 2* (David Leitch, USA, 2018); *X-Men: Dark Phoenix* (Simon Kinberg, USA, 2019).
31 Rick Berman and Michael Piller, USA, 1993–9, seven seasons.
32 Regarding *Babylon V* see Balleste, 'The Earth Alliance Constitution'.
33 *Guardian of the Galaxy Vol. 1*, James Gunn, USA, 2014; *Guardian of the Galaxy Vol. 2*, James Gunn, USA, 2017.
34 *Episode VII: The Force Awakens* (J.J. Abrams, USA, 2015); *Episode VIII: The Last Jedi* (Rian Johnson, USA, 2017); *Episode IX: The Rise of Skywalker* (J.J. Abrams, USA, 2019).
35 *Episode IV: A New Hope* (George Lucas, USA, 1977); *Episode V: The Empire Strikes Back* (Irvin Kershner, USA, 1980); *Episode VI: Return of the Jedi* (Richard Marquand, USA, 1983).

All these movies share what Chapaux accurately describes as a bio-centred view, whereby each species has both 'the right to exist and the obligation not to destroy the other species' and in so doing replicate at a wider scale the liberal ethos of international law, part of the Kantian ideal of peace through law. Nevertheless, in the endless imaginary of science fiction authors, there are situations where the international law concepts no longer seem applicable. As a negative, they show the limits of the plasticity of international law.

The limits of the liberal ethos and the inoperability of international law

In his chapter, Benatar concludes alongside Koskenniemi[36] that international law is intrinsically ambivalent. International law needs to find balance in seeking conflicting aims of order and autonomy, protection and freedom, peace and self-protection, equality and human- (or bio-)centred view. But what happens when the balance tilts too far in one direction? When the society depicted is all about order or self-protection? When such scenarios are envisaged in science fiction cinema, international law ceases to be an operative explanatory framework. Two extreme situations can be used to illustrate this: the disappearance of the international (inter-planet, intergalactic, etc.) and self-preservation as the sole motive for action. But beyond this, what international law ultimately rests upon is the capacity for actors to communicate with one another. A liberal world cannot function without communications which can be understood by humans. These limits remind us of some of the key assumptions on which international law is founded.

Inoperability through the end of the international

If it is possible to see within the 'world government trope' (Benatar), the final extension of the constitutionalist mindset and thus still a project stemming from international law legal theory, this is no longer the case for other types of organisation. When projecting at the global level the structures of dictatorship or empire, the international law analogy no longer functions. In *Nineteen Eighty-Four*,[37] the dystopian movie based on the famous eponymous book, the relationships between the various group members are

---

36 Martti Koskenniemi, *From Apology to Utopia: The Structure of International Legal Argument* (Cambridge: Cambridge University Press, 2006).
37 Michael Radford, UK, 1984.

solely sustained by means of coercion and constant monitoring. Only the vertical link of domination remains. Likewise, in *Star Wars*, when most of the galaxy is controlled by the (evil) Empire, there is not much international law has to say. Orders from the Emperor are non-negotiable; life is cheap for rebels and subordinates alike. For instance, one of the major plot lines of *Star Wars: The Empire Strike Back* sees the Empire seeking to establish full control by developing a weapon, the 'Death Star', that can instantly annihilate planets. No rules, only power, can stop its use. Again, the relations between the various groups, the Empire or the rebellion, or even the neutral parties, cannot be seen to rely on any form of recognizable international law. The Empire seeks the total destruction of the Rebels. Neutrals can only stay neutral up to the point that they do not hinder any of the aims of the Empire; otherwise they must submit as the famous betrayal of Lando Caldrissian, the administrator of a seemingly independent and neutral cloud station, reveals (*Star Wars: The Empire Strikes Back*). In both instances, there is no longer an international to speak of, only a vertical relationship of control backed by military might. It is all about power and self-interest. From the perspective of relations between States, this has led Morgenthau, the international relations realist scholar, to deny the relevance of international law.[38] Many other science-fiction dystopian movies have described societies of this type: economic oligarchies for *Robocop*[39] or *Blade Runner*,[40] fake equality in *Total Recall* (2012),[41] caste type control in *Gattaca*,[42] etc. These examples underline that the international law metaphor cannot extend to non-liberal forms of governance. Another limit of the plasticity of international law resides in the importance of biocentrism.

Inoperability through the end of biocentrism

There are other situations where the international law analogy no longer seems to apply. This is especially the case with movies depicting violent encounters with alien species, where 'we're fighting for our right to live' (Chapaux). When survival is at stake then the internal rules (common rules regulating various groups whether human or human with non-humans) and

---

38 H.J. Morgenthau, *Politics Among Nations: The Struggle for Power and Peace* (New York: A. Knopf 1948).
39 Paul Verhoeven, USA, 1987.
40 Ridley Scott, USA, 1982.
41 Len Wiseman, USA, 2012.
42 Andrew Niccol, USA, 1997.

external rules (rules regulating the encounter with violent others) no longer follow any of the recognized patterns of international law.

On the internal front, survival necessities demand full allegiance of the various groups where refusal of common rules cannot be tolerated. For instance, in *Ender's Game*,[43] parents must give away their most talented children to be trained as warriors, even though they may be severely injured or even die during this training. Ender Wiggin, the hero of the movie, is such a child. He will learn to maim (and kill) children to keep his position in the Fleet school. Human rights are rescinded for the greater good.

On the external front, the survival of humanity ends any rights for the opposing force, up to xenocide.[44] In *Independence Day*,[45] the initial doubts of human leaders (typically the US president) regarding the use of nuclear weapons are wiped, as we (conveniently) learn that aliens are only there to fully exhaust the Earth's resources. They fail to care about any local life forms. Moreover, they have done so previously against many other civilizations. Thus, the valiant and inventive utter annihilation of the aliens can only be understood as good overcoming evil. Non-liberal action stops from enabling a protection stemming from (liberal) international law. To a similar extent, in *War of the Worlds*,[46] the invaders also do not look at having interactions with humans, but they are only defeated through the unforeseen help of local viruses rather than through human resilience and cleverness. Finally, in *Ender's Game*, after the first attack by the Formic, the alien civilization, which had cost millions of lives, there is no longer room for negotiation. Rules of war are no longer applicable, nor is humanitarian law. There is no right or wrong in the use of weapons of mass destruction including the annihilation of the aliens' home planet. Ender Wiggin is tricked into using a weapon of mass destruction known as the 'Little Doctor', as he under the impression that the war he and his team are waging is only a simulation. But the moment in which the xenocide is completed is a time of celebration, for victory has come. This depiction matches the concept of the 'public enemy' developed by Carl Schmitt,[47] one of the most prominent Nazi legal scholars. In his non-liberal view, there is no peace possible with an enemy, 'war follows from enmity'.[48]

---

43 Gavin Hood, USA, 2013.
44 Term coined by Orson Scott Card, the author of *Ender's Game*, and adapted from genocide to describe the extermination of an alien race
45 Roland Emmerich, USA, 1996.
46 *The War of the Worlds* (Byron Haskin, USA, 1953); *War of the Worlds* (Steven Spielberg, USA, 2005).
47 C. Schmitt, *The Concept of the Political* (G Schwab tr, Chicago: University of Chicago Press, 2008).
48 Schmitt, *The Concept of the Political*, 28.

In the two dimensions of the 'end of the international' either through the production of a strong vertical hierarchical link backed by the law, or in a vision of encounter with aliens through the lens of the fight for survival, the major substantive principles of international law cannot apply. The flexibility of international law therefore finds its limits.

Inoperability through the impossibility of communication

To move from a world of international relations best represented by the realist view to the constructivist view, it is imperative to move from a zero-sum game to a positive-sum game.[49] However, as explained by game theory, communication is essential to make that jump.[50]

In *Independence Day*, communication was not really the issue as the aliens were working on a zero-sum game assumption: only one species can use the Earth; *Ender's Game* differs fundamentally. In the former, as we saw, aliens are intrinsically un-redeemable by completely refusing any sort of interaction with others. In the latter, the war leading to the extermination of the aliens is mostly stemming from miscommunication. The Formic queen has actually tried to bridge that gap by attempting to talk to Ender via a game he has been playing whilst training, hence the title, *Ender's Game*. The movie does not end with the destruction of the Formic home planet but with Ender being shown by the Formic queen where to find the very last Formic cocoon. This reveals how the nature of communication of relation can only be seen from humanity's perspective. Aliens cannot dictate the terms through which communication will happen. If they are too different, because of their telepathic abilities or other radically different forms of communication, then it does not matter; xenocide is still legitimate.

A similar type of questioning has been proposed in *Arrival*.[51] The movie has been relatively successful at the box office and has impressed the critics with its thoughtful imagining of a first encounter with an alien species. As in *Independence Day*, the alien vessels 'land' in several parts of the world. But the similarities stop there. Indeed, they do not behave aggressively, on the contrary they open the door to interactions at every one of their twelve landing sites. This is where the main hero, a US professor of linguistics, intervenes as she tries to understand how to communicate with a species

---

49 Anne-Marie Slaughter, 'International Law in a World of Liberal States' (1995) 6 *European Journal of International Law* 503, 507.
50 See, for instance, R.M. Dawes, 'Social Dilemmas' (1980) 31 *Annual Review of Psychology* 169, 185.
51 Denis Villeneuve, USA, 2016.

with a radically different language structure. Slowly she gathers vocabulary, enough to reach the point of asking the aliens what their purpose is. War against them is nearly started because their answer can be interpreted as either 'use weapon' or 'offer weapon'. China opts for 'use weapon' and gets ready for war, whereas the linguist believes in 'offer weapon' as a tool to help humanity. This reminds us of the key dilemma seen as a starting point of modern international law: the encounter between the Spanish conquistadors and the local civilizations. The communicative nature of the encounters finally pushed Charles V to heed the advice of Las Casas on the inclusion of the 'Indians' within humanity. This choice of communication with foreign groups led to some of the earliest formulations of international legal principles by the Spanish scholars Vitoria and Las Casas.[52]

Conclusion: the nature of international law through the lens of science fiction cinema

A brief analysis of science fiction cinema has helped us rediscover both the flexibility of international legal concepts as well as its limits. Some conclusions can be taken from this. The first is the most obvious. Science fiction cinema can be a great didactic tool which could be used in class to show the operation of some key aspects of international law. It has been noted that current students of international law are more likely to be familiar with events depicted in recent science fiction cinema than they are to know about the history of the twentieth century or even the twenty-first century. Worlds such as *Star Trek* are full of legal material which reasonably mimic international legal concepts to be useful in that regard. It is sufficient reason for international legal academics to be interested in science fiction cinema. However, it would be quite thin from a legal scholarship perspective. Stimulatingly, sci-fi cinema offers a much more vivid landscape than the traditional hypotheticals used by the doctrine as it 'presents an inconceivable situation, or it takes a modern-day problem and stretches it to allegorical dimensions, free of the limitations of nonliterary reality' (Benatar). This is partly what Benatar and Chapaux have tried to do.

This chapter tried to 'boldly go'[53] where the doctrine has not gone before, by discussing key features of international law through the lens of science

---

52 Antony Anghie, 'Francisco De Vitoria and the Colonial Origins of International Law' (1996) 5 *Social & Legal Studies* 321; Martti Koskenniemi, 'Empire and International Law: The Real Spanish Contribution' (2011) 61 *University of Toronto Law Journal* 1.

53 The original *Star Trek* television series famously started with a voiceover stating that the aim of the *USS Enterprise* was to 'boldly go where no one has gone before'.

fiction cinema. It proposes that some core aspects of current international law are not actually essential for the international law language to function and continue to resemble the 'Earth international law' that we know. Despite the State-centrism of many features of international law, the State concept is not central to the survival of international law whereas sovereign equality still matters. If a form of equality amongst the various social groups cannot be ascertained then the main features of international law inspired by a liberal view are no longer operational.

Likewise, human speciesism matters less than the preservation of what science fiction authors imagine what is to be human, the liberal ethos of humanity. It is made easier through anthropomorphism, by aliens or AIs being given human traits. But what is necessary is that from the point of view of humans, for a group to be extended a status of subject of 'interstellar' law, the other group needs to be able to communicate their acceptance of the international liberal order which demands the preservation of human lives as well as the capacity for humans to stay independent.

In that sense, science fiction serves as a useful reminder of the foundations of international law. Indeed, most cinematic science fiction worlds have embraced a worldview similar to the one upon which international law is based, a liberal world of equal communities created to benefit the individuals composing these communities. And when they depict a non-liberal world, such as some experienced by humanity, then international law no longer functions.

The imagination of new worlds represented in science fiction cinema is a fertile ground for reflecting on the nature of international law and of international legal concepts. By stretching the conditions of operation, assumptions of international law can be further tested. International law argumentative structure makes it quite flexible, maybe more flexible than first appears, but it nevertheless demands fidelity to some features of the liberal ethos to continue operating at a conceptual level. There is scope to think much further about international law with science-fiction cinema.

9

War on film: gender trouble in Siddiq Barmak's *Osama*

Gabrielle Simm

Film is a widely accessible medium for communicating ideas about international law.[1] Popular culture, including film, influences law students, politicians charged with the responsibility of committing troops to war, soldiers, anti-war protesters and the general public on questions such as the legality of the use of force. Most writing at the intersection of international law and film is implicitly aimed at an audience of international lawyers. This may be because the field of film studies, emerging out of sociology, semiotics, psychoanalysis, literary and cultural studies, addresses concerns other than those that animate international lawyers. As consumers of popular culture, international lawyers are not immune from the influence of film in shaping our imagination of what international law is or should be.[2]

The chapters by Olivier Corten and François Dubuisson provide a methodology and examples for analysing how international law on the use of force is represented in film.[3] This law and its application to the Israeli–Palestinian conflict are much debated amongst international lawyers. However, the novel contribution of Corten and Dubuisson is their attention to the representation of relevant aspects of international law in film and

---

1 Cinema and film are interpreted broadly to include television programmes and teleseries.
2 See, for example, Wouter G. Werner, 'Justice on Screen: A Study of Four Documentary Films on the International Criminal Court' (2016) 29 *Leiden Journal of International Law* 1043; Immi Tallgren, 'Come and See? The Power of Images and International Criminal Justice' (2017) 17 *International Criminal Law Review* 259; Kirsten Ainley, Stephen Humphreys and Immi Tallgren, 'Introduction: International Criminal Justice on/and Film' (2018) 6 *London Review of International Law* 3: special issue and the references cited therein.
3 Olivier Corten, 'Mais où est donc passée la Charte des Nations Unies? Représentations et sous-représentations des règles sur l'usage de la force dans les films d'action' and François Dubuisson, 'Le conflict israélo-palestinien: une saga cinématographique' in Olivier Corten and François Dubuisson (eds), *Du Droit International au Cinéma* (Paris: Pedone, 2015).

television. A key contribution is introducing the rich variety of French language scholarship on international law and film to a new audience. While offering new readings of the films and tele-series discussed, the chapters go much further. The breadth and depth of the material surveyed instils confidence in the representativeness of the claims made about international law in film. The chapters share a common understanding about how to categorize approaches to the relation between international law and film that will prove useful to other scholars to adopt, test against particular films, genres or themes, and potentially react against or modify in the context of the existing scholarship on international law and film with a focus on the use of force.

Informed by these chapters, my aim here is to explore how films can bolster or undermine claims about the legality of the use of force. I begin by drawing out three themes of the contributions of Corten and Dubuisson that I consider important to discussions of international law and films. They are: genre, interpretation and interdisciplinarity. Next I offer some suggestions for further research in this field; chiefly, panning out to take in world cinema; investigating the material conditions in which films are produced as relevant context in their interpretation; and using Third World Approaches to International Law (TWAIL) and feminist approaches to analyse the representation of international law in film. Finally, I explore the status of women as providing a justification for the US military intervention in Afghanistan in 2001 through a close reading of the film *Osama*.

Genre, interpretation and interdisciplinarity

Genre is key to film studies because viewers have a set of expectations about a genre on which filmmakers rely. Part of the pleasure of watching a film is seeing those expectations fulfilled. By contrast, some viewers may rate a film more favourably if it subverts expectations of the genre or successfully crosses or combines genres to create hybrid genres (e.g. docu-fiction). The war film is an established genre; however, documentary films, propaganda films, and their counterpart, anti-war protest films, are other genres in which the legality of war comes into focus on film. Further, war can form the pretext for or backdrop to spy movies or gangster movies[4] and Westerns replay wars of colonial conquest. However, Corten explicitly selects action movies

---

4 See Jacobo Ríos Rodríguez, 'Jack Bauer, 007 et OSS 117: quelles répresentations du droit international?' in Olivier Corten and François Dubuisson (eds), *Du Droit International au Cinéma* (Paris: Pedone, 2015) 187.

to examine the use of force where international law appears as an irritating bureaucratic hurdle to be overcome; the hero succeeds by ignoring the rules. This contrasts with war movies, where the fog of war blurs clear lines between right and wrong.[5] Dubuisson's discussion of the Israeli–Palestinian conflict covers a range of genres, including the checkpoint movie, thrillers, romance and comedies. By focusing on a wider range of genres than just war films or documentary films, international legal scholars can addresses film primarily as a form of entertainment that is seen by far larger audiences, whether in the cinema or on television, than those who frequent the lecture theatres where international law is taught and increasingly video-recorded as part of online teaching or university engagement with the general public.

In French, another meaning of genre is gender. In Western film studies, genres have long been recognized to be associated with particular genders. In her 1991 article, Linda Williams argues that low-brow films mostly ignored by academia, which she terms 'body films', make a spectacle of the (usually female) body caught in the grip of excess emotion, whether sexual arousal, fear or sadness.[6] Such body films are gendered in relation to their target audiences. So melodramas or 'weepies' have a target audience of women; pornography, of men, and horror films, adolescents whose sexual identity is still under development.[7] The gender of the protagonists in films and the viewers' ability to identify with the protagonist is to some extent structured by psychoanalytic concepts of active masculinity and passive femininity, but such concepts are not determinative. While action films and war films are assumed to target male audiences and romance films female audiences, teenage boys may identify with the female victim of horror films, for example. The association of genre with gender is important for later arguments in relation to the genre of the film *Osama*, in which a girl (cross-)dresses as a boy in an attempt to escape the gendered oppression of the Taliban in Afghanistan.

Interpretation of films is the second key issue discussed here. The idealist/critical dichotomy around which Corten and Dubuisson's contributions are organized offers a useful way of generalizing about the portrayal of international law in a large number of films. At the same time, it risks simplifying and closing down the range of potential readings of film. After all, films capable of diverse interpretations are often considered the richest and most rewarding. They can pass the test of multiple viewings, eliciting different responses from different viewers or different responses from the same viewer over time. Some of the films discussed may not be capable of sustaining multiple interpretations. For example, the pop culture genre of

---

[5] Ainley et al., 'Introduction'.
[6] Linda Williams, 'Film Bodies: Gender, Genre and Excess' (1991) 44 *Film Quarterly* 2.
[7] Williams, 'Film Bodies', 4.

action movies is rarely ambiguous about its heroes and villains. As Corten argues, Hollywood films that present the use of force as the only viable option thereby naturalize the automatic recourse to force, rather than seeing it as governed by international law as the last in a series of dispute resolution mechanisms and only available in certain defined circumstances. Corten's contribution here lies not just as an international lawyer but in exposing the ideology and identifying the politics of cultural texts. Dubuisson notes the portrayal by Israeli and Hollywood directors of the creation of the State of Israel as characterizing the dominant 'nationalist heroic' stream of cinema, which is, however, subject to challenge from a counter-current of critical Israeli cinema. Dubuisson further acknowledges the possibility of multiple interpretations of films that do not fit neatly into the idealist/critical dichotomy.

The film *Lemon Tree* (dir. Eran Riklis 2008) is emblematic of not two but three approaches to international law depicted in film. As Dubuisson explains, the film shows the legal battle between a Palestinian widow, Salma Zidane, and the Israeli Defence Minister who moves next door to her on the border between the West Bank and Israel. The Israeli Intelligence Service deems Zidane's lemon grove to be a security threat that interferes with its protective surveillance of the minister. Zidane takes her fight to the Israeli Supreme Court, which makes the unprecedented decision to order only half the grove to be uprooted. According to Dubuisson, three potential interpretations are embodied here. The Court decision signifies that the Occupation is regulated by law and hence legitimate. For Zidane, who inherited the lemon trees from her father, the personal impact of the decision demonstrates the futility of resort to law. Finally, the Palestinian lawyer who takes the case for strategic reasons sees it as a symbolic first step towards greater rights for Palestinians.

An undercurrent that Dubuisson does not discuss is the relationship between the minister's wife, Mira, and Zidane. Mira sympathises with Zidane, asks her husband to overturn the decision to uproot the lemon trees and eventually leaves her husband. An empathy exists between the two women who never speak as they share no common language. The film personalizes the impact of the continuing Israeli Occupation; however, a gender analysis might also consider whether presenting two women as peacemakers falls into stereotyping women as naturally peaceful.[8] Such arguments have been made about the Women, Peace and Security Resolutions beginning in 2000 with Resolution 1325 passed by the UN Security Council.[9]

---

8 Hilary Charlesworth and Christine Chinkin, 'Are Women Peaceful? Reflections on the Role of Women in Peacebuilding' (2008) 16 *Feminist Legal Studies* 347.
9 UNSC Res 1325 (31 October 2000), UN Doc S/RES/1325.

Another potential interpretation is that seeing women as peaceful ignores the role of the minister's wife in supporting her husband who leads Israel's military repression of Palestinians. These interpretations do not go strictly to the issue of whether or not the use of force is lawful in this context. But while focusing on the gender dynamics of the film and its portrayal of the Israeli–Palestinian conflict, they implicate international law's attempts to harness gender legitimacy for the Security Council in passing the Women, Peace and Security resolutions.[10]

The third issue to be addressed here is the question of interdisciplinarity. Interdisciplinary work in international law is increasingly popular.[11] Funding agencies place increased value on interdisciplinary work, perhaps seeing it as better placed than single disciplines to solve complex problems.[12] Interdisciplinary work may offer a greater range of research methods, overcome barriers to communication through familiarity with specialized terminology and highlight the blind-spots of individual disciplines. In this context, what benefits does scholarship on international law and film in particular offer? International lawyers can be relied on for high level skills in textual analysis; less so for our visual literacy skills, which tend to be uneven depending on individual interests in art, photography and so on.[13]

---

10 Dianne Otto, 'The Security Council's Alliance of Gender Legitimacy: The Symbolic Capital of Resolution 1325' in Hilary Charlesworth and Jean-Marc Coicaud (eds), *Fault Lines of International Legitimacy* (Cambridge: Cambridge University Press, 2010) 239.

11 For example, Gerry Simpson, 'Duelling Agendas: International Law and International Relations (again)' (2004–5) 1 *Journal of International Law and International Relations* 61; Matthew Craven, Theorizing the Turn to History in International Law' in Anne Orford and Florian Hoffmann (eds), *The Oxford Handbook of the Theory of International Law* (Oxford: Oxford University Press, 2016) 21; Ekaterina Yahyaoui Krivenko, 'International Law, Literature and Interdisciplinarity' (2015) 9 *Law and Humanities* 103; Anne van Aaken, 'Behavioural International Law and Economics' (2014) 55 *Harvard International Law Journal* 421; see further August Reinsich, Mary E. Footer and Christina Binder (eds) *International Law and ... Select Proceedings of the European Society of International Law, vol. 5, 2014* (Oxford: Hart Publishing, 2016).

12 Michelle Burgis-Kasthala, 'Introduction: How Should We Study International Criminal Law? Reflections on the Potentialities and Pitfalls of Interdisciplinary Scholarship' (2016) 17 *International Criminal Law Review* 227, 230.

13 See e.g. Hilary Charlesworth, 'The Art of International Law' forthcoming Collected Courses of the Hague Academy of International Law; Daniel Litwin, 'Stained Glass Windows, the Great Hall of Justice of the Peace Palace' in Jessie Hohmann and Daniel Joyce (eds), *International Law's Objects* (Oxford: Oxford University Press, 2018) 463; Aoife Duffy, 'Bearing Witness to Atrocity Crimes: Photography and International Law' (2018) 40 *Human Rights Quarterly* 776.

Yet it is imperative for international lawyers to develop such skills, as visual communication through digital media grows in importance. These chapters promote not so much technical skills in film, but rather provide a model of how to analyse the stories films tell through visual language about international law.

Despite the promise of multiple benefits, interdisciplinary work faces challenges. First is the challenge of credibility. An initial observation is that filmmakers do not seem to regard expertise in international law as necessary or relevant to the credibility of their product. Judging by the lack of acknowledgement in the credits and the errors that go unnoticed, international lawyers are rarely consulted in filming scenes in which their expert knowledge could be relevant. This contrasts with the practice of seeking advice from medical experts on the veracity of scenes involving surgery, for instance, or from scientists on relevant aspects of film.[14] Second, can an expert in one discipline attain sufficient expertise in another to be recognized as competent by experts in the second discipline, or will she be regarded as an amateur? Film studies scholars and cinematographers can point to the inability of counsel and judges in international criminal trials to notice when film has been edited. Such cinematic illiteracy could have important implications where film is relied on as evidence, which seems to be the most frequent way in which film becomes an issue in international law in practice. As for research, does international law and film scholarship do more than 'remain grounded in one discipline while dabbling in the theory and methods of another'?[15] In short, whether it lies across disciplinary boundaries or demarcates its own territory within international law, international law and film scholarship is welcome for what it teaches us about viewing war on film and analysing the power encoded in cinematic representations of international law.

Future research directions

The chapters by Corten and Dubuisson offer a methodology by which international lawyers can critique the depiction of international law in film. Their contribution goes well beyond that of international lawyers as experts

---

14 E.g. 'Expert Medical Consulting for Film and Television' www.doctorsonset.com, accessed 30 April 2019; 'Being a Hollywood Science Consultant isn't Exactly Glamorous', *Wired magazine* (19 January 2019).

15 D.W. Vick, 'Interdisciplinarity and the Discipline of Law' (2004) 31 *Journal of Law & Society* 163, 171 cited in Burgis-Kasthala, 'Introduction', 236.

pointing out the errors in popular representations of international law. Instead they make visible the framing techniques that usually remain hidden by presenting counter-arguments to the understanding of international law implicit in much mainstream cinema, for example, the stereotyping of Palestinians as terrorists rather than presenting them as rights-holders. Here I suggest three main areas for further research, inspired by the insights and methods of Corten and Dubuisson.

First, much could be gained by panning out to capture a broader vision of world cinema. As Corten explains, much of his argument about the downplaying of international law as a restraint on, or as simply irrelevant to, the use of force is based on an analysis of Hollywood action films. This is understandable given Hollywood cinema's dominance of Anglophone and, indeed, Western film and television production. Although Hollywood remains the largest in terms of box office revenue and film financing, Bollywood and Nollywood, the Indian and Nigerian film industries, are the largest and second largest in the world respectively by number of films produced, and China is growing in importance for audience size and related revenue.[16] Would the same conclusions be reached about the Hollywood portrayal of international law as weak, if not irrelevant to, decision-making on the use of force if Bollywood, Nollywood or Chinese cinema were the subject of analysis?[17] It may be that those film industries have a different take on the conflicts that repeatedly appear in Hollywood films; or that they focus on different wars: Bangladesh, Sri Lanka or Kashmir; West African conflicts in which Nigeria plays regional superpower; or East Asian hot and cold wars? International lawyers with the linguistic and cultural competence to analyse these films would do well to undertake this work. Perhaps these cinemas are interested in other issues implicating international law, such as poverty, climate change, foreign investment or access to medicine. The regional and global success of these other film-making industries potentially overshadows national or local film-making, which is also important to investigate for its portrayal of international law. In this vein, Dubuisson's rich exposition of the Israeli–Palestinian conflict considers mainstream and counter-currents in Hollywood, Israeli and Palestinian cinema. Analysis by international lawyers of Iranian cinema, for example, would help to reveal the extent to which the wars that feature in Hollywood cinema are

---

16 Kate Hodal, 'Nollywood's New Generation in the Spotlight at Film Africa in London', *Guardian* (2 November 2020).
17 E.g. Oishik Sircar, 'Bollywood's Law: Collective Memory and Cinematic Justice in the New India' (2015) 12 *No Foundations: An Interdisciplinary Journal of Law and Justice* 94.

represented and how mainstream or government-sponsored productions differ from independent films.[18]

Second, the contributions point to the potential for analysis of ideology of both cinema and international law in terms of a 'military-cinematographic complex'. Corten refers to the film *Wag the Dog* as a prescient portrayal of the tendency of governments to use film as political propaganda to justify war. His reference to the military-cinematographic complex suggests James Der Derian's 'military-industrial-media-entertainment network'. Der Derian argues that 'there has been from the very first a close "link" between the military, simulation, the development of the computer and the entertainment industry'.[19] Long before the embedded film-making with which we are familiar from films justifying the global war on terror, Hollywood directors were promoting the war effort in films about the Second World War.[20] If close relationships exist between the government or defence ministry and the film industry, independent or critical visions of the legality of the use of force are difficult to sustain. Much attention is paid to the symbolic meanings of film; further attention to their material production and the financial undergirding of this expensive enterprise would no doubt influence how we interpret both cinema and its portrayal of international law.

Third, the films discussed are also open to interpretation from TWAIL and feminist perspectives in ways that connect with broader debates in international law. For example, Corten refers to how Michael Moore's film *Fahrenheit 9/11* represents the people of Palau as naked and primitive savages. Moore's film thereby brackets the history of US colonialism in the Pacific and Palau's exercise of self-determination through a compact of free association with the United States. Dubuisson refers to several films that include female protagonists in counter-stereotypical roles in the Israeli–Palestinian conflict. For instance, Anna, the Israeli police officer in *Room 514* who investigates her military colleagues' treatment of a Palestinian family, and *Miral*, which stars a Palestinian girl brought up in an orphanage who falls in love with a political activist, are a far cry from the five wealthy young women, archetypal victims

---

18 On an Iranian government sponsored film on the Tehran Hostages, see Thomas Erdbrink, 'Film to Present Iran's View of "Argo" Events', *New York Times* (10 January 2013), www.nytimes.com/2013/01/11/world/middleeast/as-academy-snubs-affleck-for-argo-iran-plans-own-movie.html, accessed 30 April 2019.
19 James Der Derian, *Virtuous War: Mapping the Military-Industrial-Media-Entertainment Network* (Boulder: Westview, 1st edn, 2000) 89.
20 E.g. Régis Dubois, *Une histoire politique du cinéma, Etats Unis, Europe, URSS* (Arles: Editions Sulliver, 2007) 64–70; cited in Corten, 'Mais où est donc passée la Charte des Nations Unies?'; Lewis Jacobs, 'World War II and the American Film' (1967–8) 7 *Cinema Journal* 1.

of kidnapping by Palestinian terrorists, on the yacht *Rosebud* in the film of the same name. Feminist film theory and international legal scholarship on the laws of war and the use of force have the potential to yield new insights into the ways in which power is configured in both film and law.

Watching the war on women/the war in Afghanistan

This section considers the legal justifications for the US bombardment and military presence in Afghanistan and how films about Afghanistan relate to such legal arguments. The official justification that the United States offered at the time it started bombing was that it was responding in self-defence to an armed attack, namely the 9/11 terrorist attacks, which the Taliban government of Afghanistan had enabled by providing Al-Qaeda with a safe haven on its territory. As the war wore on, the US government offered another justification to the public, namely that the Taliban's 'war on women' required the ouster and removal of the Taliban from power. At the time, images of Afghanistan in Western countries were dominated by women wearing *chadaris*, referred to as *burqa* in Arabic, which were interpreted as silencing and imprisoning them. By contrast, the 2003 film *Osama* depicts a girl forced to dress as a boy and work to feed her family, due to the Taliban's prohibition on women's work and restrictions on their movement. I conclude this section with a reading of *Osama* in the context of other films about Afghanistan that aims to evaluate whether the film provides additional visual justification for the US war or challenges the picture of women in Afghanistan as irretrievably oppressed.

The first, and official, justification provided by the United States for the war in Afghanistan was that it was acting in self-defence. In a letter to the president of the Security Council, the US permanent representative to the United Nations in New York referred to the Al-Qaeda hijackings of four passenger aircraft on 11 September 2001 as an armed attack.[21] Under article 51 of the Charter of the United Nations, States must immediately report 'measures taken in the exercise of this right to self-defence'.[22] At international law it was and remains disputed whether an attack by a non-State actor can constitute an armed attack giving rise to a right to self-defence.[23] Further,

---

21 Letter dated 2001/10/07 from the Permanent Representative of the United States of America to the United Nations addressed to the President of the Security Council, UN Doc S/2001/946.
22 Charter of the United Nations, art. 51.
23 Daniel Bethlehem, 'Self-Defense against an Imminent or Actual Armed Attack by Nonstate Actors' (2012) 106 *AJIL* 770; Elizabeth Wilmshurst and Michael Wood,

it remains controversial whether such an attack can justify a response in self-defence against a State which is 'harbouring' them, especially when it is unclear whether the State knew of or could have prevented such an attack.[24] Even assuming that a right to self-defence arises in response to an attack by non-State actors, the international law of self-defence imposes requirements of necessity and proportionality.[25] These requirements do not justify the overthrow of the government of the 'safe haven' State, as occurred in relation to the Taliban in 2002.

In addition to self-defence, the US government attempted to convince the public that its military response was justified on another ground, namely, the abuse of women's human rights in Afghanistan under the Taliban.[26] In November 2001, Laura W. Bush delivered her husband President George W. Bush's weekly radio address, arguing that 'the fight against terrorism is also a fight for the rights and dignity of women'.[27] Her address was based on a State Department report released the same day titled 'The Taliban's War Against Women'.[28] Dianne Otto described this publicity as whipping up a 'gender panic' which 'helped to justify the continuing muscularity of the military occupation of Afghanistan as a means of rescuing Muslim women from the barbarism of their culture, in the face of waning popular support for the occupation in the West'.[29] However, the fact that Mrs Bush held no official government position could be interpreted to mean that 'the position of women in Afghanistan is women's business and not a serious international concern'.[30] The United States had failed to raise the issue of

---

'Self-Defense Against Nonstate Actors: Reflections on the "Bethlehem Principles"' (2013) 107 *AJIL* 390.

24 Olivier Corten, 'The "Unwilling or Unable" Test: Has it Been, and Could it be, Accepted?' (2016) *Leiden Journal of International Law* 777; Ntina Tzouvala, 'TWAIL and the "Unwilling or Unable" Doctrine: Continuities and Ruptures' (2016) 109 *AJIL Unbound* 266.

25 *Military and Paramilitary Activities in and against Nicaragua* (Nicaragua v United States) Merits 1986 ICJ Rep 14 [194].

26 Sari Kouvo, 'The Beginning of a New Era? Thinking about Feminism, Law and Being Left Alone' (2017) 7 *feminists@law* 1, 2.

27 Radio Address by Mrs Laura W. Bush, 17 November 2001, www.bushcenter.org/publications/articles/2013/02/radio-address-by-mrs-laura-w-bush-crawford-tx-november-17-2001.html, accessed 1 December 2019.

28 Report on the Taliban's war Against Women, https://2001-2009.state.gov/g/drl/rls/6185.htm, accessed 1 December 2019.

29 Dianne Otto, 'Decoding Crisis in International Law: A Queer Feminist Perspective' in Barbara Stark (ed.), *International Law and Its Discontents* (Cambridge: Cambridge University Press, 2015) 115, 125.

30 Hilary Charlesworth and Christine Chinkin, 'Editorial Comment: Sex, Gender and September 11' (2002) 96 *AJIL* 600, 602.

abuse of women's rights in the five years of Taliban rule up until that point. It remained silent about repression of women by the warlords who preceded the Taliban and later re-formed to become the Northern Alliance after the overthrow of the Taliban.[31] Likewise, the United States did not object to women's second-class status in similarly repressive States that were also US allies, such as Saudi Arabia and Kuwait.[32] The inconsistency in advocating for women's rights suggest that the United States instrumentalized the issue at that time to counter flagging support for its war in Afghanistan.

The plausibility of mobilizing violations of women's rights to justify the use of force in Afghanistan was aided by already circulating media representations of Afghan women as 'victims of Islamic Oppression'[33] whose most iconic image was of the pale blue *chadari*. Matthew Kearns contends that the close-up portrait-style images of women would normally signify equality; but the focus on the *chadari* removed the subject from her context, dehumanizing and subordinating her.

> A central component of this was an intense visual emphasis on the burka ... Such visualizations possess a substantial history in western discourse, in which the burka signifies the threatening otherness and inferiority of Islam.[34]

These images of faceless women suffering under the Taliban were juxtaposed with those of Western women and with Afghan women following regime change. After the overthrow of the Taliban government, images of women throwing off their burkas were depicted 'as a collective subject liberated from Islamic oppression'.[35] Kearns cites George W Bush: 'One of the most joyous things for me is to *see the faces* of the Afghan women as they have been liberated ... we're freeing women and children from incredible oppression.'[36]

The United States could have deployed other legal justifications to support the legality of its use of force in Afghanistan. Humanitarian intervention is usually framed as a response to mass human rights violations.[37] International lawyers disagreed over whether the 1999 US-led

---

31 Matthew Kearns, 'Gender, Visuality and Violence: Visual Securitization and the 2001 War in Afghanistan' (2017) 19 *International Feminist Journal of Politics* 491, 500.
32 Charlesworth and Chinkin, 'Editorial Comment', 602.
33 Kearns, 'Gender, Visuality and Violence', 495.
34 Kearns, 'Gender, Visuality and Violence' (references omitted), 495.
35 Kearns, 'Gender, Visuality and Violence', 496.
36 George W. Bush, 'Remarks on Signing the Afghan Women and Children Relief Act of 2001', 12 December 2001, Kearns, 'Gender, Visuality and Violence', 500 (Kearns' emphasis).
37 Anne Orford, *Reading Humanitarian Intervention: Human Rights and the Use of Force* (Cambridge: Cambridge University Press, 2003).

NATO bombing of Serbia to stop its attacks on ethnic Albanian Kosovar insurgents could be justified as humanitarian intervention.[38] The type of human rights violations required to ground a right to humanitarian intervention is unspecified but the justification has been invoked in relation to mass violations discriminating against groups primarily on the basis of their ethnicity, religion or nationality, or a combination of these.[39] While these violations have included mass sexual violence, for example, in West Pakistan in 1971, protecting the human rights of women has never been the primary justification for humanitarian intervention.[40] Even in Afghanistan, the clearest example of the instrumentalization of women's rights to justify the use of force, the United States did not refer to humanitarian intervention, perhaps because humanitarian intervention is the most controversial exception to the prohibition on the use of force.

Further, the Women, Peace and Security agenda might have been raised in relation to Afghanistan. This series of resolutions was not made under Chapter VII of the UN Charter and is therefore not binding. However, the resolutions have provoked strong, if divergent, responses from feminists. For example, in 2016 the former Afghan Minister for Women, Dr Sima Simar, argued that '[t]he women's rights situation in Afghanistan, Syria, Iraq and a lot of other countries shows the uselessness of these resolutions'.[41] By contrast, Gina Heathcote considers that 'the women, peace, and security framework supports and legitimates the use of force'.[42]

In this context, the film *Osama* is important as it can be read as either a call for American firepower to stop the Taliban's abuses against women, or alternatively, as a rejection of the portrayal of Afghan women as faceless, voiceless victims of Islamic oppression. Directed by Soviet-trained Afghan filmmaker Siddiq Barmak and released in 2003, *Osama* narrates the story

---

38 Hilary Charlesworth, 'International Law: A Discipline of Crisis' (2002) 65 *Modern Law Review* 377, 379–81.
39 E.g. Gregory H. Fox, 'The Vietnamese Intervention in Cambodia-1978' and Dino Kritiotis, 'The Indian Intervention into (East) Pakistan- 1971' in Tom Ruys, Olivier Corten and Alexandra Hofer (eds), *The Use of Force in International Law: A Case-Based Approach* (Oxford and New York: Oxford University Press, 2018).
40 Bina D'Costa, '*Birangona*: Rape Survivors bearing Witness in War and "Peace"' in Elysse Bemporad and Joyce W. Warren (eds), *Women and Genocide: Survivors, Victims, Perpetrators* (Bloomington: Indiana University Press, 2018) 159.
41 Sima Simar, 'Keynote Address: On Women, Peace and Security' in Susan Harris Rimmer and Kate Ogg (eds), *Research Handbook on Feminist Engagement with International Law* (Northampton: Edward Elgar, 2019) 17, 24.
42 Gina Heathcote, 'Feminist Perspectives on the Law on the Use of Force' in Marc Weller (ed.), *The Oxford Handbook on the Prohibition on the Use of Force* (Oxford: Oxford University Press, 2015) 114, 115.

of a twelve-year-old girl who lives with her mother and grandmother. The Taliban's raid on hospitals prevent her mother from working, so the girl's grandmother crops her hair short, dresses her in her deceased father's clothes, and sends her to work in a tea shop of a friend of her father to try to feed the family. The Taliban conscript her into a madrassa where she, along with many teenaged boys, is forced to rote learn the Quran in Arabic and to learn how to fire weapons. Renamed Osama, she manages to pass as a boy, even entering the bath house and being instructed by the middle-aged mullah in the correct Islamic way to wash male genitals. However, her biology betrays her when a trickle of menstrual blood flows down her leg and she is expelled from the madrassa and punished for her transgression by being forced to become the youngest and newest unwilling wife of the mullah. The film ends with the image of the girl dressed in her father's clothes skipping rope inside the jail, a memory that signifies the freedom within, before the rape that is soon to inaugurate her marriage.

Osama could be read as belonging to several genres. Mark Graham reads it as

> essentially a horror movie. Its monsters, though not supernatural, are terrifying just the same ... the film's narrative bears many gothic hallmarks, most notably the lone heroine trapped in a shambling ruin, menaced by religious fanatics and sexual predators.[43]

Graham also sees it as fitting into 'the Hollywood Eastern'[44] along with Rudolph Valentino in *The Sheikh* and *Lawrence of Arabia*, and as a war story which is 'always a horror story'.[45] Drawing on Williams' discussion of related genres, the term melodrama does not fit easily to *Osama*, because the girl's sufferings are not the stuff of which first world problems portrayed on daytime television are made. Yet the melodramatic aspects highlight the fictional aspects of this docudrama, while the use of amateur actors and neorealist techniques suggest authenticity and a documentary quality.[46]

Osama is worthy of analysis because its ambiguity is the basis for contrasting views about whether it can be read as propaganda for the US war against the Taliban's war against women or alternatively as presenting Afghan women as capable of protest and resistance. Mark Graham convincingly paints *Osama* as the former.

---

43 Mark Graham, *Afghanistan in the Cinema* (Urbana: University of Illinois Press, 2010), 89.
44 Graham, *Afghanistan in the Cinema*.
45 Graham, *Afghanistan in the Cinema*, 94.
46 R. J. Cardullo, 'An Afghan is a Woman: Siddiq Barmak's Osama' in R. J. Cardullo (ed.), *Teaching Sound Film* (Springer, 2016) 293, 302.

Like horror movies with their damsels in distress, *Osama* followed the formula of narrative films like *Kandahar* and documentaries like *Afghanistan Unveiled*.[47] With its sympathetic female lead, it pitched the Afghan conflict as a war for sexual liberation against the fanaticism of Islam. Was the U.S. invasion right or wrong? Did it do more harm than good? Did innocent people get bombed? Were feminists cynically manipulated by warmonger politicians? Who cares, Jane Smiley wrote in the December 2, 2001, *New York Times Magazine*. The end justified the means, because 'the Afghan women took off their burkas'.[48]

Yet the film resists Western expectations of Afghan women. The opening sequence of mass demonstrations of women against the Taliban and the way in which a woman fights back against the Talib locking her into a chicken coop are not the stereotypical scenes of powerless women imprisoned by their religion.[49] Despite the signs they carry, 'We are not political', these loud, brave women demanding justice correct the Western image of oppressed, veiled Muslim women.[50]

Most importantly, it is not the veiling of the girl that provides the narrative tension, but rather her transvestism and passing as a male.[51] Her entry into male-only spaces, such as the madrassa and the inner sanctum of the bath house, enables her to witness what women are prohibited from seeing. Much feminist film theory is built on the observation that films assume a male viewer. However, in the bath house, the girl 'exposes the male voyeur. For it becomes painfully obvious that the dirty old man instructing them is the male gaze itself, watching the boys as she watches him'.[52] Hence, *Osama* is a film that generates conflicting interpretations as to whether it should be read as propaganda for the US intervention in Afghanistan or as a depiction of Afghan women's political agency.

The financing and circumstances of production of the film also inform its interpretation. As noted earlier, filmmaker Barmak trained in Moscow, although he immediately joined the mujahideen on his return to Afghanistan.[53]

---

47 *Kandahar* (dir. Mohsen Makhmalbaf, 2002) tracks the journey of an Afghan-Canadian woman's search for her sister. *Afghanistan Unveiled* (dir. Brigitte Brault, 2003) was filmed by fourteen Afghan women trained by a French filmmaker (Brault) with funding from the US State Department and other international sources: US State Department, https://2001-2009.state.gov/g/wi/rls/38610.htm, accessed 1 December 2019.
48 Graham, *Afghanistan in the Cinema*, 94 (quotes omitted).
49 Graham, *Afghanistan in the Cinema*, 96.
50 Gohar Siddiqui, 'Docudrama's Blurred Boundaries: Truth and Fiction in Afghani Cinema' (2019) 59 *Jump Cut: A Review of Contemporary Media*.
51 Graham, *Afghanistan in the Cinema*, 97.
52 Graham, *Afghanistan in the Cinema*, 100.
53 Randy Kennedy, 'From Guerrilla to Director: Siddiq Barmak's Road to "Osama"', *New York Times* (11 February 2004).

When the Taliban came to power, he and his family fled to Pakistan where they lived for six years.[54] A Dari-speaking Tajik, he chose a Tajik lead (Marina Golbahari).[55] Barmak was assisted financially and encouraged by Iranian filmmaker Mohsen Makhmalbaf, who directed *Kandahar*. *Osama* received funding from investors from Japan and Ireland and from UNESCO, but not from the Afghan government. The lack of political, historical and cultural context for the Taliban and the lack of critique of the alternatives, such as the Northern Alliance (which includes Tajiks), is problematic.[56] In short, the interpretation of all *Osama*, like other films, cannot escape the material conditions of its production and resulting biases.

Conclusion

International law is rarely cast in a starring role, either as hero or villain, in films dealing with war. Questions of genre and the possibility of multiple interpretations are key to analysing how films portray the relevance and substance of international law. In 2001 the United States claimed that self-defence was the legal basis for its intervention into Afghanistan; however, later it built on images of oppressed Afghan women already circulating in the media to argue that the war on terror was the answer to the Taliban's war on women. The film *Osama* gives rise to potentially conflicting interpretations, with its disavowal of historical context enabling it to be read as propaganda for the US military intervention on an alternative, visual rather than legal, basis. At the same time, the film presents rare images of Afghan women demonstrating against the Taliban. Crucially, the lead character transgresses gender boundaries by dressing as a boy, even if forced to do so out of desperation. Hence, the panorama of world cinema provides broad scope for fresh new perspectives on the intersection of international law and cinema.

---

54 Maryam Maruk and Maggie Loescher, 'Osama and Afghan Cinema: An Interview with Siddiq Barmak' (4 March 2004), www.openDemocracy.net, accessed 1 December 2019.
55 Graham, *Afghanistan in the Cinema*, 106.
56 Graham, *Afghanistan in the Cinema*, 105.

10

Shut the fuck up, Suarez! Necroethics and rights in a world of shit

Mario Prost

Films often resonate in deep and fruitful ways with complex philosophical questions. Several chapters in this book[1] provide a rich and engaging analysis of films as an artistic medium for thinking about a dominant theme of contemporary legal philosophy: the subversion of law under extreme conditions.[2] Specifically, they examine how films have historically expressed and represented the tension between law, war, military violence and human rights and counter-terrorist operations. The authors adopt a similar approach, drawing a typology of films based on how they interpret and resolve this tension, often to the benefit of military necessity and national security. They draw similar conclusions too: whilst films (principally Western and predominantly American) often acknowledge the presence of legal constraints on the use of force, they typically justify their setting aside on utilitarian grounds or in favour of competing normative principles under some Agambenian state of exception argument.[3] Films, they argue, don't generally take rights very seriously, often depicting them as expendable or at any rate impractical and ill-suited to govern warfare.

In what follows, I want to complicate this line of argument by examining some of its underlying assumptions about films, law and warfare. I start by raising some preliminary questions about what films do and difficulties involved in interpreting and categorizing cinematic works. I move on to argue that, rather than advocating the setting aside of humanitarian principles in the name of some vitally important ends, many of the films reviewed are perhaps best understood as depicting the moral dilemmas raised by the implementation of rights in extreme conditions and reflecting

---

1 See in particular Chapters 4 (Olivier Corten), 5 (François Dubuisson) and 7 (Martyna Fałkowska-Clarys and Vaios Koutroulis).
2 For a recent take on this theme, see Thomas Eger, Stefan Oeter and Stefan Voigt (eds), *International Law and the Rule of Law under Extreme Conditions* (Tübingen: Mohr Siebeck, 2017).
3 Giorgio Agamben, *State of Exception* (Chicago: University of Chicago Press, 2005).

on some of the profound shifts which have recently occurred in the law and ethics of warfare. I conclude with some final thoughts on the role of films in de-sanitizing war in a context where law often serves the opposite end.

Film as resource and film as source: cinema as the 'ultimate pervert art'

Films can be approached from a variety of theoretical perspectives. Often, they are apprehended as a narrative source. Films are used to tell stories about law, war, terror and interrogate the meaning of specific doctrines. They provide plotlines and examples that are mobilized to think through conceptual arguments, ideas and questions, following a rich philosophical tradition. Scholars have long used movies as support for giving abstract concepts or theories concrete meaning, from the question of 'doing the right thing' in *Force Majeure*[4] to genetic determinism in *Gattaca*[5] or the nature of the self in *Memento*.[6]

However, law and films intertwine in deeper ways too and are engaged in complex relations of reciprocal insight and influence. Films – and popular culture more generally – play an essential role in forming our affective landscapes. They provide the signs, images, stories, metaphors, plotlines and characters with which we make sense of our lives and the world around us. As such, they create a framework from which we view particular situations and a set of justifications or reasons for particular course of action. In the introduction to Sophie Fiennes' *The Pervert's Guide to Cinema* (2006), Slavoj Žižek asserts that 'cinema is the ultimate pervert art. It doesn't give you what you desire, it tells you how to desire'. For Žižek, there is nothing natural about our desires. Our desires are artificial constructs and, in the social construction of our desires, films have a potent presence. Amongst other things, this imaginative potency shapes our demands, expectations, values and beliefs as socio-legal agents, what we may call our collective legal consciousness.[7]

---

4 Ruben Östlund, France, Norway, Sweden, 2014.
5 Andrew Niccol, USA, 1997.
6 Christopher Nolan, USA, 2000. See e.g. Julian Baggini, Christine Korsgaard, Ursula Coope, Peter Singer, Susan Haack, Kenneth Taylor and Slavoj Žižek, 'I Watch Therefore I Am: Seven Movies that Teach Us Key Philosophy Lessons', *Guardian* (14 April 2015). See also Mary M. Litch, *Philosophy Through Film* (London: Routledge, 2nd edn, 2010).
7 See generally Richard K. Sherwin, *When Law Goes Pop: The Vanishing Line Between Law and Popular Culture* (Chicago: University of Chicago Press, 2000); Lawrence M. Friedman, 'Law, Lawyers, and Popular Culture' (1989) 98 *Yale Law Journal* 1579.

The influence of the hit TV series *24*[8] on public debates regarding torture in the war on terror offers a paradigmatic example of the role of film in shaping collective legal consciousness. The hugely popular show, which premiered only a few weeks after the 9/11 attacks, follows maverick counter-terrorist agent Jack Bauer as he runs against the clock to foil various terrorist plots against America. Bauer is brave, single-minded, ruthless and devoted. He's also not afraid to get his hands dirty.[9] Amid a background of ticking bombs and imminent catastrophes, Bauer and his colleagues from the Counter-Terrorist Unit (CTU) are constantly forced to make grim choices that pit civil liberties against security. When confronted with a choice between affording an uncooperative suspect due process or using torture to extract information, Bauer invariably chooses coercion. He snaps people's fingers, shoots them in the kneecap, electrocutes them with lamp wires. In doing so, Bauer does not discriminate: CTU colleagues and supervisors, ex-girlfriends and relatives are all tortured at one point in the show. Critically, the imposition of torture invariably and almost instantaneously forces suspects to speak truthfully about what they know. In *24*, the torture victims talk in a timely and accurate manner, divulging crucial information before the bomb goes off. They do not pass out, vomit on themselves or have psychotic breaks. Neither do they tell lies that waste time. Torture is practically infallible: it works, where orthodox legal methods have failed.

As is now well documented, *24* has had a significant role in framing public debates that erupted after the Abu Ghraib prison scandal and news of the US administration using 'enhanced interrogation techniques' in Guantanamo. The show has been especially influential in popularizing certain hypotheticals such as the 'ticking time bomb scenario' – a mind experiment with practically no real world relevance – and in rationalizing the 'by any means necessary' approach to counter-terrorism.[10] Public officials, presidential candidates, leading intellectuals and academics have cited Jack Bauer as a pertinent exemplar for thinking about the permissibility of torture.[11] Justice Scalia of

---

8   Joel Surnow and Robert Cochran, Fox, USA, 2001–10, 2014.
9   For a philosophical analysis, through *24*, of the problem of attaining good ends through morally dubious means, see Stephen de Wijze, 'Between Hero and Villain: Jack Bauer and the Problem of "Dirty Hands"' in Jennifer Hart Weed, Richard Davis and Ronald Weed (eds), *24 and Philosophy: The World According to Jack* (Malden: Blackwell, 2008).
10 Ron E. Hassner, 'The Myth of the Ticking Bomb' (2018) 41 *Washington Quarterly* 83; Olivier Corten, 'La banalisation de la torture comme un instrument de lutte contre le terrorisme: comme au cinéma?' (2017) 79 *Revue interdisciplinaire d'études juridiques* 229.
11 Kelly M. Greenhill, '24 on the Brain', *Los Angeles Times* (28 May 2007); Dahlia Lithwick, 'How Jack Bauer Shaped US Torture Policy', *Newsweek* (25 July 2008);

the US Supreme Court has defended torture by appealing to Bauer to justify the use of extreme measures in extreme circumstances.[12] In the run-up to the 2008 presidential elections, Bill Clinton told NBC's *Meet the Press* that, whilst America should oppose torture as a matter of policy and honour the Geneva Conventions, when confronted with the proverbial ticking bomb and terrorist in hand one ought to look to vigilante agents like Jack Bauer to do whatever it takes to keep the country safe and be prepared to live with the consequences.[13] Philippe Sands has described how the series gave people in Guantanamo lots of ideas and made it more difficult for people objecting to torture to stop it.[14] One commentator has even remarked that the lawyers designing interrogation techniques during the Bush administration 'cited Jack Bauer more frequently than the Constitution'.[15]

It is hard to quantify the impact of a show like *24* with any degree of certainty. Jack Bauer is as much a symptom as he is a source of America's anxieties about terror and the need to resort to the dark side to defeat it. But one thing is clear: popular culture is not merely descriptive of formal systems, concepts or categories. As ideological texts, films have the power to construct socio-legal narratives that frame our understanding of what is good, possible or necessary in given situations.[16] Like any frame, once accepted they become hard to notice or question, especially in contexts where films provide backstage access to places or practices of which viewers have no first-hand experience. Understood within the framework of legal pluralism, popular culture therefore participates in the day to day making (or unmaking) of the law. In a world where law is produced not just formally but also discursively, through the interpretation and choices of multiple actors, films are not merely fictional resources that we can mobilize to tell stories about law. By influencing how thinkers think, how judges judge, and how interrogators interrogate, they become a source of law.[17]

John Yoo, *War by Other Means: An Insider's Account of the War on Terror* (New York: Atlantic Monthly Press, 2006).
12 Colin Freeze, 'Justice Scalia Cites Jack Bauer as Example in Discussion Over Torture', *The Globe and Mail* (20 June 2007).
13 Joe Mathews, 'Bill Clinton and the Jack Bauer Exemption', *Los Angeles Times* (30 September 2007).
14 Philippe Sands, *Torture Team* (New York: Palgrave, 2008) 63.
15 Lithwick, 'How Jack Bauer Shaped US Torture Policy'.
16 On the relationship between films and ideology, see the general introduction to this volume.
17 See Desmond Manderson, 'Trust Us Justice: 24, Popular Culture, and the Law' in Austin Sarat (ed.), *Imagining Legality: Where Law Meets Popular Culture* (Tuscaloosa: University of Alabama Press, 2011).

Interpreting film: shining a light on dark deeds?

In their chapter, Fałkowska-Clarys and Koutroulis elaborate cinematic typologies based on how films interpret specific legal norms and the broader question of how law ought to respond to situations of emergency. In other words, they categorize films on the basis of their jurisprudential content. This approach raises important methodological questions, some of which are readily acknowledged by the authors, but others of which warrant some further consideration. In examining these questions, I want to focus here on the possibility of assigning fixed or stable meanings to films.

What is the content of a film? This seemingly simple question represents one of the most vexatious problems of film theory and often requires looking past the film's surface.[18] Take the example of *Zero Dark Thirty* (2012), which has given rise to numerous interpretive disputes. Kathryn Bigelow's film about the hunt of Osama Bin Laden follows Maya – a fiercely driven and socially awkward CIA agent – in her relentless pursuit of America's public enemy number one. The film has drawn heavy criticism for its alleged pro-torture stance and for creating the false impression that 'enhanced interrogation techniques' played a key role in finding Bin Laden.[19] Much of the criticism has been directed at the film's gruelling first act, a graphic depiction of the black-site interrogation of Ammar, a detainee with suspected links to Bin Laden's entourage. In the lengthy scene, Ammar is strung up by ropes, waterboarded, deprived of sleep and forced into a small wooden box. Ammar provides unreliable information about a suspected attack in Saudi Arabia but supplies clues about Bin Laden's personal courier which later prove valuable in locating his whereabouts.

Is *Zero Dark Thirty* an apology for torture? Does it provide a jurisprudential justification for the state of exception? These questions have given rise to widely different views. On one level, a crucial piece of information in Maya's investigation is elicited from a prisoner who has been tortured. Yet the actionable intelligence is not provided during the opening torture scene but later, over a relaxed meal and after Ammar is tricked into believing that he has already spoken while delirious from lack of sleep. As noted by Blistène, this scene can be understood simultaneously as showing the ineffectiveness of torture and opening the door to its

---

18 See e.g. David Bordwell, *Making Meaning: Inference and Rhetoric in the Interpretation of Cinema* (Cambridge, MA: Harvard University Press, 1991).

19 See e.g. Alex von Tunzelmann, 'Zero Dark Thirty's Torture Scenes are Controversial and Historically Dubious', *Guardian* (25 January 2013); Jane Mayer, 'Zero Conscience in Zero Dark Thirty', *The New Yorker* (14 December 2012).

redemption.[20] Intelligence is gathered through rapport-based interrogation and ruse, rather than coercion, but Ammar's cooperation happens on the back on intense sleep-deprivation and physical abuse. This ambiguity is later carried throughout the entire film, which is filled with false starts and failed leads. Torture is an integral part of the chain of events leading to Bin Laden's ultimate downfall. Yet important breakthroughs happen through painstaking intelligence work, bribing informants, surveillance, and cooperation with foreign intelligence agencies.

Bigelow and her screenwriter Mark Boal have come under intense pressure over the deep ambiguity of the film. In defending it, they have insisted that the practices shown in the film tally with what the CIA has admitted to in an important report released in 2009 documenting the interrogation techniques used in its black-sites. Torture was an integral part of US counter-terrorism policy and practices. As such, it is a central part of the story that could therefore not be ignored. The film, they argue, rejects cheap moralism and shows counter-terrorism as it is, raising difficult questions about the ethical cost of the war on terror.[21] More importantly perhaps, they have claimed that the decision to show the use of torture is not meant to be understood as advocating it, either morally or strategically. Depiction is not endorsement, claims Bigelow, and if it was no artist could ever portray inhumane practices: 'confusing depiction with endorsement is the first step towards chilling any American artist's ability and right to shine a light on dark deeds, especially when those deeds are cloaked in layers of secrecy and government obfuscation'.[22]

Whether Bigelow's authorial intent to depict torture without endorsing it removes the film's moral ambiguities is of course debatable. As noted by Fałkowska-Clarys and Koutroulis, a central question is whether a film such as *Zero Dark Thirty* can *ever* be neutral. Žižek, in a scathing critique of the film and of Bigelow's defence, raises precisely this point. To depict an act so profoundly shattering as torture in a neutral light, he argues, necessarily amounts to a form of endorsement, whatever the director's intention might have been.[23] The film normalizes torture not by showing it but because of *how* it shows it, i.e. without moral context or traumatic impact on those

---

20 Pauline Blistène, 'Torture et prisons secrètes: Zero Dark Thirty, l'insoutenable figuration du réel?', *Culture-pop et droit international* (2 March 2016), http://cdi.ulb.ac.be/zerodarkthirty, accessed 26 November 2020.
21 Melena Ryzik, 'Kathryn Bigelow Steps Up Defense of "Zero Dark Thirty"', *New York Times* (16 January 2013).
22 Ben Child, 'Kathryn Bigelow on Zero Dark Thirty: "It's Illogical to Ignore Torture"', *Guardian* (16 January 2013).
23 Slavoj Žižek, 'Zero Dark Thirty: Hollywood's Gift to American Power', *Guardian* (25 January 2013).

practising it. Here, Žižek draws our attention back to the film's narrative structure and specifically to the character of Dan, Maya's CIA partner who tortures Ammar in the film's opening act. Dan passes casually from torture to friendliness once the victim is broken, seemingly unaffected by the barbaric acts he has just perpetrated. Later in the film, Dan trades his blood-stained gloves for a desk job at Langley. To Žižek, there is something deeply disturbing in how Dan 'changes from a torturer in jeans to a well-dressed Washington bureaucrat'.[24] This, he argues, is normalization at its purest and most efficient.

What the above demonstrates is that films like *Zero Dark Thirty* defy easy categorization and invite multiple interpretations.[25] Films are often sites of intense epistemological struggle and rarely have a single fixed meaning. This renders attempts to typologize films based on their normative content (for or against torture; narrow or extensive interpretation of the principle of distinction, etc.) highly unstable and contingent upon basic assumptions regarding the film's narrative structure, aesthetic form, substance, context, authorial intent, and how these elements interact within a given socio-economic context.

Split-second ethics in the fog of war: 'They're gonna fry you if you're wrong'

There is difficulty in treating films as the product of a single, consistent creative intelligence putting forward a coherent set of ideas or arguments. More often than not, films raise issues for audiences to think about, frequently coming across as ambivalent and drawing attention to complex emotions, dilemmas, contradictions rather than articulating a fixed view. Films often work as thought experiments do, i.e. as devices of the imagination used to investigate the nature of things. Most of the films analysed by Fałkowska-Clarys and Koutroulis in their chapter on the principle of distinction are perhaps best understood in this way. Rather than taking a firm position on the principle itself, films typically draw the viewer's attention to the deep ethical complexities and conundrums – the 'moral and legal quagmire'[26] – that people making targeting decisions in war are confronted with. The thought-experimentesque nature of films is particularly pronounced in some

---

24 Žižek, 'Zero Dark Thirty'.
25 Daniel Joyce and Gabrielle Simm, '*Zero Dark Thirty*: International Law, Film and Representation' (2015) 3 *London Review of International Law* 295, 311.
26 Fałkowska-Clarys and Koutroulis in this volume, pp. 128–52.

of the works reviewed by the authors. In *Eye in the Sky*,[27] for instance, the film uses clever narrative devices – such as a miniature beetle-like surveillance drone allowing the mission operators to establish that the house occupants are suicide bombers about to cause extensive loss of civilian life – to turn some factual judgements normally covered by a veil of ignorance into clear-cut determinations, a characteristic feature of thought experiments such as trolley cases or ticking bomb scenarios.[28]

Of course, combatants who make life or death determinations on the battlefield rarely possess the sort of certainty of knowledge found in *Eye in the Sky* or the luxury to ponder the finer points of ethics and law involved in their decisions. In *Eye in the Sky*, the ethical dilemma is posed by the certainty that striking the terrorists will, without a shadow of a doubt, lead to the death of an innocent little girl selling bread outside of the targeted house. The moral quagmire arises out of what is known to be true: the identity of the targets, their unquestionable wickedness, and the absolute innocence of the civilian passerby. However, the film simplifies and dogmatizes what is often a far more complex reality, where knowledge is imperfect and combatants have little time for deliberation. The problems posed by uncertainty of knowledge are especially acute in counter-insurgency situations where warfare is not fought in pitched battles between regular armies and where a clear line of demarcation between combatants and civilians can be difficult to establish. Many films on the Iraq and Afghanistan wars touch on the inherent difficulty of making split-second ethical judgements in the fog of war, i.e. in the absence of certainty about one's enemies, one's friends and the consequences of one's actions.

American Sniper[29] – which has been met with great controversy for offering an unrepentant whitewash of America's imperial war in Iraq[30] – uses the psychological toll of having to make these hard decisions to humanize its main character. Directed by Clint Eastwood, the film centres on Chris Kyle – the most lethal sniper in US military history – during his four tours in Iraq. Several scenes in the movie show him struggle with the decision to pull the trigger. In the film's opening sequence, a woman and a

---

27 Gavin Hood, UK, 2015.
28 As noted by Marko Milanovic, 'Eye in the Sky', *EJIL Talk!* (9 May 2016), www.ejiltalk.org/eye-in-the-sky, accessed 26 November 2020.
29 Clint Eastwood, US, 2014.
30 Stephen Maher, 'Hollywood at War', *Jacobin Magazine* (22 February 2015). When asked about *American Sniper* glorifying war and snipers, Clint Eastwood replied that, to him, his film was anti-war because it shows the difficulties the soldiers deployed on the ground and their families go through; Stephen Galloway, 'Clint Eastwood Describes His Near-Death Experience, Says "American Sniper" is Anti-War (Exclusive)', *The Hollywood Reporter* (16 March 2015), www.hollywoodreporter.com/news/clint-eastwood-describes-his-death-781618, accessed 26 November 2020.

boy are approaching a US marine convoy concealing what appears to be an RKG anti-tank grenade. Perched high on a building, Kyle consults his commanding officer, who answers 'you know the ROEs; your call'. Kyle's heartbeat accelerates. His breath is racing, as his spotter mutters 'they're gonna fry you if you're wrong. They'll send your ass to Leavenworth'.[31] The kid starts racing towards the convoy. Kyle pauses upon exhale and pulls the trigger, earning the first of his 160 confirmed kills. Later in the film, Kyle kills an insurgent who is aiming an RPG at a nearby US convoy. A young kid no older than Kyle's own son approaches, setting his sight on the weapon lying on the ground. 'Don't you fucking pick it up' mumbles Kyle. The kid grabs the RPG, shoulders it and takes aim. Kyle prepares to fire, turning nauseous at the prospect of having to kill yet another child. Just as he lays his finger on the trigger, the kid suddenly discards the RPG and runs off, leaving Kyle gasping for air and biting back his tears.

The real Chris Kyle, to be sure, did not experience these ethical conflicts. 'I could give a flying fuck about the Iraqis' he wrote in his memoir, 'if you see anyone from about sixteen to sixty-five and they're male, shoot'em. Kill every male you see'.[32] The fictional Kyle, however, does draw attention to some of the problems and paradoxes of military responsibility and of ethics in war. *Jus in bello* requires professional killers to make determinations about legitimate targets of deadly violence in the most challenging circumstances. Whilst some cases may be fairly straightforward, others sit on the borderline. Often soldiers cannot be sure just who is attacking them, where the attack is coming from, and even whether they are under attack at all. Life or death decisions frequently have to be taken in confusing combat situations in which split-second decisions can lead to legitimate acts or result in a war crime.[33] This is especially true in guerrilla warfare where fighters will often deliberately take up position amongst civilians so as to render ethical determinations extremely difficult to make or entice the enemy to violate *jus in bello*. This presents the more powerful enemy with difficult choices: attack and pay a potentially high moral and political price for killing civilians, or desist from attacking and suffer potential military loss.

The difficulty of making ethical or rule-based decisions in combat is accentuated by the nature of military training. A major paradox of *jus in bello* is that it requires soldiers to act in combat as morally autonomous agents when they are trained precisely *not* to do so. People are generally reluctant

---

31 Leavenworth is a military correctional facility located in Kansas.
32 Chris Kyle, *American Sniper: The Autobiography of the Most Lethal Sniper in US History* (New York: HarperCollins, 2012) 188.
33 Eric David, *Principes de Droit des Conflits Armés* (Brussels: Bruylant, 3rd edn, 2002) 921.

to hurt other human beings, this reluctance stemming from a combination of biological, psychological, social and moral constraints. Because the core business of armies is killing, they require their personnel to act against these constraints.[34] A crucial part of training soldiers involves teaching them to ignore the limits normally placed on the use of deadly violence so that in the right circumstances they will not hesitate and will kill the enemy. Military training removes trainees 'from the framework of the inhibiting force that civilization has raised against killing'.[35] This is done through a process of moral disengagement where soldiers are actively taught to bypass their normal moral decision-making and release aggression when ordered to. The constant repetition of training exercises in which tasks are standardized and compartmentalized reduces the necessity of making decisions and minimizes the occasions in which moral questions arise. Through exhausting physical training and strict discipline, recruits are transformed into soldiers who submit and conform to the armed forces' ethical judgements.[36] Training affirms hyper-masculine norms of aggression, stoicism and aversion to weakness. Role effectiveness is associated with masculine potency. Failure and doubt are treated as threatening and often associated with femininity or homosexuality. This process of de-individuation can cause profound and traumatic injury to soldiers' moral centre, sometimes with tragic consequences. Kubrick's *Full Metal Jacket*[37] exposes, amongst other things, the dehumanization and loss of individuality affecting recruits as they are transformed into cold-hearted killing machines, culminating in Private Pyle's psychotic breakdown and gruesome suicide in the barrack's latrine.[38]

Military training erodes the very self-determination and free will that *jus in bello* requires. Soldiers are thus subjected to an ethical double bind where they are simultaneously required to throw off their moral inhibitions and act in a righteous way, to suppress doubt and shame whilst at the same time exercising moral autonomy and using their sovereign mind. That tension is well illustrated by the film *Good Kill*,[39] in which the characters of Egan and Suarez present the two sides of the double bind. Egan, the male pilot, follows orders, registering only mild discomfort as the CIA orders increasingly

34 Dave Grossman, *On Killing: The Psychological Cost of Learning to Kill in War and Society* (New York: Back Bay, 2009).
35 Theodore Nadelson, *Trained to Kill: Soldiers at War* (Baltimore: Johns Hopkins University Press, 2005) 43.
36 David Gee, *The Last Ambush? Aspects of Mental Health in the British Armed Forces* (London: Forces Watch, 2013) 31.
37 Stanley Kubrick, USA, 1987.
38 Rich Schweitzer, 'Born to Kill: S. Kubrick's *Full Metal Jacket* as Historical Representation of America's Experience in Vietnam' (1990) 20 *Film and History* 62.
39 Andrew Niccol, USA, 2014.

questionable strikes and dealing with his troubled conscience by hitting the bottle hard in the secret of his bathroom. Suarez, the female pilot, cannot turn off her moral outrage sensors the way Egan does. She objects to the illegal strikes ordered by her commanding officer and the pseudo-ethics of just war invoked to justify them. When she suggests that double-tapping amounts to a war crime, she is shut down, quite literally: 'Shut the fuck up, Suarez! [...] You wanna talk about all the shots we didn't take, waiting for some D.C. lawyer to come back from lunch? [...] So, fucking sue me. Later, Jane Fonda.' The reply confirms Suarez's assessment of the situation whilst rendering it inconsequential. Unwilling to ignore or rationalize the consequences of her actions the way her male colleagues do, Suarez eventually turns in her wings, conceding she is not cut out for 'battlefields and blackjack', a shorthand for masculine military culture.[40]

The new necroethics of imperial warfare

Films can be seen as reflecting the progressive transformation of the war on terror. In their chapter, Falkowska-Clarys and Koutroulis, for instance, insist on the changing nature of warfare and the challenges it poses to traditional *in bello* and human rights concepts. This angle of analysis, however, focuses primarily on the changing materiality of warfare, in particular the nature of belligerents and the unequal distribution of power amongst them. I want to suggest here that films reveal as much about the changing materiality of war as they do about the normative framework within which contemporary imperial violence is deployed. We tend to assume that modern warfare is characterized above all by profound technological changes and the increasingly asymmetric nature of conflicts.[41] But disparities of power and vulnerabilities have been a constant feature of small wars in history. Perhaps, then, the specificity of contemporary warfare has less to do with the material conduct of armed violence than with the ethical and political norms that shape and are invoked to regulate its conduct.

The regulation of war is traditionally premised on the precept of combatant liability to, and non-combatant immunity from, the effects of fighting. Combatants, as the primary agents of warfare, are permitted to

---

40 See the insightful analysis by Rebecca Adelman, 'Imperial Cry-Faces: Women Lamenting the War on Terror' in Scott Laderman and Tim Gruenwald (eds), *Imperial Benevolence: US Foreign Policy and American Popular Culture since 9/11* (Oakland: University of California Press, 2018).
41 See e.g. Herfried Münkler, 'The Wars of the 21st Century' (2003) 849 *International Review of the Red Cross* 7 (highlighting, in particular, asymmetry, demilitarization and privatization as the salient features of the 'new wars').

engage in hostilities and can lawfully be targeted by opposing forces. They can, in other words, kill and be killed. Non-combatants, on the other hand, inasmuch as they are not active participants in hostilities, cannot be lawfully targeted by belligerents. Unless they are engaged in direct combat support of the enemy's armed forces, they are in principle immune from intentional harm.[42] The regulation of war is also traditionally premised on the precept of a demarcated zone of conflict, bounded in time and in space. Though there exists no clear legal delineation of the battlefield and there is inconsistency in the writings and case law on the matter, the laws of war and the package of special rights and privileges they stipulate – including the right to kill enemy combatants at will and without process – are only intended to apply within the specific confines of an armed conflict, i.e. between identifiable belligerents and within territorially defined combat zones.[43]

As has been widely remarked, these traditional precepts have been subverted by the global war on terror to the point of being turned entirely upside down.[44] On the view that they are in an transnational armed conflict with Al-Qaeda, the Taliban and associated forces, the United States and its allies have claimed the right to pursue and eliminate anyone, anywhere, posing a threat to their national security. In the process, militarized violence has lost its traditional limits. War has become deterritorialized, borderless and ubiquitous. Armed violence is no longer confined within the limits of a demarcated combat zone and extends to potentially all corners of the earth where terrorists and their sponsors can be found, including areas far remote from any recognized 'hot' battlefield.[45] Because the ubiquitous enemy can never be fully defeated, the war has no end in sight. The 'everywhere war' is also the 'forever war', an indefinite campaign for the preventive elimination of uncivilized hostiles roaming imperial peripheries.[46]

42 Gary D. Solis, *The Law of Armed Conflict – International Humanitarian Law in War* (Cambridge and New York: Cambridge University Press, 2010) 187–8; Hugo Grotius, *The Rights of War and Peace* (Washington: Walter Dunne, 1901) 325–6 (in which Grotius defines killing or otherwise injuring the person of a public enemy the most essential 'right of war').
43 Jonathan Crowe and Kylie Weston-Scheuber, *Principles of International Humanitarian Law* (Cheltenham and Northampton: Edward Elgar, 2013) 14–15; Ingrid Detter, *The Law of War* (Cambridge: Cambridge University Press, 2nd edn, 2000) 168.
44 Frédéric Mégret, '"War"? Legal Semantics and the Move to Violence' (2002) 13 *European Journal of International Law* 361; Jason Ralph, *America's War on Terror: The State of the 9/11 Exception from Bush to Obama* (Oxford: Oxford University Press, 2013).
45 Jennifer C. Daskal, 'The Geography of the Battlefield: A Framework for Detention and Targeting Outside of the "Hot" Conflict Zone' (2013) 161 *University of Pennsylvania Law Review* 1165.
46 Derek Gregory, 'The Everywhere War' (2011) 177 *Geographical Journal* 177.

In this unbounded war, the sovereignty of other states becomes a contingent matter, conditioned on their willingness or ability to support the imperial pursuit of terrorist groups. Third World sovereignty is, in any event, assumed to be subordinate to the security interests of the imperial powers. Films such as *Eyes in the Sky* or *Zero Dark Thirty*, whilst raising important legal-ethical considerations regarding the manner in which targeted assassinations are prepared and executed, tend to obscure the deeper and perhaps more significant question of whether killing suspected terrorists on the territory of other states is appropriate at all. This uncritical embrace of extraterritorial assassination as a tool of statecraft, as noted by a commentator, says a good deal about the new normal in the era of the global war on terror.[47]

As well as reframing the spatial and temporal coordinates of war, the global war on terror completely reverses the traditional distribution of vulnerability in warfare, in which soldiers are exposed to death and civilians are protected. Contemporary forms of imperial military violence are characterized by what Chamayou calls a new principle of 'imperial combatant immunity' in which the quasi-invulnerability of dominant powers is transformed into an overarching political-ethical norm.[48] To keep the everywhere war going indefinitely, Western lives have to be preserved, as such is the condition for the public to continue supporting (and funding) imperial military interventions. For the sake of preserving Western military lives, the risk of producing civilian casualties has become more widely accepted. Explicitly articulated during NATO's intervention in Kosovo – where pilots were ordered not to fly below an altitude of 15,000 feet to keep aircraft out of reach of enemy defences, knowing that this would reduce the accuracy of air strikes and endanger the lives of those the intervention was supposed to save – a new doctrine has emerged in which combatant immunity ranks higher than non-combatant immunity. Under this new meta-legal principle, non-combatants are protected so long as this does not endanger military lives.[49]

---

47 Susan Carruthers, 'Zero Dark Thirty' (2013) 38 *Cinéaste* 50, 51.
48 Grégoire Chamayou, *A Theory of the Drone* (New York: New Press, 2013) 127.
49 This was theorized most prominently by Kasher and Yadlin, who argue against the principle of combatant liability/non-combatant immunity in favour of a simpler, overarching principle of safeguard of one's national lives according to which soldiers may impose greater risks on foreign civilians if this minimizes risks to themselves. See Asa Kasher and Amos Yadlin, 'Military Ethics of Fighting Terror: An Israeli Perspective' (2005) 4 *Journal of Military Ethics* 3. See also the discussion in Adil Ahmad Haque, *Law and Morality at War* (Oxford: Oxford University Press, 2017) 159–60.

The situation depicted in the film *The Lone Survivor*[50] – where US Navy SEALs chose to act within the traditional bounds of international humanitarian law and spare the lives of civilians, knowing that this would bring probable death and mission failure – is an outlier. The filmworthiness of this true story derives precisely from the fact that it resolves the ethical dilemma in a way that now appears remarkably unconventional. Under the new necroethics of imperial warfare, moral dilemmas that pit the life of soldiers against that of civilians are now routinely resolved in favour of the former. In the opening scene of *American Sniper*, a man stands on a rooftop talking on his cell phone as he watches a US convoy. Thinking that he may be reporting troop movement to insurgent fighters, Kyle radios in for authorization to take him down. His commanding officer replies 'if you think he's reporting troop movement you have a green-light'. Goat, Kyle's spotter, jokingly interjects that 'he could be calling his old lady'. Kyle takes a deep inhale, dips his shoulders and prepares to take the shot, on the mere suspicion that the man is a militant with presumed sympathy for Iraqi insurgents.[51]

As noted by Chamayou, drone warfare further radicalizes these normative swings by doing away with combat altogether. Drones eliminate the very possibility of reciprocation, as the enemy cannot defend itself or retaliate. By doing so, drones create a new, unconventional regime of violence in which imperial combatants can kill but cannot be killed, taking the principle of combatant immunity to new logical extremes. The very notion of war therefore enters into crisis. Without the possibility of reciprocation, war turns into militarized manhunt, the organized search and elimination of hostiles on the run.[52] By sparing imperial soldiers any exposure to death, drones completely destabilize military ethics, which traditionally value courage, self-sacrifice and readiness to die. In the last scene of *Full Metal Jacket*'s opening act (the boot camp), Gunnery Sergeant Hartman – Kubrick's infamous drill instructor – lectures his men on graduation day: 'Most of you will go to Vietnam. Some of you will not come back. But always remember this: marines die, that's what we're here for!'

If killing and being killed is the essence of warfare, drone killings, by permitting to crush the enemy without ever risking one's own skin, produce a profound crisis in military ethos.[53] Revealingly, some of the most virulent critics of drones have been Air Force pilots, who have derided drone

---

50 Peter Berg, USA, 2013.
51 The man on the roof is not shot as he hangs up and steps away before Kyle is able to pull the trigger.
52 Chamayou, *A Theory of the Drone*, 30–7.
53 Chamayou, *A Theory of the Drone*, 96–106.

operation as a cowardly activity that erodes traditional military values and is 'more akin to the practices of video-gaming joystick jockeys than that of combat soldiers'.⁵⁴ In *Good Kill*, Egan's bitterness and depression come less from the questionable morality of his actions than from a sense of dishonour and longing for genuine combat experience, having been yanked from the cockpit of his former F-16 fighter jet and placed in a trailer in Nevada: 'I am a pilot and I'm not flying [...] I miss the fear. You're up in the sky, something can happen. There's a risk, you know? [Here] we've got no skin in the game. I feel like a coward every day. Taking pot shots from half a world away in an air-conditioned cubicle. Worst thing that can happen to me is carpal tunnel or I spill coffee on my lap.'

Sacrifice and bravery are not, of course, completely absent from drone warfare. Drone pilots can experience high levels of stress, guilt and psychological trauma, from the realization of their own destructiveness and the difficulty in compartmentalizing, due to the lack of transition time between mission and regular life. Yet bravery is defined no longer by exposure to violent death but by exposure of one's psychic vulnerability to the effects of dronized homicide.⁵⁵ A stream of films have been produced since 9/11, including *Good Kill*, that depict the psychic wounds inflicted upon 'our' military men and women in the global war on terror. Critically though, the attention drawn to the imperial soldier's psychic wounds – as well as omitting the fact that drones inflict PTSD to entire populations in the Global South who suffer from constant exposure to death from the sky⁵⁶ – typically serves to confer an 'ethico-heroic aura' to a cowardly killing machine, giving it a legitimacy it could not otherwise acquire.⁵⁷

Whatever one's position on the normalizing function of films, one thing is clear: the global war on terror completely dislocates the normative framework originally designed to regulate armed conflicts. Fałkowska-Clarys and Koutroulis, in their chapter, do not fully acknowledge the difficulty of applying old *in bello* categories to the war on terror. This is problematic since, as noted by Chamayou, 'to apply norms designed for a conflict to slaughtering practices, and to be willing to pursue the discussion without questioning the presumption that these practices still stem from

---

54 Jesse Kirkpatrick, 'Drones and the Martial Virtue Courage' (2015) 14 *Journal of Military Ethics* 202.
55 Chamayou, *A Theory of the Drone*, 103.
56 James Cavallaro, Stephan Sonnenberg and Sarah Knuckey, *Living Under Drones: Death, Injury, and Trauma to Civilians from US Drone Practices in Pakistan* (Stanford: Stanford International Human Rights and Conflict Resolution Clinic, 2012).
57 Chamayou, *A Theory of the Drone*, 105.

within that normative framework, ratifies a fatal confusion of genres'.[58] Fałkowska-Clarys and Koutroulis do allude to a certain 'inadequacy' of traditional humanitarian principles to govern new forms of war. But theirs is an argument about the changing materiality of warfare, whereas Chamayou suggests something more radical: modern imperial warfare (particularly drone warfare) is not, in actual fact, warfare at all but something altogether different, a 'unilateral relationship of death-dealing'.[59] To apply *jus in bello* norms to something that is no longer *bellum* proper renders this transformation invisible and naturalizes it.

Conclusion: de-sanitizing war

By way of conclusion, I want to respond briefly to Fałkowska-Clarys and Koutroulis' assertion that, in showing atrocities committed by armed forces without taking a strong moral stance against violations of the laws of war, films risk 'trivializing' these atrocities, influencing both the public and soldiers themselves.[60] Through constant cinematic exposure to violations of humanitarian law, they argue, people may start viewing the horrors of war 'in a detached way' and become numb to – or more accepting of – certain behaviours in time of war. Whilst it is entirely plausible that films – and popular culture more generally – play a role in shaping public conscience and affect people's perception of what is right, what is possible and what is necessary in specific circumstances (as I have indeed argued earlier), this view needs to be qualified in important ways.

Films, to begin with, often depict certain practices to spark outrage and raise, rather than lower, our collective state of consciousness. Leaving aside the whole genre of human rights cinema – the main purpose of which is to raise awareness and knowledge of human rights (often with all the traits and biases of the human rights movement[61]) – feature films can play a powerful role in mainstreaming human rights violations with a degree of efficacy that historians' or victims' accounts often fail to achieve. To be clear, films can elicit inappropriate responses to atrocities, for instance numbness or perverse pleasure, be it by aestheticizing them or by transfiguring them into a thrilling spectacle. Films also tend to foreground what Žižek calls subjective violence – that carried out by identifiable evil agents (e.g.

---

58 Chamayou, *A Theory of the Drone*, 163.
59 Chamayou, *A Theory of the Drone*, 162.
60 Fałkowska-Clarys and Koutroulis in this volume, pp. 128–52.
61 See Sonia Tascon, 'Considering Human Rights Films, Representation, and Ethics: Whose Face?' (2012) 34 *Human Rights Quarterly* 864.

criminals or terrorists) – as the most visible mode of violence, at the expense of the objective violence of our economic and political systems.[62] Much depends on who is looking at whom and how, and on the film's aesthetic and narrative choices. But there is no doubt that films can elicit compassion, challenge dominant perceptions and break through spectators' ignorance, indifference or denial.[63]

Aside from these general considerations, I take issue with the notion that films ought to place greater emphasis on the role of humanitarian law as a principle of moderation in war. As Moyn has recently noted, there is a distinct possibility that sanitizing war by bringing its conduct within the bonds of legal constraints may paradoxically make it more enduring. The 'humanization' of war – a legitimate goal in the short term – makes recourse to it more tolerable in the long term, or at the very least renders its legitimation easier for various actors and audiences. Focusing on the 'hygiene' of war distracts us from questioning the propriety of aggressive warfare in the first instance.[64] The danger is that, by cleaning up war and scrubbing it of its most outrageous excesses, one renders principled opposition to it comparatively more difficult. By emphasizing the formal prohibitory aspects of *jus in bello*, lawyers and humanitarians might 'sanitize and normalize the grave reality that it regulates', thus facilitating the advent of the 'forever war'.[65]

War is, in the words of Joker in *Full Metal Jacket*'s final scene, 'a world of shit'. Whilst law can help prevent some of the worst excesses of war, it can never completely eliminate war's inherent and unredeemable shitness. Perhaps, then, films' greatest value lies not in comforting but in unsettling the liberal intuition that war can be fought humanely, by showing that the trees of a 'good kill' always conceal 'a forest of tombs'.[66] *Full Metal Jacket*'s finale is so great precisely because it symbolizes the crushing reality of war in a decidedly unheroic tone, with no redemptive resolution. A pacifist, Joker is turned into an agent of sadistic destruction and marches on in a wasteland of smoke and fire, as the Marines chant the Mickey Mouse Club theme song in an eerie funeral procession for their lost innocence. As the final images

---

62 Slavoj Žižek, *Violence* (London: Profile Books, 2008).
63 On these themes, see Shohini Chaudhuri, *Cinema of the Dark Side: Atrocity and the Ethics of Film Spectatorship* (Edinburgh: Edinburgh University Press, 2014).
64 Samuel Moyn, 'Toward a History of Clean and Endless War', *Just Security* (9 October 2015), www.justsecurity.org/26697/sanitizing-war-endlessness, accessed 26 November 2020.
65 Eliav Lieblich, 'The Facilitative Function of *Jus in Bello*' (2019) 30 *European Journal of International Law*, 321–40.
66 Chamayou, *A Theory of the Drone*, 190.

fade, we hear the Rolling Stones' 'Paint It Black' on the sound track, a final expression of Kubrick's tragic vision of history and lack of optimism about the possibility of change.

> I look inside myself and see my heart is black
> I see my red door I must have it painted black
> Maybe then I'll fade away and not have to face the facts
> It's not easy facin' up, when your whole world is black.

11

Presentations and representations of international law in films and TV series

Serge Sur

When the editors of this most interesting book invited me to comment on its chapters, I felt very much honoured and also challenged. I happen to have written essays about cinema, but in a spirit of analysis rather than synthesis. That is to say, I selected a restricted number of films, without focusing on international law per se.[1] Ever since its inception, cinema has inspired many written pieces, notably artistic or technical considerations. It has progressed, a long time ago, from the status of mere entertainment to that of art in its own right, a reflection of its time, perpetuating, in a way, the role of novels as they were in the nineteenth century. Regarding law, symposiums organized by legal scholars have proliferated during the past few years, for instance in La Rochelle or Perpignan. There, one can measure how their vision of films is detailed and precise, and the number and calibre of cinema lovers is impressive. The lens of international law is less frequent; I will go back to that matter. That said, I admire the quality of the various contributions, the writers' wit and intelligence, their culture and their insights on the immense corpus of films that may fit our theme.

To present my conclusive considerations, the best structure I could find for my chapter is a two-part plan, in accordance with a French tradition. Those two parts allow me to tackle the matter of international law in film, and, let's say it now, to gauge how much it is unknown or wrongly known there. What is the place of international law in film dramaturgy

---

1 Serge Sur, *Plaisirs du cinéma. Le monde et ses miroirs* (Paris: France-Empire-Monde, 2010), prefaced by Jean Tulard. To deal with the matter of self-quoting once and for all, I will simply indicate that while this volume regards international relations and the evolution of domestic societies, three chapters may be more closely related to the following developments: 'French History As Seen By Jean Renoir – *La Règle du jeu* (1939) – *La Marseillaise* (1938) – *La Grande illusion* (1937)'; 'Two American Reflections on Violence – *High Noon*, Fred Zinnemann, 1952 – *The Man Who Shot Liberty Valance*, John Ford (1961)'; 'Two Films by Pascal Bonitzer or Witty Plays on Dialectics – *Rien sur Robert* (1998) – *Petites coutures* (2003)'.

indeed? Most of the time, it is accessory, and more implicit than visible. One can always analyse cinema with this perspective, but international law is generally ignored or deformed. Thus, it becomes relevant to ask oneself the reasons behind such distortions and transgressions, probably connected to the constraints of storytelling for film, more concerned with disruptions than normality. They are more deeply connected to the goals of films, those goals implying to use the law as a tool rather than show it.

What is the place of international law in film?

Before we get to the heart of the matter, one can ask oneself whether film, in its current form, is dying – without international law playing any sort of part in it, fortunately. To put it simply, film's classical format of ninety minutes in a dark room is deeply threatened. This very dimension does not hold anymore, and two-hour or three-hour formats are becoming frequent. As a linear narrative has become boring, surprises and plot twists are needed – excesses that grow tiring instead of sparking more interest. A talented filmmaker, Pascal Bonitzer,[2] observed that audio-visual creativity – screenplays, direction, narrative dynamics – is found more today in British and American TV series than in film, because of stricter technical constraints and a more vibrant sequential dynamics. He adds that Hollywood no longer produces interesting new material, being limited to big guns and violence for teenagers, including disaster movies, or bland remakes. Moreover, audio-visual works are much more seen on a screen, on TV or on the Internet, than in film theatres.

That conclusion may be reached with some nostalgia, since nothing will ever replace the magic of silver screens, their animated hypnoses and the collective feelings they aroused. But nostalgia is recurring and cinema is an art in nostalgia. It has continuously evolved, from silent movies to films with sound then speech, with colour, in Cinemascope, from theatres to DVDs, and even mobile devices now ... Some filmmakers, even high-calibre ones such as René Clair or Charles Chaplin, thought that cinema died with the introduction of speech, and was diminished to the status of recorded stage-plays. The next step remains unknown, yet the question of the place of international law remains constant. It seems to me that, generally, one

---

2 Already quoted in note 1. Also, the author of *Cherchez Hortense* (Pascal Bonitzer, France, 2012), a film about identity obviously pertaining to international relations in a context of migrations and globalisation. Raphaëlle Leblanc has written a remarkable article about it: 'Identity as a Tall Tale: *Cherchez Hortense* by Pascal Bonitzer – from ID Papers to Love Letters' (2014) 66 *Questions Internationales* 115–21.

may first observe that cinema – in a broad sense, implying all audio-visual creations – and international law share a sense of imagination and staging. Law, indeed, belongs to the realm of imagination, even if it aspires to a performative imagination and not merely speculative, unlike film. Here, we must confront these imaginations and their staging.

Imagination and dramaturgy in film

Most of the time, when films are built around an organized narrative, the imagination and staging of film rely on classical rules of performance, where the horizontal shooting set, then the vertical screen, replace the stage. A comparison with theatre is unavoidable, but the cinematic form, which integrates a musical dimension and a less visible choreographic one, is certainly closer to opera, the richest and most complete show. One of the epitomes is the *Godfather* saga,[3] a true opera as well as a treatise in political science, where law also plays a part. You'll remember that in the first *Godfather*, a meeting is organized at the top of New York mafia's 'five families' to settle their feud peacefully. How can one not think of the UN Security Council and its five permanent members, eternal rivals, yet condemned to cooperate if they want to avoid confrontation? An implicit reference to international law is made, then an arrangement is found. Is this a metaphor? Was it on Francis Ford Coppola's mind? A specialist in international law cannot but conflate both images.

This type of staging rests basically on a drama between three archetypes: passion, reason, rules – and this is where law comes in. It is another dimension of the classical rules of three unities. Passion stands for irrationality, the impulses and human wanderings that make the trials and tribulations; here it must be reminded that it is not a detail, but the drive within the work, the 'pitch' according to a now familiar vocabulary. Reason means the logic of events, the order of things that forms the frame of action but also the strategy that will allow characters to defuse or appease passions. Rules stand for social order, whether it should be maintained or re-established. Thus, in a crime film, the killing impulse disrupts public order; the investigation, then the arrest of the murderer, restore harmony.

---

3 *The Godfather* (Francis Ford Coppola, USA, 1972) based on a novel by Mario Puzo, featuring Marlon Brando, Al Pacino, James Caan, Robert Duvall, Diane Keaton; *The Godfather: Part II* (Francis Ford Coppola, USA, 1974), same cast except Marlon Brando, also featuring Robert de Niro; *The Godfather: Part III* (Francis Ford Coppola, USA,1990) same cast without Robert Duvall and Robert de Niro, also featuring Andy Garcia. Nino Rota composed the score of all three instalments.

This three-character dialectics is excellently summarized in the last verse of Corneille's *Le Cid*: 'Rely on time, your valour, and your king' (translated by A.S. Kline, 2007). Time stands for reason, valour for passion and the king for the law. When passion prevails, disorder and suffering will take the first seat and the story will be a tragedy. When reason does, the story becomes comedy and when the law prevails, the story is both comic and tragic with a happy ending.

Imagination and dramaturgy in law

For their part, imagination and dramaturgy in law rely on standards, explicit or implicit rules, on the law itself as mentioned, that is to say in its broader sense. Indeed, all standards do not pertain to law in the narrow sense of positive law. They may pertain to natural law, and conflicts between those two types of standards are an active dramatic device. The notion, then, needs to be broadened. Thus, an important dimension of Western-style films is to illustrate the transition from a state of nature to a state of society with the rule of public law, and at the very least their conflict. Standards may also pertain to morals and religion. They can even be extended to logic, the rational strategy that commands the efficiency of behaviours, including the use of tricks of reason: indirect means. It is the well-known Weberian opposition between ethics of belief and ethics of responsibility. Yet these standards for rational behaviour do not keep us in this framework, since they pertain to reason as acting device, not as law. Law-involving dramaturgy involves conflicts between standards, either between same-category standards or different-category ones, yet still belonging to the legal universe in its broader sense.

It is worth mentioning an illustration of these conflicts between norms with *The Bridge on the River Kwai*,[4] a film that Olivier Corten and François Dubuisson analysed with great subtlety.[5] It shows the radical opposition between two conceptions of the law of war and military honour, the Japanese one being *bushido*. For Colonel Saito, prisoners are no longer soldiers since they failed and surrendered, they should have got themselves killed or killed themselves, particularly officers. For Colonel Nicholson, the Geneva Conventions prescribe that prisoner officers cannot be forced to work – as an aside, Japan is not party to any of these Conventions. Such is the explicit, on-screen conflict. But as one knows, film knows on-screen and off-screen,

---

4 *The Bridge on the River Kwai* (David Lean, UK, 1957) based on a novel by Pierre Boulle and featuring amongst others William Holden, Alec Guinness, Sessue Hayakawa.
5 See Chapter 1 of this book.

and what goes on off-screen might be the most important part. Thus, as a phantom thread behind this normative conflict lies implicit conflict between civilization and barbarians, the United Kingdom being civilized and Japan barbaric here, and the civilized West will show barbarians that they cannot build the bridge without the active, yet voluntary contribution of British officers. Order is restored and, fundamentally, reason, when the bridge, once finally completed, is destroyed by a commando led by an American officer.

We are here at the intersection between on-screen and off-screen. Yet we must go further, since the reality of off-screen is different. It opposes three, not two, types of norms. The third and last type, the one that prevails, is that of *jus ad bellum*, active war, that commands the bridge be destroyed. It wins over *jus in bello*, passive and, in this context, defeatist. It is not by chance that the commando is led by an American officer. The message of the film dismisses both the Japanese and the British, Japanese imperialism and British colonialism, two hierarchical societies, equally archaic, each wanting to dominate the other: by building the bridge, British prisoners will show the Japanese they will do better. By destroying their common work, the film states that this confrontation belongs to the past and justifies American order, at least as it perceives itself, that of the world to come, both lawful and rational, and in the present moment that of war, warring war if I may say so, that of the fight against aggression. The commando may have been organised by the British commandment, but the decisive role of American officer Shears is triggered when, as a prisoner himself, he evades, showing that the pursuit of war must prevail over the status of prisoner.

Cinema as an art of representation and law as a technique for forging concepts

In this respect, the two fields veer apart. Representation belongs on-screen, forging concepts belongs off-screen. Contributions to this volume have largely been devoted to off-screen, since this is the field that fosters commentary, understanding of films, even beyond their intentions. After all, their teachings may exceed the deliberate intents of filmmakers, all the more that a movie is a collective work gathering together multiple contributions, sometimes the written work that inspired it, screenwriters, directors, larger cultural context, and viewers add their personal interpretation, imbued with their own conceptions. And it is just and proper that off-screen should not irrupt on-screen, because the risk is to simplify and deplete meaning. Characters find themselves constrained in pre-made interpretations, reduced to the role of mere puppets with all-too-visible strings. This is one of the reasons why international law can only with difficulty appear as a main actor in film, because the fact that it is a concept sends it, for logical and dramatic reasons, off-screen.

Merging off-screen and on-screen results in attrition, as shown by science fiction movies, a genre in themselves. One may disagree, but I stand by my opinion: on the whole, its image-illustrated conceptualization may be dramatic, filled with film virtuosity and special effects, but intellectually, they are poor, especially as they are more and more imbued with the mechanical and impulsive violence of video games, which are loved by teenagers all over the world. In broader terms, science fiction films are the movie equivalent of photo-novels. It is known that photo-novels magnify passions. The audience is projected into a fantasy world with which the average reader identifies: the nurse marries the brilliant doctor, the CEO falls in love with his assistant, the pilot falls for the stewardess, after various tribulations and upheavals. In the same vein, the imaginary world of science fiction in film is restricted, and the utopia and anticipation it purports to illustrate really are a nod to the past. It belongs to heterotopia more than utopia, by transferring known information, unremarkable anticipation, recycling in a supposed future stories that have already been lived.

Robots, aliens, unlikely monsters and hidden benefactors, intergalactic conflicts fought with impressive spaceships confer a cosmic dimension to earthly disputes: the array takes us back to the past and effects human self-aggrandizement. Back to the past: *Star Trek*[6] has been mentioned, this multiform saga brimming with simplified normative conflicts.[7] When they evoke a conflict beginning by a dispute on a frontier river, the adventures of the Federation of United Planets nod, for instance, to the history of Rome and a legal dispute around a treaty. Thus began the Punic wars according to Polybius, who wrote in the second century BC.[8] Utopia is everything that did not happen in the history of the Roman people, it has been said. Science fiction often rests on the transposition of Roman-Greek Antiquity. Magnification: either we are confronted with 'augmented men'[9] ('enhanced

---

6 A series of films, between 1979 and a future where man has never gone before, prolonging *usque ad nauseam* a TV series (1969–79) and the tribulations of the Federation of United Planets, for the repetitive enjoyment of a young audience.

7 See Chapter 2 in this volume.

8 Polybius (approx. 208–126 BC). Politician, military and diplomat, political theorist and historian. A Greek who fought against Rome, then a hostage allied to Rome and a conciliator between Rome and Greece. Fascinated by the Eternal City's rise to power, author of a monumental *General History*, of which only a fragment subsists. His method is close to Thucydides'.

9 The theme is that of augmenting human capacities with neotechnologies and protheses, and is at the heart of a debate on humanism, consciousness, freedom. See, for instance, Bernard Claverie, *L'homme augmenté. Néotechnologies pour un dépassement du*

man') saved and improved by robotization, in a technologic normativity based on *RoboCop*[10] dissolving law and liberty – which doesn't belong to fiction but anticipation – or to a variant: more or less human-like extraterrestrials.

The victories of this superior humankind in such normative conflicts are never final, since the eternal struggle between Good and Evil must be maintained, and the next instalment must be prepared. This naively didactic reduction, a bit amended by humour, is so obvious that it loses any other interest than entertainment. I will make an exception, not for the illustration of international law but for cinematographic quality, for the series *Men in Black*[11] which belongs to science fiction as parody by being an open satire of contemporary US society, its obsession for social control, conspiracy and secret dominance. On the reverse, the best films do not present a visible message, and particularly not a single message, they remain in open-ended ambiguity. To quote François Jullien,[12] 'a wise man has no opinion'. Let us compare *The Bridge on the River Kwai* to Renoir's *Grand Illusion*.[13] The latter illustrates Renoir's quip: everyone has their reasons, and it is frightening. There, too, prisoners do evade to resume fighting, but nobody is judged, everyone follows their own standards and the audience chooses theirs.

International law as an unlikely cinematographic object

It seems that we have strayed far from law. But it is also true that international law does not easily become an object for film. It can be understood since, if international law is properly and wholly enforced, fulfilling its goal, it

---

   corps et de la pensée (Paris: L'Harmattan, 2010). The term 'augmented man' is a neutral choice in contrast with the original phrase 'enhanced' man which hints at an improvement.
10 *RoboCop* (Paul Verhoeven, USA, 1987), starring Peter Weller and Nancy Allen. Followed by *RoboCop* 2 (Irvin Kershner, USA, 1990) and 3 (Fred Dekker, USA, 1993); in a way it is a reinterpration of Frankenstein's creature.
11 *Men in Black* (Barry Sonnenfeld, USA, 1997) starring Tommy Lee Jones and Will Smith. Sweet satire of films milking, in a frightening way, the theme of invaders, but also of conspiracy theories that suppose the presence of world dominators hidden behind daily appearances – in point, protective and well-meaning ones. Followed by *Men in Black* II (2002) and III (2012).
12 François Jullien, philosopher and Sinologist, expert in analysing differences between Western and Eastern thinking: *Le Détour et l'accès, Stratégies du sens en Chine, en Grèce* (Paris: Grasset, 1995); *Traité de l'efficacité* (Paris: Grasset, 1997); *Un Sage est sans idée, ou l'autre de la philosophie (L'ordre philosophique)* (Paris: Seuil, 1998).
13 See note 1 above.

regulates peaceful relations and allows to settle potential disagreements in peace and quiet: a minimal dramaturgy of sorts. It moderates passions and frustrations, be they historical or other, brings reason to interactions and behaviours, and produces harmony. Films are about catharsis or excitation and peace has no history. Diplomatic negotiations, discussions pertaining to drafting a treaty, nuances in picking terms for a settlement may be compelling to experts that can appreciate their stakes; the greater audience would fall asleep, and not many would stay until the end. Reading the General Lessons in International Law by The Hague Academy may be enlightening, rich in teachings, stimulating for the mind, but it is no thriller. Doctrinal conflicts do not set audiences on fire and do not translate well into film. The disputes arising from them, in the meaning of rhetorical *disputatio*, tend to happen in the quiet, friendly context of volumes like ours.

Thus, cinema struggles to use international law as an interesting dramatic device. A movie like *Quai d'Orsay*,[14] largely dealing with the UN debate about the planned US intervention in Iraq in 2003 and the French-US opposition against the Security Council, practically leaves out international law. Negotiation, an object of literature,[15] with its finer points, discussions, delays, hidden depths, hardly lends itself to the quickness and aggregation of meanings of film. It can only be tackled with shortcuts or metaphors. Here again, *The Godfather*,[16] especially the first two instalments, is a model. Negotiation is permanent, underpinned by the use of force and threats – offers you cannot refuse – leading to an infinitely precarious balance. Partners are always virtual allies and potential enemies, they nurture old grudges and frustrations, betrayal is always in sight, and failures end in armed violence. This is a classical depiction of inter-State relations. As for neutrality, *La bataille du Rio de la Plata*[17] shows us the German juggernaut Graf von Spee chased by British ships in 1939. It finds shelter in a Montevideo haven, which it must leave because Uruguay is a neutral country. The diplomatic manoeuvres of British and French ambassadors to Uruguayan authorities are less dramatic than the spectacular naval fight scenes and the ultimate deliberate flooding of the ship.

War, war against each and everyone, to exist, to make one's place under the sun, every conscious being seeks for the death of the other. Taking this logic

---

14 Bertrand Tavernier, France, 2013, starring Thierry Lhermitte, Raphael Personnaz, Niels Arestrup, Julie Gayet.
15 See for instance Francis Walder, *The Negotiators* (New York: McDowell, Obolensky, 1959).
16 See note 3 above.
17 *The Battle of the River Plate* (Michael Powell and Emeric Presslanger, UK, 1956) starring John Gregson, Anthony Quayle, Peter Finch.

to the extreme, one might argue that international law can only be shown as a shadow, either when it is absent, or when it is distorted, transgressed, violated. The absence of international law equates anomia, a lawless world devoid of rules, adding to the loneliness of its inhabitants. 'There is no such thing as society',[18] to quote Margaret Thatcher's famous Hobbesian quip. If there is no specific international society, there is no international law either. But Hobbes eventually coined the Leviathan, which, at least, ensures security at the price of slavery. Such is not the case on an international level: if there is a Leviathan, films prefer to show hidden conspiracies, clandestine domination, invisible masters, predatory and driven by foul intentions, general insecurity.[19] Distortions, transgressions and violations underline the inconsistencies, lack of relevance, powerlessness of international law. Between the two stretches the vast domain of espionage films, which do not deny this law but ignore it, since it sort of takes a backseat, as espionage is not forbidden by international law.

One exception, a response to transgressions and violations, might be the court film, which stages and represents legal proceedings and a final court settlement with strong stakes: the freedom or very life of the accused, but also the resolution of a puzzle – the *whodunit* mocked by Alfred Hitchcock.[20] A trial, with its ritualized proceedings, its drama, is a whole cinematic genre largely exploited by US film, thanks to the accusation procedure, and mostly internal trials, those urban and civilized variants of the duel. They are the offspring of the duels that were one of the main devices in Westerns. In both cases, there is are legal rules for the face-off, and in trial law provides both the framework and the instruments for confrontation. Resources are much more scarce on an international level. The Nuremberg and Tokyo trials were mainly the subject of memorial documentary films.[21] The development of international criminal justice, with international criminal

---

18 From an interview with *Women's Own Magazine*, 31 October 1987: 'Who is society? There is no such thing! There are individual men and women and there are families and no government can do anything except through people and people look to themselves first. It is our duty to look after ourselves'.
19 An otherwise minor film gives an instance of this classical theme: *The Adjustment Bureau* (George Nolfi, USA, 2011) starring Matt Damon and Emily Blunt. See Serge Sur, '*Le vote à l'écran: The Man Who Shot Liberty Valance*, John Ford—*The Adjustment Bureau*, George Nolfi—de la construction de la démocratie à l'illusion démocratique' (2012) 21 *Politeia* 48–58.
20 See the conversations between Alfred Hitchcock and François Truffaut, *Hitchcock-Truffaut, édition definitive* (Paris: Gallimard, 2003).
21 Two miniseries were nevertheless devoted to these international trials: *Nuremberg* (Yves Simoneau, Canada/USA, 2000); *The Tokyo Trials* (Pieter Verhoeff and Rob W. King, Japan/The Netherlands/Canada, 2016).

tribunals established by the Security Council and the International Criminal Tribunal created by the Rome statute are still too recent to nourish a genuine subcategory of the genre.[22] In Polanski's *The Ghost Writer*[23] for instance, the shadow of the Criminal Court, rather than its reality, is evoked.

Distortion and transgressions of international law according to films' classification

Here, one must remain within the boundaries of what has been presented and discussed, even when allowing oneself a few incursions at the edges. It is clear that one could only give a starring role to a few elements in a huge cinematographic corpus, about a theme extremely vast in itself. In this exploration, very diverse film genres or registers have been evoked. Those discussed most frequently belong to different genres. Is international law perceived and presented differently according to these registers, and how? First, one should give a few precisions on the genres or registers thus considered, then keep and illustrate those that seem the most relevant within our context, that is to say propaganda films, militant films and parodies.

A few examples of classification

One can reject the distinction between *humdrum* and *ham-dram films*, not because it would be purely subjective but because it hardly seems useful here. The equalizing effect of screen and camera may lead to a confusion. Humdrum films, a rather colloquial but useful term, designates films devoid of interest, originality, boring, badly acted, that seem to have been interpreted and filmed out of a sense of duty, not conviction, or devoid of talent. To each their own. For a cinephile, especially when rushed or tired, they make analysis easier because they simplify or caricature, and through their own clumsiness show better the devices, tricks and seams of film. Good films are complex, rich, ambiguous, discretely open to multiple interpretations, where humdrum films are first drafts, often pretentious at that.

---

22 However, some recent films and series evoke the activities of international criminal courts (see, amongst others, *Sometimes in April* (Raoul Peck, HBO, Rwanda, France/United States, 2005); *Storm* (Hans-Christian Schmid, 2010); *Largo Winch II – The Burma Conspiracy* (Jérôme Salle, France/Belgium/Germany, 2010); *Black Earth Rising* (Hugo Blick, BBC Two & Netflix, UK, 2018)). See also Anne Lagerwall's chapter (Chapter 6) in this book. Whether this will lead to the production of a specific subgenre remains to be determined.
23 Roman Polanski, France/Germany/UK, 2010; starring Ewan McGregor, Pierce Brosnan, Kim Cattrall.

Ham-dram films, on the contrary, possess a certain unpretentious charm, a peculiar atmosphere, both old-fashioned and light-hearted. They can be, and often are, minor works in the filmography of major authors, either because of their small budget or their thin scenario. In the same spirit, they're often interpreted by good actors having some fun at hamming it up. They have no international career. Like small wines, they don't get exported, which adds to their idiosyncratic character. To take an example, one might think about Claude Chabrol's minor period, with his espionage or action films around the character of the Tiger, *Le Tigre aime la chair fraîche* or *Le Tigre se parfume à la dynamite*.[24] His magnum opus in this regard seems to be *Marie-Chantal contre Dr Kha*,[25] staging the somewhat ridiculous disappearance of the Tiger. US ham-dram films are most of the time B-movies, often noir, illustrating the violence of US society: thus, ham-dram films are in sync with a national *ethos*.

Let us, precisely, do without *films' national spirit*. Indeed, there are different national spirits in film, even though Hollywood was the melting pot of multiple cultures, enlivened by directors trained in Europe and elevated by a great number of Jewish filmmakers fleeing anti-Semitic persecution in Europe. Many of the films mentioned and analysed here have been made in the United States, and the domination of US film is overbearing. Very far behind, British, French and few other films – notably Israeli – have been evoked. One can but notice the scarcity of references to Italian cinema, which was one of the richest and most remarkable in the world. *Was*, unfortunately, not *is*; Italian excellence now seems to reside within the origin of some of the best US filmmakers. Why such scarcity? Maybe because Italian films are turned more towards their society than the outside world, sign of a national spirit that shed its international ambitions after fascism.

There now remains a third mode of classification for genres and registers, between *propaganda films*, *militant films* and *parodies*. Such is the distinction we will cultivate here. These three categories do not pertain to any national tradition, but propaganda films are particularly developed in the United States, as we will see later. To summarize it all, propaganda films praise, in one way or another, force and the passions it sets free, blending

---

24 *Le Tigre aime la chair fraîche (Code Name: Tiger)* (Claude Chabrol, France, 1964) starring Roger Hanin, Maria Maudan, Stéphane Audran; *Le Tigre se parfume à la dynamite (Our Agent Tiger)* (Claude Chabrol, France, 1965) starring Roger Hanin, Michel Bouquet, Roger Dumas.
25 *Marie-Chantal contre Dr Kha (Blue Panther)* (Clause Chabrol, France, 1965) starring Marie Laforêt, Stéphane Audran, Francisco Rabal, Serge Reggiani, Charles Denner, Roger Hanin.

the group together and elevating its values. Militant or ideological films focus more on the universal and, in the logic of Antigone, claim for apparent weakness at the service of justice – thus, law, but is it positive law? Parody films mock propaganda more or less openly; they subvert it. They rather belong to reason, disenchanting and putting into perspective – and here, we meet again our three actors under a different perspective: passion, law, reason. What of international law? It is diverted by propaganda, sublimated by ideology and ignored by parody.

Propaganda films

Propaganda films are not only from the United States. All countries, particularly in times of war, are led to use cinema to justify their cause and embellish their pursuit of conflict. More broadly, State intervention always tends, in one way or another, to leverage film as an instrument. Propaganda is a form of lying, and Stendhal observed very perceptively that power lies, now and always.[26] Only the quality of lies is subject to change, he wrote. Cheap lies are for everyman, silver sterling lies will persuade the upper middle class and golden lies will fool a few gentlemen. Hollywood certainly perfected the technique, both under the influence of the State – it is know that the Pentagon has an office in Hollywood and has an interest in screenplays – and more generally that of civil society. Norman Mailer, the screenwriter, wrote that all of US cinema is propaganda and explains it by the end of the Frontier: as it reached the Pacific barrier, the American adventure found shelter in dreams of grandeur and now tries to spread them around the whole world.[27]

This propaganda revolves especially around armed force, violence and war. It is famously perceived much more favourably in the United States than in Europe. It permeates popular US culture, not least cinema and video games, with Militainment, a conglomeration of militarization and entertainment.[28] As for individual violence, it is the salvation and remedy of a lonely individual, abandoned by all, threatened by powerful enemies, without the helpful contribution of absent or corrupt public authorities.

---

26 Stendhal, *Lucien Leuwen*, unfinished novel, written in 1834 and published posthumously (Paris: Le Divan, 1894).
27 Norman Mailer, *Oswald's Tale: An American Mystery* (New York: Random House, 1995).
28 About this concept and its applications, see David Grondin's very enlightening article: 'L'étude des objets, espaces et sites de sécurité de la vie quotidienne: enquête sur la militarisation de la vie américaine par le biais de la culture populaire' (2013) *Etudes internationales* 453–70.

High Noon,²⁹ a Western masterpiece, is a metaphor with a broad scope, both internal and international, individual and collective. This is precisely former presidents Bill Clinton and George W. Bush's favourite film, according to their own words. During the Iraq war in 2003, US papers have compared reluctant Europeans to the population of Hadleyville, turning away in cowardice from Gary Cooper as Sheriff Kane.³⁰ Where there is no law, the state of nature and natural right to self-defence prevail. Thus, force is self-justified, and generous, but, as an effect of propaganda, it is also actually usurped in its presentation, and even self-criticized by US films that preserve, by their self-criticism and this plot twist, a form of purity.

Self-justified force. As is well known, preventive or preemptive legitimate defence as appreciated by the United States for themselves was the doctrine of the George W. Bush administration, reminding one of Bismarck or his disciple von Bülow, chancellor of the Wilhelmian empire, who wrote to the emperor in 1905.³¹ 'To be right or wrong is of no consequence in relationships amongst nations, except if the man who violates the law is not powerful enough to free himself of scruples.' Belgium witnessed the consequences of this perspective in 1914 and 1940. Countless US films implicitly justify US war actions, praising fighters' courage and demonizing the enemy! The theme of invaders is a common one in this type of film, *Aliens* or others, and the prevailing rule is that of their destruction.³² This is an illustration of the conception of Carl Schmitt, for whom the history of international law is but the history of the concept of war.³³ US cinema mostly adheres to this conception, even as the United States has contributed, with the UN Charter, to consecrating a more lawful conception of the use of armed force, a more Kantian one in a way.

29 *High Noon* (Fred Zinnemann, USA, 1952) starring Gary Cooper and Grace Kelly. See note 1.
30 Words by James Woolsey, former CIA director, to the *Wall Street Journal* (25 February 2002): 'It's *High Noon* for the civilized world—Let timorous Europeans go home to their kids.'
31 Guillaume II *in Correspondance secrète de Bülow et de Guillaume II*, foreword by Maurice Muret (Paris: Grasset, 1931).
32 In the famous TV series *The Invaders* (Lorry Cohen, ABC, USA, 1967–68), the ordinary American citizen David Vincent fights almost alone against human-shaped extraterrestrials. The only way out is to destroy them, a metaphor that can be adapted to all exterior perils threatening US isolationism. A more recent example of this US theme is *World Invasion: Battle Los Angeles* (Jonathan Liebesman, USA, 2011) starring Aaron Eckhart and Michelle Rodriguez. A band of heroic Marines saves the city from the attack of mysterious enemies.
33 Carl Schmitt, *Le Nomos de la Terre* (Paris: PUF, 1950).

Generous force. The use of armed force is often presented as an altruistic act, not only destined to individual preservation but also to loftier goals. It is no longer *High Noon*, even though Sheriff Kane saves the town from the predation of a band of wrongdoers, but as a collateral of him defending himself. It is more aptly illustrated by *The Man Who Shot Liberty Valance*,[34] a film in which eliminating a gangster protects a regular citizen but also allows establishing the rule of law: violence acts at the same time as protection, correction and foundation. This force knows how to protect its own – *Saving Private Ryan*[35] depicts a US army that cares about sparing a family that has already been through a lot. It generally fights not only for the United States, but also to protect or set free captive populations. For instance, excerpts have been shown where Bruce Willis, as a faultless warrior, knew how to inspire renewed motivation in his peers at the service of a cause greater than themselves.[36] He did not impose anything, but each and every one determined their own fate freely after his call.

Usurped force. US film is rather fond of attributing to the United States the will to use armed force for altruistic causes, when the reality is rather different. For instance, the champion of freedom did not ratify the Versailles Treaty, when they initiated it. President Wilson wanted peace based on international law, when Clemenceau wanted peace based on security. The pair dialogues during dinner: Clemenceau shows the roasted chicken on the table and quips: 'See this chicken? It believed in international law.' *Se non è vero* … The United States has left European democracies alone to confront Nazi Germany, and it is Germany that declared war on the United States in December 1941. It did not, contrary to a film's propaganda,[37] decrypt German code *Enigma*, since the British and the Polish did it. A film like *Mars Attacks!*[38] depicts a ridiculous French president, ready for a cowardly compromise with little invading green men, and a clear-sighted and brave American president. But, in the recent Syrian affair, the United States renounced to an intervention notably desired by France.

Self-criticism of force. As a caveat to the aforementioned, it is fair to note that US film knows, more and better than others, how to criticize some

---

34 *The Man Who Shot Liberty Valance* (John Ford, USA, 1961) starring James Stewart, John Wayne, Lee Marvin and Vera Miles.
35 *Saving Private Ryan* (Steven Spielberg, USA, 1997) starring Tom Hanks and Matt Damon.
36 See the commentary, in Chapter 5 of this collection, on the film *Tears of the Sun* (Antoine Fuqua, USA, 2003) with Bruce Willis and Monica Bellucci.
37 *U 571* (Jonathan Mostow, France/USA, 2000) starring Harvey Keitel, Bill Paxton and David Keith.
38 Tim Burton, USA, 1996; starring Jack Nicholson, Glenn Close, Annette Benning, Pierce Brosnan and Danny DeVito.

excessive uses of force, either in their principle or in their methods. For instance, the Vietnam war gave rise, very quickly after defeat, to a rush of US films showing the vacuity and the cruelty of this conflict.[39] Compared to the relative scarcity of French cinema about the Algerian war – a film such as *La battaglia di Algeri*[40] had to be produced in Italy and was censored in France for a long time – there is, here, an undeniable superiority of US democracy, founded on the First Amendment and freedom of expression. It is, in a way, the autonomy of civil society manifesting against the State. The same applies, to a lesser degree, to Afghanistan after 2001 and the war in Iraq after 2003.[41] Yet this self-criticism only had limited effects, since excesses like clandestine jails, illicit transfers of inmates without a conviction or even illegal abductions or torture have received no punishment, while the detention centre at Guantanamo is still operational.

Militant cinema

These are films calling on a more elevated conception of law and justice, opposed to the brutal and sometimes immoral logic of States, or even of non-State stakeholders, for instance transnational firms. Their goal is to engage public opinions, they are like the eye of Cain addressing silent reproach to criminals, a vehicle for the spirit of humanitarian or human rights NGOs. They are the weak claiming their own against the strong, in the name of law based on universal values, internalized as much as it is international. One can interpret them as an implicit criticism of positive international law, since this law protects State sovereignty and only imposes minimal obligations on transnational firms. This type of film likes to use emotion as a plot device; they go for the heart. A US film such as *The Constant Gardener*,[42] based on a British novel and directed by a Brazilian director, is an efficient denunciation of the abuse perpetrated by pharmaceutical multinational companies. Concerning States, one of the messages behind *The Interpreter*[43] is the denunciation of the UN's indifference towards dictatorships. In a more

---

39 Amongst the most famous, *Apocalypse Now* (Francis Ford Coppola, USA, 1978); *The Deer Hunter* (Michael Cimino, USA, 1978); *Platoon* (Oliver Stone, USA, 1986); *Full Metal Jacket* (Stanley Kubrick, USA, 1987).
40 *La Battaglia di Algeri* (Gillo Pontecorvo, Italy/Algeria, 1965) starring Jean Martin and Yacef Saadi.
41 Films by Michael Moore are an example of this type of committed political cinema.
42 Fernando Meirelles, USA, 2005; based on John Le Carré's novel of the same name (2001), starring Rachel Weisz, Danny Huston and Bill Nighy.
43 *The Interpreter* (Sydney Pollack, USA, 2004) starring Nicole Kidman, Sean Penn, Catherine Keller and Yvan Attal.

subtle manner, *Wag the Dog*[44] illustrates the fabrication of a US war, but it also belongs to parody, verging on burlesque.

Parodic films

With their irony, the way they do not let themselves be fooled by propagandas or militantism, parodic films represent the return of reason, and a return to reason. They target cinema itself, when it takes itself seriously and wants to grab audiences with passion or glorified values. Its message might pass as disenchantment, the expression of merry pessimism, but it is the more adult, the one that expresses resistance of the mind against disguise. It could find its inspiration from what de Harlay, the *Premier Président*, said to young magistrates bedecked in clothing and ribbons reminiscent of those of aristocrats at the King's Court: 'Masks, I know you for what you are!'.[45] This genre is difficult. As is famously known, it is difficult to make good people laugh and much easier to make them cry. Thus, parodic films number a great many ham-dramas along masterpieces. The greater films in all registers do have a slightly satirical dimension, some distance with their subject. Hitchcock, Kubrick, amongst others, have directed films that do not rely on humour, but their masterpieces contain a slight smile.[46] In all forms of art, comedy is the most challenging and the most accomplished.

We may limit ourselves here to three types of parodic films: French, British and American. It might be too a way of coming back to a national film spirit, since humour does not rely on the same drives, whether it be American gags, British wit, French vaudeville to simplify matters. For the French, let's study the recent OSS 117, a character based on Jean Bruce's espionage novels[47] from the 1950s and 1960s. These two films[48] mock the

---

44 *Wag the Dog* (Barry Levinson, USA, 1998) starring Dustin Hoffman, Robert De Niro, Denis Leary and Anne Heche.
45 Anecdote told by Saint-Simon, *Mémoires* (Paris: Gallimard, coll. Pléiade, 1958).
46 Think, for instance, about *North by Northwest* (Alfred Hitchcock, USA, 1959) or *Lolita* (Stanley Kubrick, USA, 1962). In *North by Northwest*, it is worth noting in passing that the United Nations is presented as a nest of spies.
47 Jean Bruce (1921–63) created the character of Hubert Bonisseur de la Bath, US agent for OSS, an intelligence service before CIA, based on a real agent bearing the actual OSS 117 ID.
48 French films by Michel Hazanavicius. *OSS 117: Cairo, Nest of Spies* (2006), starring Jean Dujardin, Berenice Bejo, Aura Atika, François Damiens and Claude Brosset; *OSS 117: Lost in Rio* (2009), starring Jean Dujardin, Pierre Bellemare, Louise Monot and Rüdiger Vogler.

country's pretentious bid to play in the major league. There is, nevertheless, a certain ambiguity, since in Jean Bruce's novels OSS 117 is a US agent, and in *Le Caire nid d'espions* he gives a Saddam Hussein lookalike a speech worthy of George W. Bush and the neoconservatives, praising a Westernized and democratic Greater Middle East. Since the action takes place just before the Suez expedition in 1956, there is the feeling of a dual target, since the US intervention in Iraq in 2003 is a sort of repetition of this operation's mistakes fifty years after. Moreover, the gag-like humour of these films has a sort of American flavour. It is a parody at times of Spielberg's *Indiana Jones*,[49] a rather satirical character himself.

In another facet of self-criticism, US film also has a parodic register. Thus, Quentin Tarantino's *Inglourious Basterds*[50] mocks the extravagant heroism of war propaganda films, as well as some rosy-coloured excesses of the French Resistance. Yet, it is uncertain whether this satirical dimension was perceived by all spectators, who may have been offended by the excessive violence that is, once again, a parody of US action films. *The Tailor of Panama*,[51] in a way a US-British film – US film, British hero invented by John Le Carré, in a satire of Graham Greene's novels – is a parody of James Bond, like Michel Hazanavicius's OSS 117. As for British cinema, James Bond movies themselves are very ambiguous, being on the one hand a nostalgic glorification of the British Empire and Rule Britannia, on the other hand a rather funny message with its very anachronism and exaggerations. But *The Avengers* series,[52] a contemporary of 007, is deliberately on the side of pastiche.

We may conclude with three examples that summarize it all: the American Jack Bauer, of the TV series *24*,[53] often mocked, takes himself very seriously,

---

49 Steven Spielberg's Indiana Jones saga starring Harrison Ford is composed of four films: *Raiders of the Lost Ark* (1981); *Indiana Jones and the Temple of Doom* (1984); *Indiana Jones and the Last Crusade* (1988); *Indiana Jones and the Kingdom of the Crystal Skull* (2008). This character has had many adaptations in other media, TV series and comics.
50 Quentin Tarantino, USA/Germany, 2009; starring Brad Pitt, Christoph Waltz, Mélanie Laurent, Jacky Ido and Diane Kruger.
51 *The Tailor of Panama* (John Boorman, USA, 2001) based on John Le Carré's novel, starring Pierce Brosnan, Jamie Lee Curtis and Geoffrey Rush. After the Cold War, spies are bored and deal in their own shams. Pierce Brosnan has famously played the part of James Bond.
52 *The Avengers* (ABC Television, UK, 1961–69) then *The New Avengers* (ITV, UK, 1976–77), British TV series around the character of John Steed (Patrick Macnee) and his successive collaborators.
53 Fox, USA, 2001–10, then from 2014 onwards; with Kiefer Sutherland, Canadian-British actor, son of actor Donald Sutherland.

regularly saves the country and develops moral rules for illegality; 007, an aristocrat and a thug, exercises playful transgression of the rules at the service of a lost Empire; OSS 117 is ridiculous, but his assignments are ultimately successful. An Egyptian's interrogation about him is on point: he is either very clever or completely stupid. What more is there to be said? Whatever it was, it was a good show.

12

Cine-legality: international law at the movies

Gerry Simpson

I once heard someone say – in a retrospective on I.A. Richards (the author of *Practical Criticism*) and his concerns with textual interpretation – that *Hamlet* could be about an infinite number of matters but it could not be about the 1984 British Miners' Strike.[1] There was, then, a limit to how much mapping or analogizing one could do. This was not a problem of temporality (we are all happy to accept that Freud is now one of the major influences on *Hamlet*) but was related instead to the question about what a text or a film could, interpretively speaking, bear.[2] There will be international lawyers who might wonder, then, how on earth cinema might speak to their own field of practice. International law is the study of international legal texts (broadly understood to include the practice and psychological bearing of states) or it is what international lawyers do but can it really be what *filmmakers* or the producers of television do?

Well, as this volume makes clear, there have been, at the very least, an impressively considerable number of filmic representations of international law. Indeed, the book begins with a direct encounter between international law and cinema in *The Bridge on the River Kwai*, where Lieutenant Colonel Nicholson (representing rigid formalism, imperial hubris) and Colonel Saito (representing a *bushido* code of honour, political realism) clash over the appropriate interpretation of the Hague Rules and Geneva Conventions as they apply to the use of prisoner-of-war labour. It is these sorts of representations (and the idea of representation is central to the concerns of this book) of international law that are a feature of much of the writing found here.

---

1 In fact, of course, it *could* be about the Miners' Strike.
2 Shakespeare hadn't read Freud when he wrote *Hamlet* (though, presumably, he was subject to the sorts of complexes that Freud later gave a name to) but our readings of *Hamlet* today are impossible without Freud.

But films do not always, or even very often, literalize international law in this way. To take a film I am very fond of, Werner Herzog's 1972 film, *Aguirre: Wrath of God*, what we have is not in any direct sense, a cinematic account of, even a gloss on, international law or international criminal justice. Indeed, *Aguirre* may not be about international law in any indirect sense either. For me, it merely suggests some possibly unusual or heterotopic ways of thinking about the field of international law (ways of thinking to which I have a predisposition in the first place). Needless to say, I am also very disposed towards the work of this sort – and there is much of it – found in this collection of fine chapters.

Before I say something about these, I want to acknowledge that this is a *zeitgeist* moment for international law and visual representations. There have been recent books on international law and its objects, on international criminal law and its artefacts, on international law and art, on the aesthetics of international law. More specifically, we have had a turn to cinema: a symposium in Australia, a European Society of International Law panel in 2014. And there have been publications: Olivier Corten's 2015 book on international law and cinema, Aeyal Gross's and Ruti Teitel's essay on film and transitional justice and Deborah Whitehall's work on Hannah Arendt and film as well as a smattering of essays about film and international law more generally in *The London Review of International Law* and elsewhere.[3] Alongside all of this, there is also, apparently, a series of international legal representations of film (according to Benatar in Chapter 2, the ICJ has been treated to allusions and references to everything from *Alice in Wonderland* to *Game of Thrones*).

Much of this is new but it is not as if this preoccupation with the visual has emerged from nowhere. The ground was cleared some time ago by both those who worked on the aesthetics of law more broadly (Douzinas, Manderson, Goodrich) and those who took an early interest in the documentary or visual aspects of international law (often international

---

3 E.g. Olivier Corten and François Dubuisson (eds), *Du droit international au cinéma. Présentations et représentations du droit international dans les films et les séries télévisées* (Paris: Pedone, 2015); see Daniel Joyce and Gabrielle Simm, 'Zero Dark Thirty: International Law, Film and Representation' (2015) 3:2 *London Review of International Law* 295–318; Kirsten Ainley, Stephen Humphreys and Immi Tallgren (eds), 'International Criminal Justice on/and Film' (2018) 6:1 *London Review of International Law*; Immi Tallgren. 'Come and See? The Power of Images and International Criminal Justice' (2017) 17:2 *International Criminal Law Review* 259–80; Immi Tallgren, 'Watching *Tokyo Trial*' (2017) 5:2 *London Review of International Law* 291–316; Wouter Werner, 'Justice on Screen: A Study of Four Documentary Films on the International Criminal Court' (2016) 29 *Leiden Journal of International Law* 1043.

criminal justice) from *Nuremberg* through to *Lubanga* (Lawrence Douglas' book *The Memory of Justice* is a notable antecedent in this regard).[4] Accompanying this is a recent popularization of aspects of international legality whether it be the *Kony Affair* and its 15 milliseconds of fame, or the references to the Rome Statute dotted around in feature films and television mini-series. So, to take some very obvious examples, one episode of *The West Wing* contained a sub-plot about Head of State immunity while the adaptation of Bernd Schlink's *The Reader* asked us to accept Kate Winslet as a war criminal. Meanwhile, Roman Polanski's *The Ghost Writer* (discussed in some of these chapters) based on Robert Harris' novel, *The Ghost*, featured an ex-British Prime Minister, Adam Lang (a bit like Tony Blair and played by a convincingly slippery Pierce Brosnan), who has ordered the invasion of a country (a bit like Iraq) and who is now holed up in a modernist masterpiece on Cape Cod writing his autobiography – with the help of a softly spoken ghost writer with a very loosely cockney accent (Ewan McGregor) – and taking advice from international lawyers about how likely it is that he will stand trial at The Hague where he is accused of having committed 'crimes against humanity'. This is a film that took itself so seriously that Article 7 of the ICC Statute was actually mentioned in the dialogue. But then Robert Harris had, after all, consulted international criminal lawyers in London as he was researching the book. In one scene, after the Lang/Blair character is described as a 'war criminal', one of his advisers – taking even 'Joint Criminal Enterprise III' a little too far – warns the ghost writer that he himself has become an accomplice to crimes against humanity simply by helping out with the Lang/Blair autobiography (Ewan McGregor has the good grace to adopt a look of surprise when confronted by this claim).

Elsewhere, we have had feature films like *The Interpreter*, *Blood Diamonds* and *Hotel Rwanda* and heavily praised – perhaps overpraised – documentaries such as *The Act of Killing*. It has now got to the point where somebody like Adolf Eichmann – perhaps because he was filmed so assiduously – has generated his own mini-industry of films from *The Specialist* to *The House on Garibaldi Street* to *Labyrinth of Lies* to Margarethe von Trotta's film about Hannah Arendt (with its immortal tag-line 'The woman who saw banality in evil').

As far as origins are concerned, lawyers love to point to *Judgement at Nuremberg* as the *echt* source of all of this. And then they especially like to point out that this was not a film about the *IMT Trial* at all but about a later trial of jurists, known as 'The Justice Trial'. So, this tale of lawyers, and

---

4 This scholarship is usefully described in Corten's and Dubuisson's opening chapter here on methodology.

film and filmic representations of lawyers prosecuting other lawyers, is one place where the whole law/cinema story originates. But as Immi Tallgren and others have shown, the *Nuremberg Trial* itself relied on film as a way of provoking reaction, and, in a double-cinematic moment, the reaction to film footage of the liberation of the camps was itself filmed. And this double cinematic moment was an inversion, both literal and figurative. The film, intended to persecute the persecutors, was shown upside down and made them laugh instead; this laughter then became somehow confirmation of their moral disability and guilt.

Cine-legality performs itself in a number of different modes, then, as this deft collection of chapters – with its editorial commitment to 'pluralism' – amply demonstrates. Quite a few of the chapters do this by documenting and examining the appearance and reappearance of international law across a variety of cinematic (televisual and filmic) moments. In Olivier Corten's chapter on the use of force, for example, he points to the tendency on the part of protagonists in films and television to adopt either an expansive interpretation of the exceptions to the norms prohibiting the use of force or a moral code operating autonomously of those norms and permitting some sort of humanitarian action in violation of the law (viewed as insensitive to human suffering). Interestingly, this is true of both Reaganite action movies (*Rambo*, *Red Dawn*, *Invasion USA*) and liberal-progressive productions (*The West Wing* (President Bartlet here often seen bending the rules of international law in the name of justice); *Three Kings*).

There are exceptions to this belligerent tendency though these tend to come in the guise of pacifist or absurdist critiques of war (*Dr Strangelove* being the most potent) or historical dramas (Corten points to an episode in *The Crown* where a breach of international law is explicitly invoked in an episode in which the Queen reprimands Anthony Eden and Harold Macmillan for their role in the 'unlawful' Suez intervention of 1956). Corten neatly disentangles the ideological dimensions of all of this and the establishment of what he calls, aptly, the 'military-cinematographic complex'.

This idea of an international law perpetually ignored or sidelined is a feature, too, of François Dubuisson's careful deconstruction of the cinema arising out of the Palestine-Israel conflict, a conflict he divides into three phases (the 1948 war and its aftermath, the 1967 war and Palestinian activism, and the contemporary phase of post-Oslo pessimism and hopelessness). In each phase, according to Dubuisson, there is a movement between idealistic and critical conceptions of international law. Yet, interestingly, neither approach seems to offer much solace to Palestinian conceptions of selfhood. In the early phase, the cinema is dominated by a heroic-nationalist style of film-making (Otto Preminger's *Exodus* is the example offered here). Later there is a focus on Palestinian intransigence (if only 'they' would accept the outcomes of international treaty negotiation) and Black Septemberist violent opposition (usually built around a call for compromise by the 'terrorists'). But for Palestinians, international law is either complicit (in its idealistic mode) or irrelevant (in its critical mode).

If Dubuisson writes about the concrete circumstances of a charged political circumstance, in Marco Benatar's essay, by contrast, we have a kind of inter-galactic international law with conventions forbidding the use of Warp Gas, clashes over sovereignty (between the Klingons and the Federation in *Star Trek*), inter-planetary councils issuing ineffectual edicts, and a continual movement between three classic images of the international diplomatic order: constitutionalism (*Battleship Galactica*), idealism (*Star Trek*) and, again, realism (mostly, the law is cruelly neglected in science fiction films (diplomats are shot in the back causing their bodies to dissolve, conventions are torn up ...)). In some respects, though, there is a lot of law here. One sometimes gets this impression from Benatar that the *Star Trek* series has been a litany of territorial disputes including, in one episode, the invocation of a compromissory clause in a treaty. In the end, though, even science fiction cannot escape the iron cage of utopia and apology.

Vincent Chapaux also takes up the question of science fiction but this time from the perspective of interspecies relationships and the spectre of anthropocentrism in international law and sci-fi. Here the curiosity lies in the dominance of an 'anti-specieist' credo in many of the popular science fiction movies (at least those that go beyond the survivalist paradigm) of the last forty years or so. According to Chapaux, films like *Avatar*, *ET*, *District 9* and *Blade Runner* are arguments against the current disposition (in which humans dominate other species and naturalize that domination) and in favour of what Sundhya Pahuja has called a law of encounter.[5]

In his commentary on these chapters by Marco Benatar and Vincent Chapaux, Nicolas Kang-Riou asks what exactly legal scholars can bring to bear on the question of film and law. As he points out, a very common way to approach science fiction is to notice parallels between 'earth international law' (Chapaux) and the alternative universes portrayed in sci-fi film. These worlds may aspire to radical difference but the old practices persist (federation, sovereignty, world government, rebellion) and these familiar legal types can be teased out through forms of analogical reasoning. But Kang-Riou cautions us against adopting only this perspective.

Are there, then, limits to cine-legality, or, perhaps another way to put this is to ask, can cine-legality encompass the disappearance or transcendence

---

5 Sundhya Pahuja, 'Laws of Encounter: A Jurisdictional Account of International Law' (2014) 1:1 *London Review of International Law*.

of international law altogether? Kang-Riou argues that this sometimes happens in a dystopian register when inter-sovereign legality is consumed by centralizing or imperial tendencies (*1984*, *Star Wars*) or where the vision offered is so bleak as to leave little room for the play of legalism (*Robocop*, *Blade Runner*) or where there is a lack of inter-operability of legal rules or communication itself. In such cases, liberal international law becomes, for him, an impossibility.

But, and to return to earth as it were, we might want to ask what sort of restaging film produces when it confronts the present crisis of legality? In some respects, when jurisprudential debates are rehearsed (as with Anne Lagerwall's *Black Earth Rising* exchange between the Prosecutor and a young black man) these seem rather crude juxtapositions between what Lagerwall calls 'romanticized images' (a fiercely moralistic prosecutor, a court with an apparently limitless jurisdictional range) and 'apologetic representations' (state inaction, government cynicism) of international criminal justice. These often feel clunky especially when transcribed. Sometimes, the facts and the law are wrong (*The Ghost Writer* just misstates the number and variety of states that have ratified the Rome Statute, and features a set of rendition crimes that would be unlikely to fall within the court's jurisdiction in any event).

There is a certain cheesiness, too, in the way prosecutors (played by Sharon Stone, say) are always invoking justice or the demands of victims (e.g. by carrying pictures of murdered or violated children in their pockets). And, as Lagerwall points out, there is a whole host of films and documentaries about the international criminal tribunals that seem frankly propagandistic (e.g. *The Reckoning: The Battle for the International Criminal Court*; *In Search of International Justice*; *Hunt for Justice*). In the case of *The Interpreter*, it turns out that the filmmakers promised Kofi Annan that there would be nothing in the film that might embarrass the UN.

Occasionally, films will offer a more fundamental, nuanced critique of international criminal justice. Here, Lagerwall invokes *Hannah Arendt* (2012) (justice as spectacle), *The Emperor* (2012) (a vaguely postcolonial take on the Tokyo Trial), *The Tokyo Trial* (2016) (where the judges are seen thrashing out questions of juridical propriety), *The Reader* (with its sympathetic depiction of a concentration camp guard (played by Kate Winslet)), *L'œil du cyclone* (2015) (in which the figure of the perpetrator-victim is handled with a certain degree of ambiguity); *A War* (2017) (where private kindness and public brutality are set in conversation with each other) and *War Don Don* (2010) (where the sentences handed out to Sierra Leonean war lords are portrayed as punitive and unjust).

When it comes to filmic representations of the cognate field of international humanitarian law, Fałkowska-Clarys and Koutroulis distinguish between those productions that make overt reference to international humanitarian law (surprisingly few, as it turns out) and those with a set of more implicit allusions to the laws of war. When it comes to explicit invocations most of them involve a set of international humanitarian law rules that appear cumbersome and compromising with television and film reflecting, perhaps, the pervasive view of international humanitarian law as having become an antique, unworkable, illusory set of rules.

Fałkowska-Clarys and Koutroulis, though, begin with a rather remarkable film: Peter Berg's *The Lone Survivor* (2013) in which a group of US Navy SEALs decide to strictly comply with the laws of war by refusing to kill three unarmed Afghan goatherds carrying a radio transmitter in the sure knowledge that their own whereabouts will be exposed (it is, and they are all killed after a gun battle with Taliban forces). In other films sympathetic to international humanitarian law, the laws of war are used in a post-hoc fashion to place in question a violent or disproportionate act (an attack on a funeral party (*Snowden*) or a group of first aid responders (*Good Kill*)).

Most treatments of the laws of war in film are much more implicit. In films like *Full Metal Jacket* or *Platoon* we are encouraged to condemn the killing of civilians in Vietnam, or, at least, understand the culture that produces such killing without the benefit of any specific reference to international humanitarian law. But, as Fałkowska-Clarys and Koutroulis point out, other films such as *The Mark of Cain* (2007), *Battle for Haditha* (2007), *In the Valley of Elah* (2007) or, more equivocally, *Apocalypse Now* in effect erase the distinction between combatants and civilians. Indeed, Francis Ford Coppola said recently of the latter: 'this is not an anti-war movie'.[6]

In Chapter 9, Gabrielle Simm returns to some of the ideological questions taken up in the introductory chapter. For her, the film *Osama* can be subjected to a number of different interpretations (an apology for US intervention, a rare example of gender visibility, a white-washing of the Taliban's internal enemies), and this is true of most of the films considered in the book in general. Simm shows us how questions of genre operate to situate the films in question in a particular mode of political engagement but she also notices that the material conditions for film and television production can be important (or at least highly influential) in determining the ideological commitments embedded in these artefacts of cine-legality. Just as important, though, is the interdisciplinary framing undertaken by scholars themselves. The vast majority of films and televisions shows considered in this collection are American (or Western). Simm makes a plea

---

6 www.theguardian.com/film/2019/aug/09/francis-ford-coppola-apocalypse-now-is-not-an-anti-war-film, accessed 1 December 2019.

in her chapter for a productive reframing of the archive to take into account the cine-legalities of the South.

In Chapter 10, Mario Prost makes the very good point that films and television are at their best when they bring out the moral dilemmas at the heart of international law and war. As he puts it:

> Films – and popular culture more generally – play an essential role in forming our affective landscapes. They provide the signs, images, stories, metaphors, plotlines and characters with which we make sense of our lives and the world around us. As such, they create a framework from which we view particular situations and a set of justifications or reasons for a particular course of action.

Shows like *24* produce in the end a 'collective legal consciousness' by constituting the grounds of a legal politics (remaking the sphere of the acceptable, displacing conventional legal rules, becoming sources of juridical authority). They have enormous ideological power, to take up the principle theme of the collection. But Prost also reminds us that films do not have fixed meanings. He is not the first scholar to think into this subject through *Zero Dark Thirty* but he gives us an original reading of the text of the film, with its ambiguities and its complicities. In the end, he points to the aesthetic and moral functions of film, functions that may not be especially closely aligned to the requirements of 'disseminating' the laws of war. To be sure, films 'can elicit inappropriate responses to atrocities, for instance numbness or perverse pleasure, be it by aestheticising them or by transfiguring them into a thrilling spectacle … [as well as foregrounding] … what Žižek calls subjective violence – that carried out by identifiable evil agents (e.g. criminals or terrorists) – as the most visible mode of violence, at the expense of the objective violence of our economic and political systems' but they are not incapable of capturing the truth of a moral-juridical event or dilemma.

In the end, we have a capacious and immensely promising newish discipline of cine-legality, represented in this collection. The archive – what Gabrielle Simm calls 'the panorama of world cinema' – is immense. Let the work begin.

Index

007 215
24 67, 75–6, 82, 177, 183–4, 215, 224
9/11 attacks 74, 130, 135, 145, 148, 183

A War 122, 127, 140, 143, 222
Abu Ghraib prison 183
Abu-Assad, Hany 91
Abyss 47, 55
The Act of Killing 219
Act of Valor 148
Afghanistan Unveiled 179
aggression, threat of, military, crimes of 26, 45, 48, 65, 112–13, 122, 190, 203
Aguirre: Wrath of God 218
Air Force One 64
Al Bashir, Omar 108
Al Qaeda 69, 136, 174
Algerian National Liberation Front (FLN) 140
Algerian War of Independence 140
Alice in Wonderland 22, 218
Alien 47
Aliens 55, 163, 211
Al-Shabaab 149
American Sniper 147, 151, 188, 194
Anaconda 45
The Animatrix 33, 35, 38
Annan, Kofi 125, 222
anthropocentrism 42, 54, 221
anthropomorphism 34, 165
Apocalypse Now 70, 142, 144, 223

apology 39, 151, 185, 221, 223
Arachnophobia 45
Arafat, Yasser 103
Argo 75, 173
armed conflict 70, 114, 129, 133, 135, 145, 147–8, 150, 152, 192
arrest 107–8, 112, 115–16, 119, 201
Arrival 48, 163
artificial intelligence 20, 37
Artificial Intelligence: A.I 158
Asimov, Isaac 158
Avatar 40, 44, 48, 55, 57, 221
Avengers: Infinity War
Avengers series 34, 215

Babylon V 157, 159
Barbie, Klaus 115, 126
Barmak, Siddiq 177
La bataille du Rio de la Plata 206
The Battle of Algiers 140, 148
Battle Beneath the Earth 65
Battle for Haditha 70, 143, 145, 148, 223
Battlestar Galactica 24, 35, 37, 154, 157–8
Bauer, Fritz 115
The Beast 71
belligerents 29, 136, 191–2, 220
Berg, Peter 134, 223
Bigelow, Kathryn 151, 185–6
Bin Laden, Osama 185–6
biocentrism 44, 46, 49, 161
Black Earth Rising 104–5, 222

Black Hawk Down 143, 149
Blade Runner 52, 57, 161, 221–2
Blair, Tony 107, 219
Blistène, Pauline 185
Blood Diamonds 219
Boal, Mark 186
Bombardier 147
Bonitzer, Pascal 200
Brave New World 36
Breaker Morant 148
The Bridge on the River Kwai 1, 2, 9, 12
British Miners' Strike 217
Bruce, Jean 214
Brüno 99, 100
Bullfrog films 124
The Burma Conspiracy 109
Bush, George W. 69, 145, 175, 211, 215

Le Caire nid d'espions 215
Cameron, James 40, 55
camp (concentration) 118, 222
Canaan, Ben 79
Canticle of the Stones 89
Captain America: Civil War 34
capture 1, 88, 134–5, 141–3, 149
Casualties of War 70
Central Intelligence Agency *see* CIA
Chabrol, Claude 209
Chamayou, Grégoire 193–7
Chaplin, Charles 200
chemical attack 62
chemical weapon 20
Cheney, Dick 145–6
child soldier 118, 127
CIA (Central Intelligence Agency) 88, 107, 113, 128, 136–8, 185–7, 190
Le Cid 202
civilians 14, 72, 92, 122, 129, 130, 138–9, 139, 140, 142–5, 148–9, 152, 188–9, 193–4, 223
  civilian casualties 140, 193
  civilian character of objects and persons 129

civilian deaths 127
civilian installations 129
civilian population 113, 130
Clair, René 200
Clemenceau, Georges 212
Clinton, Bill 184, 211
Close Encounters of the Third Kind 48
Cloud Atlas 50, 55, 57
Cohn-Bendit, Daniel 124
Cold War 37, 63, 66
colonialism 173, 203
colonization 29, 90
combatants 134, 137–38, 141, 143–4, 152, 188, 192–4, 223
compromissory clause 29, 221
conduct of hostilities (rules) 129, 131, 133, 138
conquest, colonial 83, 85, 87, 167
The Constant Gardener 213
constitutionalism 22–3, 25, 35–739, 221
cooperation (States cooperation) 73, 108, 112
Coppola, Francis Ford 201, 223
Corneille, Pierre 202
Corten, Olivier 202, 218
crimes against humanity 51, 107, 111, 112, 113, 219
Critical Legal Studies 4, 101
  critical approach to international law 80, 84, 87, 91, 102, 173, 220
  critical conception of international law 79, 85
Crossing Lines 112–13
The Crown 73, 220
Cultural Legal Studies 3, 5

David, Eric 2, 189
The Day the Earth Stood Still 25–6
Dayez, Bruno 3
De Vitoria, Francisco 164
del Ponte, Carla 124
Delcourt, Barbara 6
Delta Force 66
democracy 27, 32, 213
Der Derian, James 173

diplomatic law 5, 27, 32–3
discrimination 83–4
dispute settlement 27, 30, 34, 38
distinction principle 129, 131, 133, 140, 143, 148, 150–1, 187
District 9 53, 56–7, 221
Divine Intervention 103
Doctor Strangelove 67, 73
Doctor Who 31, 37
double-tap strike 137–8, 191
Douglas, Lawrence 219
Douzinas, Costas 218
Dr Sima Simar 177
drone, pilot, strike, operation, warfare, killings 128, 136, 138, 149, 150, 188, 194–6
Dubuisson, François 6
dystopia 55

E.T. the Extra-Terrestrial 47
Eastwood, Clint 147, 151, 188
ECOSOC (UN Economic and Social Council) 37
Eichmann in Jerusalem 119
Eichmann, Adolf 115, 119, 120, 219
Emperor 10, 38, 120–1, 161, 222
Emperor Hirohito 10, 120
Empire of the Ants 45
Ender's Game 162, 163
enhanced interrogation techniques 183, 185
Enigma 212
equality 79, 81, 83–4, 158, 160, 176
 rights 81, 156
 sovereign equality 165
Exodus 78, 80, 84, 220
expulsion (Palestinian population) 83, 85, 90
extraterritorial assassination 193
Eye in the Sky 149, 150, 188

Fahrenheit 9/11 69, 173
failed state or rogue state 66
Fail-Safe 67, 73
Fassbender, Bardo 24

Fauda 93, 102, 143
feminist approaches 167
Fiennes, Sophie 182
Firefly 158
Force Majeure 182
forced labour 51–3
Forgiveness 92
Foxtrot 103
Framed: Women in Law and Films 3
freedom of expression 213
From Apology to Utopia 151
Full Metal Jacket 70, 139, 143–4, 190, 194, 197, 223
Futurama 25

Galafilm 125
Game of Thrones 22, 218
Gattaca 161, 182
Gavras, Costa 86
Generation Kill 70, 139
Generous force 212
Geneva Convention (III) relative to the Treatment of Prisoners of War 9
 Article 27 1, 12
Geneva Convention (IV) relative to the Protection of Civilian Persons in Time of War
 Article 53 94
Geneva Conventions 116, 152, 184, 202, 217
genocide 51, 112, 117
Ghost in the Shell 32
The Ghost Writer 208, 219, 222
Go tell the Spartans 142
Godfather 201, 206
Good Kill 129, 136, 190, 195, 223
Göring, Hermann 126
Graham, Mark 178
Grand Illusion 205
The Green Berets 75, 147
Greene, Graham 215
Gross, Aeyal 218
Guantanamo 183, 213
Guardian of the Galaxy 159
Gundam Wing 25

Hague Regulations on the Laws
   and Customs of War on Land
   (1907) 90
   Article 6, Article 44 10, 90
Hamas 93, 100, 144
Hamlet 217
Hannah Arendt 119, 218, 222
Hannah K 86
Harris, Robert 107, 219
Hartmann, Florence 124
Hausner, Gideon 119
Hazanavicius, Michel 215
Head of State immunity 219
Heathcote, Gina 177
Heinlein, Robert A. 24
heroic-nationalism 80, 82, 87, 89, 220
Herzog, Werner 218
High Noon 211, 212
hijacking 60, 88
Hill 24 Doesn't Answer 82
Hitchcock, Alfred 207
Hobbes, Thomas 207
Holocaust 80, 118
Homeland 75–6
hostage 88, 204
   American hostage in Tehran 75
Hotel Rwanda 219
The Hour 73
House of Cards 60
The House on Garibaldi Street 219
human rights 5, 6, 21, 23, 27, 53, 62,
   70, 90, 93, 150, 157–9, 175–7,
   181, 191, 196, 213
humanitarian intervention
   responsibility to protect, right of 62,
   64, 68, 177
Hunt for Justice 107, 111, 125, 222
The Hunting Party 116, 126
The Hurt Locker 132, 142, 151
Hussein, Saddam 69, 215
Huxley, Aldous 36

I Am Not Your Negro 127
ICC (International Criminal Court)
   58, 104, 105, 107–9, 112, 114,
   124, 166

ICJ (International Court of Justice) 102,
   103, 218
ICJ Adv. Op. on *the Legal
   Consequences of the Construction
   of a Wall in the Occupied
   Palestinian Territory* 102
ICTR (International Criminal Tribunal
   for Rwanda) 117
ICTY (International Criminal Tribunal
   for Former Yugoslavia) 107, 111,
   123, 124
Idealism 18, 22, 26, 27, 31, 35–9, 68,
   72, 79, 80, 83–9, 101, 155, 221
ideology 5, 7, 8, 13, 16–7, 37, 60, 75,
   77, 154–5, 169, 173, 184, 210
IDF (Israel Defense Forces) 103, 144
imminent threat 59, 128
impunity (fight against) 105–7, 109,
   116, 125
In Search of International Justice 222
In the Valley of Elah 143, 223
Independence Day 44, 67, 162–3
Indiana Jones 215
Inglourious Basterds 215
insurgency 177, 189, 194
interdisciplinarity 9, 167, 170
international community 34, 68,
   77, 102
International Court of Justice *see* ICJ
   102–3, 218
international crimes 117–8, 123, 127
International Criminal Court *see* ICC
   58, 104–5, 107–9, 112, 114,
   124, 166
international criminal justice v, 7, 31,
   104–7, 109, 110, 112, 114–17,
   119–25, 127, 166, 207, 218–9,
   222
international criminal law 27, 122, 218
International Criminal Tribunal for the
   Former Yugoslavia *see* ICTY 107,
   111, 123, 124
International Criminal Tribunal for
   Rwanda *see* ICTR
international criminal tribunals 125,
   208, 222

international humanitarian law (also IHL and law of armed conflicts) 2, 5, 10, 27, 129, 130, 141, 158, 222, 223
International Law Centre (Law Faculty of ULB) 2, 6, 7
international legal order 5, 22–3, 25, 68, 71
International Military Tribunal for the Far East 120–21
international organizations 23, 68, 116
international peace and security 34, 59
international relations *see* IR
international trade law 41
The Interpreter 107, 125, 213, 219, 222
interspecies relations 40, 43, 44, 46–7, 54–5, 56
interspecies slavery 52
interventionism 62, 76
invasion 58, 179, 219
Invasion USA 65, 220
I-Robot 52, 158
IR (international relations) 3, 4, 6, 7, 8, 13, 21, 26, 31, 59, 60, 68, 72, 74, 161, 163
Israel Defense Forces *see* IDF
Israeli–Palestinian conflict 79, 87, 89, 94–7, 100, 102, 166, 168, 170, 172–3
It Must Be Heaven 102

Jackson, Robert 126
JAG 58, 59, 64, 135
Jarhead 70
Joint Criminal Enterprise 219
Judgement at Nuremberg 219
Jullien, François 205
Jurassic Park 46
Jurassic World 46, 55
Jurassic World: Fallen Kingdom 46
jurisdiction 31, 106, 108, 112–3, 222
jus ad bellum 27, 203
jus in bello 70, 189, 190, 196–7, 203
Justice et cinéma 3
Justice League 112

The Justice Trial (IMT Trial) 219
Justice Pal, Radhabinod 121–2
Justice Scalia, Antonin 183

Kandahar 179, 180
Kant, Immanuel 36
Karadzic, Radovan 126
Kearns, Matthew 176
Khirbet Hiza'a 85
Khleifi, Michel 89
Kony Affair 219
Korean War 69
Koskenniemi, Martti 39, 151, 160
Kouchner, Bernard 124
Krigen 140, 143
Kubrick, Stanley 139, 190, 194, 198, 214
Kyle, Chris 147, 188–9

L'œil du cyclone 118, 127, 222
La Fontaine, Henri 23
Labyrinth of Lies 115, 219
Largo Winch II 109
Las Casas, Bartolome 164
Lawrence of Arabia 178
Lean, David 1
legal dogmatics 9, 10, 12, 15
legal formalism 11, 12, 125, 217
legal pluralism 24
legal positivism 11
Lemon Tree 94–5, 169
Leviathan 207
Lévy, Bernard-Henri 6
liberal world and non-liberal world 160, 165
Loevy, Ram 85
The London Review of International Law 218
The Lone Survivor 134, 148, 194, 223
The Lord of the Rings 43
Lumumba 127

Macross 25
magnissima charta 23
Mailer, Norman 210
Makhmalbaf, Mohsen 180

The Man Who Shot Liberty Valance 212
Manderson, Desmond 218
Marie-Chantal contre Dr Kha 209
The Mark of Cain 70, 142–3, 223
Mars attacks! 72, 212
Martens clause 152
Massé, Jacques 124
Matrix 33, 50, 55, 57
mediation 30, 98, 100
Memento 182
The Memory of Justice 219
Men in Black 37
Mengele, Josef 115
Middle East 33, 79, 97, 99, 215
military intervention 58–9, 62, 66, 167, 180
military objectives 129, 134–5
military-cinematographic complex 74, 75, 173, 220
military-industrial-media-entertainment network 173
Milosevic, Slobodan 107
Miral 99, 103, 173
Mladic, Ratko 116, 126
modern warfare 130, 133–4, 140, 143, 150, 191
Monsters 48
Moore, Michael 69, 70, 173
Mossad 115, 119, 120
Moyn, Samuel 197
Munich 102

national security 68, 181, 192
National Security Agency *see* NSA
NATO (North Atlantic Treaty Organization) 66
NATO peacekeeping 62, 177, 193
natural law (*jus naturalism*) 6, 12, 50, 202
negotiation 40, 73, 89, 96–8, 100, 162, 221
Neon Genesis Evangelion 25
Niccol, Andrew 136
Nineteen Eighty-Four 160

Nixon, Richard 25
non-combatant immunity 191, 193
non-intervention principle 28, 62–4, 68
North Atlantic Treaty Organization *see* NATO
Nos amis les terriens 49
Nos chers criminels de guerre 124
NSA (National Security Agency) 138
nuclear war 67, 73, 162
Nuremberg 10, 126, 138–9, 207, 219
Nuremberg Military Tribunal 10

occupation, military, occupied territory, occupying power 30, 51, 70, 79, 81, 87, 89, 90–6, 101–2, 175
Okja 50
Omar 91, 108
On Wings of Eagles 75
Only Human 100
The Open Conspiracy 36
Operation finale 119
Operation Thunderbolt 60
Osama v, 167–8, 174, 177–9, 180, 223
Oslo Accords 79, 89, 96, 98
OSS 117 214–6
Otto, Dianne 175

The Pacific 148
Pacific Rim 38
Pahuja, Sundhya 221
Paint It Black 198
Palestine Liberation Army 88
Palestine Liberation Organization *see* PLO
Palestine Stereo 95
Paradise Now 102
participation (direct participation of persons or objects in hostilities) 129, 130, 148
peaceful coexistence 24, 44, 157
Peck, Raoul 127
The People versus Fritz Bauer 115
The Pervert's Guide to Cinema 182
philosophy of law 9, 11
Piranha 3D 45

Piranhas 45
Pirates of the Caribbean 22
Pitch Black 45
Plaisir du cinéma: Le monde et ses miroirs 6
Planet of the Apes 51, 53, 57
Platoon 70, 139, 143–5, 223
PLO (Palestine Liberation Organization) 87, 89, 96, 99
Polanski, Roman 208, 219
Pollack, Sydney 125
Polybius 204
Pontecorvo, Gillo 140
pop culture 2, 17, 132, 168
POW (prisoners of war) 1, 9, 10, 217
power relations 4, 12, 28, 32, 79, 84, 87, 97
Practical Criticism 217
Predator 46
presumption of civilian character in IHL 136
prisoners of war *see* POW
The Promise 102, 139
proportionality principle 94, 130, 138, 140, 175

Quai d'Orsay 206

Raid on Entebbe 60
Rambo: The Fight Continues 64
Rambo III 71
The Reader 118, 126, 219, 222
Reagan, Ronald 75
realism 22, 31, 34–5, 37, 68, 136, 155, 217, 221
Realpolitik 33
rebellion 118, 127, 161, 221
reciprocity principle 34, 141
The Reckoning: The Battle for the International Criminal Court 222
Red Dawn 65, 220
Redacted 70, 132
Reel Justice: The Courtroom goes to the Movies 3

Renoir, Jean 205
Report on The Taliban's War Against Women 175
The Rescuers 64
Resolution 819 111, 116, 124, 126
Resolution UNGA
    Resolution 181 83
    Resolution 194 95
    Resolution 194 (II) 83
    Uniting for Peace 60
Resolution UNSC
    Resolution 1325 169
    Resolution 242 98
    Resolution 476 98
    Resolution 480 98
    Women, Peace and Security Resolutions 169, 170
revolution 53, 66
Richards, I.A. 217
right of return of refugees 83, 86–7
right to live 40, 42, 44–5, 65, 67, 161
right to self-determination, 101, 157, 173, 190
right to subdue weakest species 40, 52
Riklis, Eran 94, 169
Rise of the Planet of the Apes 53
Robocop 161, 222
RoE (rules of engagement) 63, 92, 134, 135, 150, 157, 189
Rolling Stones 198
Rome Statute 108, 112, 208, 219, 222
    Article 5 112
    Article 7 113
Room 514 92, 173
Rosebud 88, 174
rule of law 76, 212
rules of engagement *see* RoE
The Russians are coming, the Russians are coming 73

Salt of this Sea 86
Sands, Philippe 184
sanitizing war, de-sanitizing war 182, 197
Saving Private Ryan 212

Schlink, Bernd 219
Schmidt, Hans-Christian 124
Schmitt, Carl 162, 211
Screamers 45
SCSL (Special Court for Sierra Leone) 125
Second World War 1, 38, 55, 74, 114, 118, 120, 126, 132
self-defence 44, 58, 60–2, 65–8, 174, 180, 211
Serenity 158
sexism 57, 177
The Sheikh 178
Simon Konianski 100
Six-Day War 87, 97
Skylight pictures 124
Snowden 138, 223
sociology of law 9
Sohn, Louis B. 23
Sometimes in April 117, 127
sovereignty 23, 25, 28, 34, 60, 62, 66, 97, 103, 150, 155, 157, 193, 213, 221
Special Court for Sierra Leone *see* SCSL
The Specialist 219
speciesism 42, 46, 57, 155, 157, 165
Spielberg, Steven 48, 55, 215
Spies Like Us 73
Star Trek 27–31, 35–6, 43, 154, 156–9, 164, 204, 221
Star Trek: Deep Space Nine 30
Star Wars 37, 154, 157–9, 161, 222
    The Phantom Menace 158
    The Last Jedi 159
    The Empire Strikes Back 159, 161
Stargate SG-1 34
Starship Troopers 24, 35, 48, 53
State borders 81–3, 85, 96, 112
State practice 19, 39
Stendhal 210
Stone, Oliver 138, 144
Storm 110, 116, 124
subjective violence 224
Suez crisis 13, 73, 215, 220
Suleiman, Elia 83, 102–3
The Sum of All Fears 61
Supreme Court of Israel 94

Sur, Serge 6
surrender
    act of 84
    conditions 84
    rule of 11, 72–3, 108

The Tailor of Panama 215
Tajiks 180
Taliban 129, 130, 134, 137, 138, 140, 143, 168, 174–9, 180, 192, 223
Tallgren, Immi 220
Tarantino, Quentin 215
Tarantula 46
Tears of the Sun 63
Teitel, Ruti 218
teleological interpretation 30, 36, 158
The Terminator 37, 55
terrorism 61, 66, 74, 76, 79, 87, 88, 140, 149, 174, 175
Thatcher, Margaret 207
Them! 45
theory of law 9
Third World Approaches to International Law *see* TWAIL
Three Kings 64, 220
ThunderCats 20
ticking time bomb scenario 184, 188
Le Tigre aime la chair fraîche 209
Le Tigre se parfume à la dynamite 209
The Time that Remains 83
Tokyo Trial 121, 222
Top Gun 75
torture 41, 76, 126, 141, 145–6, 149, 183–7
Total Recall 161
Transformers 38
transitional justice 218
Transparent 100
Traoré, Sékou 127
La Traque 115
Trevorrow, Colin 55
Tutsis genocide 117
TWAIL (Third World Approaches to International Law) 167, 173
Twelve Monkeys 53
Twelve O'Clock High 147

UN (United Nations) 22, 24–6, 33, 37, 38, 58, 65, 78, 80, 82–3, 92, 101, 107, 125–6, 174
UN Charter 23, 59, 60, 65, 68–71, 74, 76–7, 211
  Article 33 98
  Article 51 61, 65, 174
  Articles 43 *et seq.* 26
  Chapter VII 177
UN Covenants on human rights 90
UN Economic and Social Council *see* ECOSOC
UNESCO (United Nations Educational, Scientific and Cultural Organization) 180
UNGA (UN General Assembly) 24, 60, 64, 78, 102, 103
UN General Assembly *see* UNGA
UNIT (United Nations Intelligence Taskforce) 37
UN Partition Plan for Palestine 78, 80–3
UN resolutions 95, 98, 102
UNSC (UN Security Council) 26, 33, 63, 98, 102, 107, 111, 170, 174, 201, 206, 208
UN Security Council *see* UNSC
United Nations *see* UN
United Nations Educational, Scientific and Cultural Organization *see* UNESCO
United Nations Intelligence Taskforce *see* UNIT
US Navy SEALs 134, 194
US Supreme Court 184
use of force 59, 61, 68, 71, 75–6, 166–9, 170, 172–4, 176–7, 181, 206, 220
Usurped force 212
Utopia 39, 55, 151, 155, 204, 221

Valentino, Rudolph 178
Van Hamme, Jean 109
Versailles Treaty 212
Vice 69, 145
Victory at Entebbe 60
Vietnam War 69, 70
von Bismarck, Otto 211
von Bülow, Bernhard 211
von Trotta, Margarethe 219
Le Voyage dans la lune 43

W 69
Wachowski, Lana 55
Wag the Dog 74, 173, 214
war crimes 107, 112–4, 116, 118, 137, 140, 145, 189, 191
War Don Don 125, 222
War Horse 55
War of the Worlds 38, 40, 43–4, 162
war on terror 66, 74–5, 77, 114, 143, 150, 180, 183, 186, 191–3, 195
war on women 174, 180
Wayne, John 75
weapons of mass destruction 58, 69, 72, 162
Wedding in Galilee 89
welfarism (animal welfare) 46
Wells, H.G. 36
Werber, Bernard 49
The West Wing 61, 64, 71, 97, 98, 219, 220
Whitehall, Deborah 218
Williams, Linda 168
Wilson, Thomas Woodrow 212
Wingfield, Thomas C. 156
women's rights 176, 177
world government 24–5, 36, 37, 160, 221
World Peace Through World Law 23

X-Men 52, 56, 57, 159

Zero Dark Thirty 151, 185–7, 193, 224
Zionism 78, 80–1, 102
Žižek, Slavoj 182, 186–7, 196, 224

EU authorised representative for GPSR:
Easy Access System Europe, Mustamäe tee 50,
10621 Tallinn, Estonia
gpsr.requests@easproject.com